*Communication
and
Human Values*

Global
Communication
in Transition
The End of Diversity?

Hamid Mowlana

 SAGE Publications
International Educational and Professional Publisher
Thousand Oaks London New Delhi

For information address:

 SAGE Publications, Inc.
2455 Teller Road
Thousand Oaks, California 91320
E-mail: order@sagepub.com

SAGE Publications Ltd.
6 Bonhill Street
London EC2A 4PU
United Kingdom

SAGE Publications India Pvt. Ltd.
M-32 Market
Greater Kailash I
New Delhi 110 048 India

Printed in the United States of America

Library of Congress Cataloging-in-Publication Data

Mowlana, Hamid, 1937-
    Global communication in transition: The end of diversity / by Hamid Mowlana.
        p. cm. — (Communication and human values)
    Includes bibliographical references and index.
    ISBN 0-8039-4318-0 (cloth: acid-free paper). — ISBN 0-8039-4319-9 (pbk.: acid-free paper)
    1. Communication, International. 2. Communication—Social aspects. 3. Communication and culture. 4. Communication and technology. I. Title. II. Series: Communication and human values (Newbury Park, Calif.)
    P96.I5M67   1996
    302.2—dc20   95-41801

This book is printed on acid-free paper.

96 97 98 99 10 9 8 7 6 5 4 3 2 1

Sage Production Editor: Astrid Virding

Contents

To the memory of my grandfather
Ayatullah Hajj Seyyed Muhammad Mowlana (1877-1944),
scholar, teacher, and community leader

Acknowledgments

The following articles of mine which were published originally in journals and readers are incorporated and reprinted in this book with the kind permission of the publishers: "Shapes of the Future: International Communication in the 21st Century," in the *Journal of International Communication*, Vol. 1, No. 1, June 1994, pp. 14-32; "The New Global Order and Cultural Ecology," in *Media, Culture, and Society*, Vol. 15, No. 1, January 1993, pp. 9-27; "Communication, Ethics and the Islamic Tradition," in *Communication Ethics and Global Change*, Thomas W. Cooper with Clifford G. Christians, Frances Forde Plude and Robert A. White, eds., White Plains, NY: Longman Press, 1989, pp. 137-146; and "Civil Society, Information Society, and Islamic Society," in *Information, Society and Civil Society: Contemporary Perspective on the Changing World Order*, Slavko Splichal, Andrew Calabrese, and Colin Sparks, eds., West Lafayette, Indiana: Purdue University Press, 1994, pp. 208-232.

I have been assisted in the preperation of this book by the careful efforts of Ginger Smith, Elizabeth Fox, Stanley Burgiel, Cynthia Dowdell, and Julia Brown. I thank them for their contributions.

Introduction

International communication is neither a discipline nor a precise science. Because human behavior reflects personal choices, international communication, in various times and places, is significantly different and subject to varied conceptual definitions. As a field of inquiry and research, international communication, or global communication as it is more commonly labeled nowadays, is in a state of ferment and evolution. In its human dimension, international communication is altered by the rise of modern political systems, the interactions as well as confrontations of various cultures with one another, and the profound development and expansion of social organizations. In its technological sense, international communication is now accompanied by the attempts of transnational actors to create a new global information infrastructure that can be compared with the two major changes that occurred during the 19th century—the establishment of railroad systems and the expansion of telegraphic lines that made rapid mobilization possible. The concept of sovereignty, so valued and honored for centuries, has now moved from geopolitical to spatio-cultural dimensions.

Most books on communication in general, and international communication in particular, treat the subject matter from an orthodox perspective that is rooted traditionally in the history and growth of communications disciplines. Many of the texts, treatises, and monographs are usually covered, classified, categorized, and discussed on the basis of the diversity and functions of the media—for example, newspapers, magazines, radio, television, telecommunications—and a variety of technological innovations and their social, political, and cultural impacts on society. The subject matter typically is treated along the lines of issues or issue areas, such as news flow, the legal aspects of communication, the New World Information Order, human rights, the privacy of transborder data flow, and a variety of other items.

There are also tendencies within the field to separate theoretical essays from more practical and everyday phenomena. Consequently, the students of communication, like any other social science disciplines, are encouraged to ask themselves whether they are engaged in theoretical discourse or practical and policy discussions. The fact that there are direct relationships between theoretical propositions and the practical aspects of everyday life cannot be denied.

The problems of the study of communication in all its dimensions are further complicated by the very nature of the sociology of knowledge as well as the academic background from which the students, researchers, and scholars have emerged. For example, within the tradition of mass communication research in the United States, the influence of journalism, political science, social psychology, and sociology cannot be denied. In the field of intercultural communication, one can observe the more distinct influence of such disciplines as anthropology, linguistics, and even, to a degree, philosophy.

In the European tradition, the study of mass communication has been influenced less by the tradition of journalism than sociology. Although political economy has been a major trend in the study of communication discourse in Europe, the disciplines of political science and international relations have not yet assumed a paramount position as has been the case in the United States. Although mathematical and quantitative models are more prevalent in all social sciences including communication in the United States, within Europe and even broader cultural and geographic areas such as Latin America and Asia, the disciplines of history, political thought, literature, and criticism have been more prevalent and pronounced.

In a number of geographical areas in the world, such as the Middle East and North Africa, where the modern communications methodologies and research are not yet well rooted in the traditions of the United States and Europe, the tendency has historically been to analyze communications questions in relation to the humanities and such specific areas as literature, poetry, philosophy, mysticism, and religion. Yet, despite these different perspectives, there remains the fact that today, more than ever, one can observe a number of high-level generalizations and concepts in all the social sciences that are of interest to everyone.

This book attempts to steer away from these traditional and orthodox ways of organizing material into either media categories or issue areas. It instead attempts to search for a number of basic concepts around which the phenomena of global communication can be analyzed. Within such concepts as history, power, community, legitimacy, and language, atte▪ have been made to bridge the gap between theory and practice, poter▪ and actuality. Efforts also have been made to incorporate a v▪

contemporary issues and policies in national, regional, and global communications to illustrate the vitality of the field, with the hope of throwing light on the complexity of the discipline. The classification and organization of the subject matter within these conceptual frameworks has an additional advantage. It allows both the writer and the reader to entertain these concepts within and across national and cultural boundaries. Such a perspective also has the advantage of making it possible to move from macro to micro analyses.

With this classification system, for example, the concept of community and legitimacy in an Islamic context can be reviewed and compared with the prevailing ideas in Western philosophy and history. The assumption here is that the political, economic, and cultural implications of communication in contemporary work cannot be analyzed unless they are discussed within the broader concepts of, say, community. The search for a community is a universal force throughout the history of world civilization. Yet, it is precisely the nature and boundaries of the community itself that are subject to disputes and contentions.

In the United States, the concept of community is usually discussed within the smaller units of society. Consequently, it is difficult for many Americans to transcend their ideas of community from an urban "real estate" community to a city as a community, or to a region as a community, or to a world as a community. This is particularly so because of the very emphasis we have given to the notion of the nation-state system and, within the American context, the notion of the union of states. It is interesting, in reviewing the history of the United States, to note that prior to the formation of the union of states, the notion of community was more of a central theme in the nation-building process, especially during the War of Independence, than in either the period after the Civil War or the modern era.

In other countries, particularly in the context of Islamic civilization and history, the concept of community transcends the smaller units and embraces nationalities, ethnic groups, and nation-states. Therefore, when the notion of community is discussed, it is perceived in a much broader geographical and cultural context. In Europe, where nationalism took its modern roots and the concept of nation-states is still strong, the postwar economic cooperation on the continent has revived the concept of community. In other geographical and cultural areas as well, such as India, China, and Japan, the relationship between the state and community is embedded in specific historical experiences.

For example, the conceptualization of the state illustrates another useful way of looking at this phenomenon. The concept of the state, as rooted in the political philosophy of Europe, varies quite a bit from that in the United States and thus influences the way we may look at the notion of civil society, that is, the relationship between the state, the community, and the individual. In this context, the concept of democracy is associated with the freedom of expression and dissemination of information; whereas in Europe, the concept of democracy takes a moral tone, with the state playing an important role in guarding not only what may be termed the public sphere but also the rights of individuals to communicate and receive information. It was therefore natural that the political transformations and upheavals of the late 1980s and early 1990s, especially in Central and Eastern Europe, were associated to a large degree with the debate over the nature of civil society and the redefinition of the relationship between the state, the community, and the individual. Indeed, it is precisely the different perceptions of democracies and civil societies that are responsible for the differentiation of communication policies within the European community and the United States, especially as may relate to the notion of the information society.

Similarly, since the late 1980s, conventional ways of looking at the concept of power have been challenged tremendously. Indeed, many of the uncertainties arising from our inability to predict international events stem from the fact that power has been and continues to be defined in orthodox and traditional frameworks. In fact, the political "realist" approach, which has dominated the international relations field since World War II, is based on a conceptualization of power that is measured almost exclusively in tangible, visible terms. Some scholars, however, have tried to break with this tradition, defining power on a more interactive level. For example, Karl Deutsch has described power as a currency in politics that can lead political theory toward the development of some form of dynamic interchange model. Deutsch acknowledged that power as a currency in interactions between political systems does indeed build on the measurability of more traditional, tangible resources, including voters, soldiers, military hardware, and manpower budgets. However, he emphasized that appropriate weighting also should be given to the intensity of support, morale, skills, and resourcefulness to estimate power in more intangible terms. More recently, Joseph S. Nye, Jr., has expanded traditional notions of power to include the influence of smaller nations and private actors such as multinational corporations in international politics.

As these examples indicate, the realist model or nation-state-centered paradigm proposed by many classical and modern scholars of international relations has been challenged by the rapidly changing environment of world politics and the global economy. Events have demonstrated that it no longer fully explains contemporary international interactions such as the demise of the Soviet Union and the emergence of new nation-states in Eastern Europe and Central Asia. It also fails to deal adequately with the turmoil of ethnicity, religious and cultural fervor, economic regionalism, and resurgent nationalism. Thus, it is becoming increasingly necessary to look at the conceptualization of power as less a question of governing and more a problem of cooperation, learning, and growth.

I should emphasize that this book is neither a descriptive nor a comprehensive text in the fields of international and comparative communication. Nor is it directed toward a given subfield of communication, such as mass communications, international development, cultural studies, or political economy, among others. Instead, it is a discursive text attempting to put a variety of issues and theoretical ideas in a conceptual framework, with the hope not only that readers will appreciate and be stimulated by these ideas but also that further observations and evaluations can be undertaken.

Every essay or book is a reflection of the author's background and orientation, and I must confess that mine is no exception. Given my own exposure over the past decades to both Western and Eastern cultures, as well as my academic career in international relations, I have a natural bias toward an interdisciplinary and intercultural approach. The reader will find some chapters tuned toward specific cultures and civilizations, such as Islam. This reflects both the changing realities of world politics and the new social and cultural forces at work.

As communication takes a prominent and central role in all institutions and aspects of contemporary national and global systems, it is hoped that this volume, by emphasizing concepts rather than fragmentary and sometimes unrelated issue areas, may be useful not only to students of communication but also to those in other social science disciplines and the humanities.

1

World Communication:
A History and Interpretation

The dramatic growth in telecommunications and communication technologies in the 1980s, the increasing sophistication of less developed nations, and the rise to supranational status of international organizations are only a few of the factors changing the face of contemporary international relations and international communication research and inquiry. It comes as no surprise that, as a result, complexity now characterizes notions of nationalism and what might be viewed as renewed efforts toward regionalism in the international system.

A look back at the 1950s through the late 1970s illuminates a period of social science research in the areas of large-scale political community formation at the national and international levels, theories of communication and control, interactive approaches to politics and society, as well as the development and use of quantitative data to test and reformulate political theories. A central theme for this period was social and political integration and the quest for an enduring world community based on social and technological mobilization of all kinds. Key researchers included such pundits as Karl W. Deutsch, Richard L. Merritt, Bruce M. Russett, and many others.

Recent studies and monographs tracing the development of mass communication research in the United States during the post-World War II period document the ways and means by which international communication research was carried out in the context of psychological warfare and U.S. foreign policy objectives. For example, Christopher Simpson (1994), in his study of the role of communication research as a tool of psychological warfare, argues that modern communication studies likely could not have emerged in their present form without large transfusions of financial assistance from U.S. military, intelligence, and propagand[...] agencies throughout the Cold War. These government agencies vie[...] mass communication as a means for persuading targeted groups dor[...] cally and abroad and as a relatively low-cost tool for widening Ar[...]

influence overseas. Similarly, Jarol B. Manheim has traced the growing reliance of foreign governments on U.S. public relations as a means of influencing U.S. foreign policy. Offering a series of case studies, including the recent efforts of the Kuwaiti government-in-exile to mold American public opinion during the Gulf war, Manheim asserts that these attempts at managing public opinion through communication efforts have become increasingly grand in both scale and sophistication.

The perception that the West was falling behind in intellectual contributions to the needs of new nations was reflected in the literature of the 1950s through late 1970s. It was acknowledged that what was needed was a wider knowledge of diverse cases to articulate probing questions of theory and the discovery or rediscovery of overlooked or neglected aspects of the nation-building process. It was hypothesized that, with the process of increased social mobilization through modernization, comes increased not decreased community building and trends toward nationalism. This makes developing countries more difficult to govern by traditional elite structures and raises the costs of foreign intervention—an issue of great import for the developed or First World tier of superpowers.

Such a perspective fostered the development of quantitative tools for elite and integration analysis in the growing series of elite studies of the times. Through both surveys of elite opinion and aggregate data on international communication in the form of international transactions (trade, travel, migration, and mail), such studies concluded that since 1957, for example, movement that had begun toward structural European integration had either stopped or significantly slowed down. National integration and nationalism in Western Europe and in communist, socialist, and developing areas were central research foci of the period. Contributors in this period contended that quantitative findings raise some of the most vital questions facing mankind, centering on the stability and quality of life and governments. These researchers attempted to measure the worldwide transfer of technologies of consumption and production among countries and among people with the thesis that such measures were acquiring crucial importance for the success or failure of national development. The result was that, on the whole, the quantitative measurement of nationalism preoccupied researchers during the 1950s through 1970s.

In this same period, however, researchers with a different vision conributed a complementary integrative paradigm for comparative mass dia production and distribution analysis, which underpins discussions e media's relationship to community building. This theme is in supthe major approach presented in this book. The topic of the interaction between ecological and social conditions, in what will be developed by the end into the notion of human or *cultural* ecology, is related to the basic premise of the interdependence and self-transformation of systems.

The Growth of
International Communication

International communication as a field of study is a 20th-century phenomenon, although international communication has occurred ever since people organized themselves into communities and began to exchange ideas and products[International communication has grown over the past several decades from a small, predominantly American area of research and inquiry into one of the most central and vital areas of international studies today. Influenced by the climate and tempo of the post-World War II and Cold War period,]the early studies of international communication by leading American social scientists established directives for future research and teaching and set the tone for U.S. international communication policy for the years to come.

This climate can be summarized into four main elements. The first is international conflict, war, and the use of propaganda. The second is the development of international organizations and diplomacy. The third is the spread of competing ideologies and the use of communication to disseminate messages. The fourth is the development of new communication technologies. Although all these elements were at work over several decades, it took time for people to realize that what these factors were giving rise to was international communication. For some, international communication was first seen as an issue of propaganda. Others saw international communication essentially as an issue of education, cooperation, and understanding.

In short, there are many factors that contributed to international communication as a field of research, policy, and study. Some of the factors central to its formation as a field both prior to World War II and following World War II follow.

Contributing Factors
Prior to World War II

- The development of communication technologies, beginning in the 19th century (photography, telegraph, telephone, submarine cables between Europe and the United States, wireless)

- The hegemony of the great European powers and their use of communication technologies and early international news agencies to enhance their powers globally and to acquire colonies and manage empires
- Industrialization and Europeanization around the world with numerous African, Asian, Latin American, and Arab societies emulating the West; the process of Westernization and secularization responsible for the creation of "modern" institutions of communication, such as the press, news agencies, radio, libraries, universities, and post, telegraph, and telephone (PTT) ministries
- The growth of international organizations and the transnationalization and integration of the field of communications (International Telecommunications Union, Universal Postal Union, the League of Nations)
- The growth of the major international news agencies in Europe and the United States and establishment of numerous national news agencies and press services
- The spread of contending ideologies—liberalism, communism, fascism, and a number of Islamic movements—and the strategic impact accorded to international communication; revolutionary movements in Iran, Mexico, Eastern Europe, and the former Soviet Union and their transnational activities through the press and communication technologies
- The realization of the psychological impact of public opinion and its importance in wartime situations; the rise of international propaganda as a result of radio technology and the bypassing of national boundaries
- The commercialization of radio in the United States; growth and expansion of cinema and film industries; development of cultural industries in Europe
- The expansion of railroads and modern navigation complete with radio technology; urbanization and industrialization contributing to telecommunications infrastructure and mass-circulated media

Contributing Factors
in the Postwar Period

It was World War II, however, and the postwar period that accelerated the growth of international communication. Specifically, the following factors were among those responsible for the expansion of the field:

- The rapid expansion of new technologies (television, satellites, computers, video, fax machines, Integrated Services Digital Networks/ISDN); the growth of dependency on international flows of specialized financial and scientific-technological information; the marriage of computer science, television, and telephone in the form of informatics

- The increased number of nation-states as major participants in political, cultural, and socioeconomic aspects of international communication and their growing role in regional, national, and international organizations
- The emergence of the United States as the dominant power on the international scene in terms of its political, cultural, military, economic, and communication influences throughout the world
- The Cold War system and its impact on international political communication through increased political legitimacy of international communication issues; the use of propaganda and international political persuasion as a major instrument of diplomacy and agenda setting; the rise of international broadcasting as a major channel of foreign policy articulation and propaganda
- The expansion of entertainment media as an export-import industry with producers, sellers, and buyers operating on a global scale; the increasing issues of copyright, intellectual property rights, privacy, and other legal concerns; the accentuated awareness of inequality and imbalance in the international flow of information
- The increased role of cultural-ideological and socioeconomic factors in the transnationalization of communication and the utility of ethnological-type studies and commissions of research, such as the MacBride Commission
- The expansion of international organizations and the international flow of information debates in the United Nations and the United Nations Educational, Scientific, and Cultural Organization (UNESCO)
- The liberation, independence, and revolutionary movements around the world, with the mobilization of populations to achieve goals using communication techniques and institutions for political and cultural impact; the emergence of the Non-Aligned Movement and the Third World's call for a New World International Information and Communication Order (NWICO); the ensuing global media debate
- The expansion of the field of development communication and the spread of the Western communication model to the Third World as a development alternative
- The increased recognition of the limitations of Western-oriented social science methods in Third World contexts; the emphasis on interpersonal and traditional communication processes; the rediscovery of the importance and involvement of the communication role of civil society versus overvaluation of the state
- The rise of transnational and multinational corporations for the production and distribution of messages and images; the creation of international telecommunications organizations such as International Telecommunications Satellite Consortium (INTELSAT) and International Maritime Satellite Organization (INMARSAT); the tremendous growth of nongovernmental organizations

- The dual processes of worldwide commercialization and deregulation of the telecommunications industry and the problems of distribution of basic communication resources (geostationary orbit and radio-electronic spectrum)
- The acceleration of international conferences, travel; the expansion of educational institutions, congresses, and seminars worldwide; the exchange of students between countries and cultures

Centers of International Communication Research

The early research and teaching of leading American social scientists strongly influenced the direction and tone of what was to become the foundation of contemporary U.S. international communication policy. The influence of these scholars and of their respective institutions is important to review in developing a history and interpretation of the field.

MIT Center for International Studies

An early center for international communication research in the Cold War era was the Massachusetts Institute of Technology's Center for International Studies, one of the most important centers of communication research in the United States during the 1950s and 1960s. The sociological techniques employed by the center focused on the control of human attitudes and behavior on a mass scale, with a key consideration of the impact of mass media on social development in the Third World.

In the summer of 1952, the Ford Foundation awarded the center an $875,000 grant for a research program in international communication. A staggering sum in its day, the allocation of this money documents the first major attempt in the United States after World War II to systematize and analyze international communication as a field of research and policy. Between 1952 and 1956, the center produced numerous studies on international communication, many involving techniques of persuasion, advertising, interrogation, public opinion polling, political and military mobilization, propagation of ideology, and related questions.

Although not publicly acknowledged, government funding through agencies such as the Ford Foundation often accounted for as much as 75% of the annual budgets of social research institutions similar to MIT. In addition, the degree of subsidy provided by U.S. military intelligence and propaganda agencies, often through institutions such as the Ford Foundation, was so great that it is unlikely that mass communication research would have emerged in its present form without it.[1] In this sense, the methodologies, literature, and institutional structure of the field of mass communication research can be seen to have tracked the growth of capitalism and mass media. With scholars such as Paul Lazarsfeld at the Bureau of Applied Social Research at Columbia, Hadley Cantril at the Institute for International Social Research at Princeton, and Ithiel de Sola Pool at MIT, the direction of government funding during this period toward certain programs had a powerful effect. It strongly influenced "the selection of who would do the 'authoritative' talking in the field; who would be recognized as leaders, and which one of several competing scientific paradigms concerning communication would be funded, elaborated, and encouraged to prosper" (Simpson, 1993, p. 316). Such action skewed communication research in favor of military intelligence and propaganda studies. Furthermore, it reduced opportunities for public debate and contributed to what might be called a communication elite among researchers and institutions that came to view mass communication research as a tool for social management and as a weapon in social conflict. It was this group that

> wrote the textbooks, enjoyed the heavy government contracts that often are necessary for professional prominence in the United States, served on the editorial boards of the key journals, and became the deans and emeritus professors of the most influential schools of communication and journalism in this country. (p. 322)

The MIT Center for International Studies was no exception. In fact, according to Simpson, during the 1950s the MIT center was funded largely by the CIA and the Air Force, often using the Ford Foundation as a cover (p. 333). The major purpose of the 1952 Ford Foundation grant, as outlined in the advisory report summary, was

> to increase scientific knowledge, but the research was to be conducted in such a way that the end product would be useful not only to the scientist but also to the statesman in his effort to preserve peace and promote understanding among men. (Center for International Studies, MIT, 1953; hereafter MIT Report)

Guidelines for the program specified that research projects "do exploratory work on communications to and from the wielders of power and influence" (MIT Report, p. vi), including the influence of middlemen operating between the mass media and their ultimate audiences. The kinds of communication, therefore, were drawn from communication elite relationships and were to be long range in nature. The underlying premise was that propaganda's effect could be amplified in conjunction "with economic development, arms transfers, policy and military training, and counter-insurgency support for U.S.-backed regimes. . . . Among sociologists, these tactics took the name 'development theory.' " Similarly, Simpson contends that terms such as "propaganda" and "psychological warfare" became supplanted with "international communication," "development," and "public diplomacy" and other more self-consciously neutral terms (MIT Report, pp. 24-25).

In this light, the MIT program's scope was to produce knowledge useful to policymakers and to scientists. Areas selected were of "highest political significance—the conflict between the Kremlin and the free world, the integration or disintegration of Europe, the rise of nationalism in Asia and Africa" (MIT Report, pp. 24-25). Research methodologies were multidisciplinary, including historical and field studies as well as laboratory experiments. This was for the expressed purpose of stimulating interdisciplinary cooperation within the behavioral sciences on an international level:

> The grant which created the program was made with the intention of stimulating research both at home and abroad—at M.I.T. and at other institutions in America and overseas. . . . Great importance should be attached to promoting cooperation research by scholars outside the United States. The study of international communication will be one-sided so long as it stems from any one country. (MIT Report, pp. 26-27)

To ensure the internationalism of the project's scope, MIT recruited scholars from a number of nations crucial to the international relations of the United States. The project proposal committee was composed of seven of the leading social scientists of the 1950s: Jerome Bruner, Wallace Carroll, Harold D. Lasswell, Paul Lazarsfeld, Edward Shils, Hans Speier (chairperson), and Ithiel de Sola Pool (secretary), with Max F. Millikan as director of the MIT center. These important thinkers were invited to gather their intellectual experience around a field called international communication. This indicates growth of the field's new and respected status and emphasizes its legitimate role "as a creative contributor to the science of international relations" (MIT Report, p. vii). The initiative for the establishment of a research program in international communication at MIT came at a time when important theoretical advances were being made in both international relations and international communication. As the MIT group saw it, "if the program lives up to the opportunities of the time, it will do much to advance scientific knowledge of human behavior at large" (MIT Report, p. vii).

Of critical importance was the new manner in which the MIT advisory report defined international communication more broadly than the media exchange formulas of the past:

> The term "international communication" in the sense intended by the [Ford] Foundation does not mean mechanical, electronic, and other physical means of conveying information across frontiers. What it means is the interchange of words, impressions and ideas which affect the attitudes and behavior of different peoples toward each other. (MIT Report, p. v)

An important new element in the MIT center's definition is that "words, acts, or attitudes" may be called international communication "whenever by design or by accident they impinge upon the minds of private individuals, officials or groups from other countries" (MIT Report, p. 1).

This definition focused on the human or social dimensions of international communication as a complex process of various interchanges using signs and symbols, the international communication process thereby became distinct from its mere technological aspects. International communication in this research context became a very broad field. It was tied to social conditions, attitudes, and institutions that influence the production or reception of "images" among peoples. Thus, the MIT research program recognized "the structure of the media through which the impulses pass, the attitudes and social circumstances of their originators, the predispositions of the receivers," and emphasized the effect and impact of the contents (MIT Report, p. 2).

Third World Elite Communication

It is important to examine the relationship of the MIT center's broadened definition of international communication in light of American overseas activities at the time. A strong correlation exists in the provisos of the advisory report between academic and socioeconomic/political goals. The launching of purely academic social science research in international communication was not the sole motive behind the Ford Foundation grant. The pragmatic policy implications of increasing American understanding of the elite communication relationships at work in the Third World was certainly another. The impact of mass media and the structure of communication systems in various other countries was a subtle but equally important research goal for the center. In addition, the backgrou climate of the Cold War can be seen as a stimulus in the research program design. By definition, international communication was to be studied and understood in socioeconomic, political, and cultural contexts.

Called "complexities of international communication," the proposal legitimized long-term studies of elite (leadership) communications and of mediation or opinion leadership by stating, "In international affairs many of the most significant communications involve leaders rather than masses, and refraction and feedback are so crucial that they cannot be disregarded" (MIT Report, p. 4).

Addressing "gaps in our scientific knowledge," the grant required that designated areas of research "should be of political significance." That this "might seem to conflict with the first criterion—that they should be of scientific merit" (MIT Report, p. 9)—was carefully considered by the center's committee members:

> The great political problems of our time offer an inescapable challenge to scientists of all kinds. There is, therefore, every reason why the program, in selecting its research projects, should keep in mind such issues of major political significance as the conflict between the Kremlin and the free world, the integration of Europe, and the rise of new nationalism in countries that have in the past been colonial areas of European powers. . . . International communication as well as the other instruments of foreign policy— economic, political, and military—in one way or another are being applied to these issues and bear upon their resolution. (MIT Report, p. 10)

The launching of an international communication social science research project at MIT correlated with the political and economic timeliness in increasing American involvement and activities in the Third World. Focusing on elite communication, research areas included the sensitivity of various elites to public communication; the background, outlook, and role of the specialists in international communication; and techniques and organization of communication between elites. A fundamental research concern was the importance attached by political elites of various nations to "negotiation as an instrument of policy in comparison with other instruments, such as economic measures, international propaganda, military force, diplomatic notes, subversive efforts" (MIT Report, p. 7).

The processes of mediation between the mass media and their ultimate audience was the focus for studies on mediation and opinion leadership. Such studies attempted to answer difficult questions, such as, who are the opinion leaders, and what is the accepted meaning of "leadership" in a given culture? To what extent is the communist message more effective than the American message because native agents diffuse it? How can channels of mediation be established in different social systems?

The socioeconomic policy implications of the Ford Foundation grant extended beyond the studies of elite communication relationships to the impact of mass media and the structure of communication systems in various countries. The language of the MIT document confirmed these policy implications by identifying the study of international communication as the study of international relations in a nonmilitary, sociocultural dimension. For example, in outlining the East-West conflict as an important potential research area, the language of the document revealed prevention of Kremlin expansion, through the communication of ideology, as the key issue:

> The conflict between the communist and the free world is of decisive importance to the balance of power and the future character of our civilization. Far from being merely a struggle for power, this conflict is also a contest of ideas and ideals for the hearts and minds of men both in the Soviet empire and in the vast "neutral" areas of the world which lie outside either sphere of influence. (MIT Report, p. 10)

Key linguistic cues in this passage include "our civilization." On whose definition will its "future character" be based? Which peoples will be eligible for a share in the "balance of power"? Which of the dominant "ideas and ideals" will win out in the "vast" areas of the Second and Third Worlds or possibly even at the core? Does "neutral" mean that these other culturally, politically, and economically diverse "areas" have no preexisting preferences for self-determination? Will their demands for self-control be respected, particularly in the increasingly important realm of communication technology and mass media production and distribution rights?

The linguistic implication in the MIT center's proposal was that these criteria were to be devised by Western authorities and "communicated" through international communication research intentionally focused on a world divided between East and West. The language appeared to emphasize the importance of the Cold War dimensions as a research element by presuming a lack of political alternatives "outside the sphere of either [Soviet or U.S.] influence" (MIT Report, p. 10).

The political dominance of the 1950s' Cold War framework also was evident in the center's selection of the Western European integration effort and its communication elites as project research areas. Again, the document's language revealed policy implications although the stated purpose is academic:

> Again, current efforts toward the integration of Western Europe are not only matters of negotiation and compromise. Beliefs and sentiments as well as interests are involved, and the success of European integration depends on the degree to which a common understanding of freedom and justice is shared by the nations involved. This is in one small measure a matter of communication across the barriers of divided interests, loyalties, and fears. (MIT Report, p. 10)

The research focus was further narrowed to the study of elites: "One elite of special significance for the program is the communications elite, i.e., the persons who exert the most influence over the content of communications in a society—such persons as authors, publishers, editors, and artists" (MIT Report, p. 4). Controllers of the mass media were singled out over political, economic, or cultural elite leadership. This research focus forecast international communication's increasingly important position in international relations. Growing U.S. and, more generally, Western concern over such issues as the free flow of information and freedom of the press influenced the direction of international communication for the next two decades. Indeed, two decades later, the 7-year evolution of UNESCO's Mass Media Declaration beginning in 1970 and the strong sociopolitical and economic reactions to its final publication in 1978 contributed to the debate over the New World Information and Communication Order (NWICO) of the 1980s.

The language of the MIT report predicted critical future issue areas. Attention to "beliefs and sentiments" are ranked higher than traditional techniques of "negotiation and compromise" in international relations transactions. "Common understanding of freedom and justice" (MIT Report, p. 10) implies achievement, from interpersonal to international levels, of complex communication processes based on two-way, feed-back-filled interactions. This is a direct challenge to the traditional one-way flow of information from developed to developing countries that has so characterized the international relations of the 20th century.

In addition, there is in the language of the document's text a conflicting assumption, perhaps a fatal one for the West, that the "communication elite, the persons who exert the most influence over the content of communications in a society" (MIT Report, p. 4) will be able to retain this control in the future. Third World publics and counterelite actors are claiming participation in international communication issues—in information technology and mass media production and distribution rights. It has become "a matter of communication across the barriers of divided interests, loyalties, and fears" (MIT Report, p. 10). Third World involvement in control over the content of communication is changing the structure of leadership.

In response to this threat, there existed in the MIT proposal an expression, almost obsession, with knowing how Third World elites were recruited and the nature of their thinking and decision making: "It takes research to learn under which social conditions mass or elite opinion decisively affects decisions. Only when the persons who make the decisions are identified, can research explore the influence of communication upon these decisions" (MIT Report, p. 5). In this context, questions , concerning "the importance and efficacy of propaganda" and "the preferences for certain types of channels or procedures" (MIT Report, p. 5) became critical research topics. It was becoming clear in the 1950s that to maintain Western control of communication content meant developing a knowledge of Third World elite training techniques. Studies would be devoted to Third World communication elites' "expectations and sentiments concerning foreign peoples, groups, and governments" (MIT Report, p. 6). Additional research questions included "What are the contacts and political influence of these specialists? How do their work relationships affect the opinions they express? What are the normal career patterns? What degree of specialization is prevalent in the profession?" (MIT Report, p. 6).

The fundamental issue in the study of elite communication focused on negotiation as an aspect of international communication: "What importance do the political elites of various nations attach to negotiation as an instrument of policy in comparison with other instruments, such as economic measures, international propaganda, military force, diplomatic notes, subversive efforts?" (MIT Report, p. 7).

Faced with the political reality of rising new nationalism in Asia and Africa, the MIT study also recognized the need to take American scientists to the field. Their role would be to conduct studies that "encompass several stages of the causal chain" rather than "isolate one stage to describe it." This research orientation was innovative in its view of "contents or media as parts of the chain of stimulus and effect" (MIT Report, p. 13). This represented an effort to preserve "the balance of power and the status of Western civilization in the years to come" (MIT Report, p. 10) against the threat of Kremlin expansion:

The West cannot be passive. Its policy cannot be merely one of economic assistance or pressure, as the case may be. It must rather take account of the cultural traditions of the areas involved which are older than that of the West and as venerable to the peoples involved as are ours to us. The task then faced by the West is to a large extent one of intelligent and sympathetic communication. (MIT Report, p. 11)

The tone of "intelligent and sympathetic communication" reflects the paternalistic, ethnocentric orientation of Western concepts of international relations prevalent in the 1950s. The content of the language was academic; the context was political and economic.

Opinion Leadership
and Long-Range Studies

After elite communication, mediation and opinion leadership were the second major research areas outlined by the MIT proposal. The third was long-range studies. The model to be employed in all projects was based on the 1948 linguistic model of Harold Lasswell, one of the MIT committee members: "Who talks to whom, how often, on what subjects, and with what influence?" (MIT Report, p. 7). The document stated that the communication process must be studied as a part of the total social system to answer such questions. This pinpointed the uniqueness of the MIT proposal in its day. Its research goals proposed precedent-setting analysis of international communication issues of the future.

The sample projects described in the MIT document related integrally to the perceived need to improve American research methodologies in overseas contexts for the purposes of foreign policy and international relations. India was selected as the area in which to examine the rise of nationalism. The subareas were to include the study of its intelligentsia (elite communication), the effectiveness of American spokesmen in India (mediation), and the origins and development of elements of the Indian image of America (long-range study). These studies met the grant "criteria of scientific relevance as well as political significance and would form a coherent program" (MIT Report, p. 15).

Results gathered from this combination of research topics on India would better inform the United States about the effects of international communication on political decision making in the Third World. "In India perhaps more than in the West, intellectuals play a major role in influencing political decisions" (MIT Report, p. 15). The relationship of overall grant objectives with this choice of fieldwork appeared strategically coordinated. An interesting concern mentioned in the long-range study proposal was Indian sensitivity to U.S. treatment of black Americans. An understanding of Indian images would enlighten American (white) decision making regarding its own internal "Third World," composed of Asian, Hispanic, and black Americans.

The research area in European unification examined business persons and their knowledge of foreign affairs (elite communication), pro-American and pro-Communist Europeans (mediation), and European attitudes toward unity (long-range study). Business persons were selected for the elite study because, "The businessmen [*sic*] engaged in international economic activities are a particularly influential elite group whose international communication might well be studied. In both Europe and America they have an important influence on the prospects of European unity" (MIT Report, p. 18). Key research questions centered around the relative effect of business, ideological, and political considerations on the formation of business persons' attitudes and opinions. Because they were instrumental in international decision making as opinion leaders, it was important to distinguish business persons' reliance on special sources of information versus mass media.

The mediation subarea of the European unity project proposed the examination of pro-American and pro-Communist mediators. What personal factors beyond social origins and early indoctrination can be identified—"intensity of drive, personal ambition, desire for comfort, idealism, and willingness to sacrifice?" (MIT Report, p. 19)—as influences on the effectiveness of either group? "What power do they have to influence decisions?" was the central question legitimizing the research (MIT Report, p. 19).

The long-range study proposed a comparison of changing attitudes toward the European defense community and German rearmament in France and Germany. The research aim was to assess "the impact of tradition, nationalism, partisanship, political organization, foreign communication, fresh events, etc., on the formation of opinion" (MIT Report, p. 19). This would be achieved by "an intensive study of attitudes and communications in one representative town in France and one in West Germany continued over two years" (MIT Report, p. 19). The study's chronology would examine four periods—the time of the first World War, the Depression, the years of Nazi ascendancy and occupation, and the years after the last war.

East-West Conflict

The first research area of the MIT document proposed study of communications in the East-West conflict. The elite communication subarea focused on diplomatic negotiations between the Soviet and Western powers in an effort to understand and overcome the "often tortuous" negotiations legacy of the past. Types and sources of information—open, such as the press; secret, such as foreign office reports—would be evaluated for perceived reliability. Negotiator views of opponents "as flexible individuals or as exponents of a fixed policy" (MIT Report, p. 20) would be analyzed for attention to nonverbal communication behaviors and underlying policy interests and publics.

The mediation subarea in the East-West conflict analysis was to be examined through non-Western interpretations of Communist and democratic news and propaganda. The research purpose was to study the influence of Asiatic ideologies and value systems on non-Western images of U.S. "intentions" (MIT Report, p. 20) in the East-West conflict. The development of "the kind of bilateral communication with the elites of Asiatic countries which will increase their understanding of our role in the East-West conflict" was to be studied in symbolic form in the structure of language and its relation to values" (MIT Report, p. 20).

The experiences of MIT field teams, at the time studying these issues in Indonesia and Central Java, were cited as possible field study bases for the Ford Foundation project. The focus was to be on the patterns and channels of communication to the local community and the processes of mediation and opinion leadership. An important additional area was the role of religion and religious institutions (especially Islam) and the social and political structure in the community. An assessment of the impact of Western communication on the views of politically and socially influen-
ims was an important research objective.

arianism and communication was the proposed long-range topic
ast-West conflict analysis. An assumption of the proposal was
itarian control placed "protracted pressures on communication"
port, p. 21). The proposal suggested examination of analogous
s as a means for studying the impact of dictatorship on commu-
behavior. Historical studies of communication behavior under
in "prison camps, rioting and martial law, and persecutions," were
analogous contexts:

The key question, however, is what happens through time? The impact of controls is a gradual one. What happens to men under continued isolation, intimidation, and hopelessness? What happens with continuous repetition of a single theme? What happens when no relief is in prospect? (MIT Report, p. 22)

The above passage is the final entry in the sample projects section of the MIT center document. Its language is sermonlike; it communicates defensiveness, almost stridency, in its pro-Western orientation. Embedded cultural, political, and economic biases are difficult to overcome. A long-range study of totalitarianism and communication must, therefore, be a cautious undertaking.

In the operational section, the MIT committee addressed this issue: "The committee has discussed this subject at some length. It believes that the future program should assume from the start a well-considered position on its relations to public policy and political issues" (MIT Report, p. 23). Recommendations based on simple conclusions were to be avoided. A desire for "forcefulness in the presentations of findings" was not to be allowed to cause the program to

forfeit in these circumstances its chance of studying political life from the vantage point of an observer who is not committed to any of the prevailing practices of changing that life. Preoccupied with the efficiency of prevailing practices, the program might neglect the study of alternative means; or preoccupied with the search for alternative means, it might neglect the consideration of alternative means. (MIT Report, p. 24)

Research topics and locations were to be based on functional (political and scientific) rather than geographical criteria. These included the following:

- The presence and availability of critical data to test the hypothesis under investigation
- The political importance of the country in world development
- The availability of social science literature on the country
- The availability of the necessary area specialists and persons with relevant skills
- The qualifications of research personnel residing in the country
- The presence of parallel studies with which costs can be shared and from which reinforcing insights can be obtained
- The cost of operation in the country

Despite the document's disclaimer, geographic criteria were of underlying research importance:

> Insofar as the program chooses to study communications aiming at unification of the free world and also on communications barriers to such unification, the program will undoubtedly wish to conduct some of its work in Western Europe, especially in France, Western Germany, and the Benelux countries. (MIT Report, p. 30)

This same reasoning was used in the report to justify work in underdeveloped areas for the study of "problems arising from the rise of new nationalisms" and "problems of communication to illiterate populations" (MIT Report, p. 30). Similarly, the study of Communist and totalitarian communication techniques would necessitate examination of the "communication within, to, and from Iron Curtain countries, perhaps using Berlin as an observation post" (MIT Report, p. 30). This reasoning also was consistent with the program's stated goal:

> We have stressed the importance of viewing international communication within the context of the international balance of power and as a part of world political processes; the importance of maintaining historical perspective and gaining historical depth; the value of experimental studies; and the desirability of field studies. (MIT Report, p. 32)

The document also referred, almost as an aside, to literature, works of art, motion pictures, novels, and linguistic studies as important aspects of international communication worthy of inclusion as potential research areas. The committee, however, did not develop these themes beyond the mere reference.

The MIT center proposal concluded with an assessment of "the present opportunity" for "exceptional achievement" and "to improve the existing body of knowledge about international communication" (MIT Report, p. 37). The beneficiaries would be statesmen and private individuals seeking guidance on technical matters. To maximize this opportunity for shared knowledge,

> It will be essential to bring into continual research association a group of specialists who have at their command the findings and methods of research upon communication. The present opportunity is to build up a program capable of contributing to a new and neglected frame of reference that cuts across

the established fields recognized in research, teaching and policy. (MIT Report, p. 37)

In sum, the MIT project underlined the interconnections of politics and communications. This connection began to attract the attention of historians and social scientists concerned with diplomacy, politics, law, military, and general social change since the end of World War I, when the study of propaganda became a field of its own. In the periods following both World War I and World War II, the paramount questions for the U.S. researchers were these:

1. To what extent do changes in the structure of world politics interact with changes in the structure of world communication?
2. To what extent does the making of foreign policy by each national participant in world politics interact with the communication process?
3. What are the strategies and tactics of communication in achieving the aims of national policy in world affairs?

The message reflected the times; the scholarly and political importance of international communication to international relations was becoming evident in the early 1950s; the magnitude of the Ford Foundation grant to MIT confirmed the increasing status of international communication. Professional endorsement of the field as a separate discipline of study, however, would require an additional 20 years.

Follow-Up to MIT Project: Political Communication Research

It took no more than a few years for the MIT researchers and their colleagues elsewhere in the United States, such as at Columbia, Chicago, and Harvard, to produce some of the early international communication research that was either designed or inspired by the MIT project. A good sample of the MIT-inspired type of research is illustrated in the special issue of *Public Opinion Quarterly* (*POQ*) (Bredemeier, 1956) that addresses political communication.

This special issue had a multiple origin. It was in part a summation, at the 2-year mark, of the pioneering international communication research program of the MIT Center for International Studies, sponsored by a $825,000 grant in 1952 from the Ford Foundation. The articles by Lewis Anthony Dexter; Frank Bonilla; Ithiel De Sola Pool, Suzanne Keller, and

Raymond A. Bauer; Harold R. Isaacs; Daniel Lerner; Claire Zimmerman and Raymond A. Bauer; and Y. B. Damle are products of the MIT program. In addition, the issue served as a forum, reflecting the increasing focus in the late 1950s on the study of international communication as political behavior by other prominent social scientists, such as David Riesman, Karl W. Deutsch, Hideya Kumata, Wilbur Schramm, Lucian Pye, W. Phillips Davison, and Alexander L. George. The work of these scholars played an important role in the expansion of international communication literature in the 1950s and 1960s and the categorization of international communication research of the time: "This issue provides a test of how much responsible empirical work is being done along with the current vigorous discussions of methodology and programmatics. The almost overwhelming response by authors is indeed a gratifying sign" (Bredemeier, p. 2). This statement was made by the guest editors of the journal—Ithiel de Sola Pool, who served as 1952-1953 secretary of the MIT project proposal committee, and Frank Bonilla, research contributor to the MIT program.

The *POQ* advisory board contained a rich complement of eminent social scientists of the period: Bernard Berelson, Jerome S. Bruner, Leonard Cottrell, Archibald M. Crossley, W. Phillips Davidson, Herbert Hyman, Harold D. Lasswell, Paul F. Lazarsfeld, Wilbur Schramm, Philip Selznick, Samuel Stouffer, Robert Strunsky, Paul Trescott, David Truman, and Elmo C. Wilson. The legitimization of international communication as a field of research in 20th-century international relations was their central concern. The editorial division of the journal contents into five major categories indicated the areas of international relations considered important in that day: (a) Communication to the Policy-Maker: Petition and Pressure; (b) International Communication: The Media and Flows; (c) Images, Definitions, and Audience Reactions in International Communication; (d) Communications and Politics in Pre-Industrial Regions; and (e) Communication in the Global Conflict. The sense of excitement that comes with the opening of a new frontier of intellectual development can be detected not only in the editorial prefaces to each of these sections but also in the tone of the articles themselves.

Communication to the Policy-Maker

Articles by Dexter, Bonilla, and Riesman were among those included in this section examining persuasive communication at the policy level. Dexter and Bonilla's work was sponsored by the MIT Center for International Studies, and Riesman's by the Foundations' Fund for Research in

Psychiatry. Their research springs from the augmented definition contained in the MIT Planning Committee Advisory Report that "words, acts, or attitudes" as well as technology may be called "international communication . . . that by design or by accident they impinge upon the minds of private individuals, officials or groups from other countries" (MIT Report, p. 2). Dexter and Bonilla's interest was the communication effect of constituency mail on congressmen and women, particularly that of American businesses and institutions. Riesman examined the influence of exposure to education, work, and travel on attitudinal openness or tolerance of political elites.

In his study, "What Do Congressman Hear: The Mail," Dexter indicated that the institutional setting in which letters flow to members of Congress shapes the message these letters convey and that on the whole the mail is considered civically important. Using reactions to the 1953 Reciprocal Trade Act, Dexter found that a large proportion of the mail is organized and sent by a few sources urging protection for particular industries. Given industries tend to have their own recognizable communication characteristics. Reflecting a lack of understanding of the elaborate and technical nature of congressional procedures, most letters recommend things that members of Congress cannot do, or the message is unclear as to what is being recommended. Because business persons and their representatives respond to the news, their response often comes too late, when a bill is already out of committee and difficult to amend.

Frank Bonilla, in "When Is Petition 'Pressure?'," sharpened Dexter's analysis by comparing the viewpoints of legislators with the main interest group in communication with them (business persons). Bonilla compared viewpoints regarding the substance of the issues at stake, the principal motives of the contenders, and the values appropriate to the issue. Like Dexter, Bonilla used reactions to the Reciprocal Trade Act tariff. Bonilla's findings supported the contention that appeals from the business community for intervention on tariff problems are experienced by members of Congress as legitimate demands from constituents rather than as efforts to exert pressure. Reciprocally, business persons are inclined to feel that legislators are quite responsive to demands from the business community: "For this group of legislators, then, communications on the tariff issue that came from industry were found less offensive than appeals from other groups and were rarely perceived as attempts at 'pressure' " (Bredemeier, p. 46). This is because the two parties share similar views regarding the fundamental issues at stake and principal motives on both sides.

Riesman's article, "Orbits of Tolerance, Interviewers, and Elites," contributed to the reintroduction of considerations of social structure into communication and public opinion research, a process giving "new vitality and new relevance for the study of public policy" (Bredemeier, p. 49). Riesman examined the communication of interviewers with elite members and the interviewing process itself as a form of social rhetoric. Riesman found the social rhetoric of the interview process to be facilitated by the existence of an interviewer/respondent subcultural shorthand.

Although he was not part of the MIT group, Riesman's work contributed to the MIT center's research concern "with identifying the influentials, tracing their patterns of communication, and plotting their community centered versus cosmopolitan identifications and contacts" (Bredemeier, p. 49). His focus was on the variables, such as education, work, and travel, that form an ecology of tolerance among political elites for political and cultural dissent. His underlying assumption was that the existence of these variables dictates a division between a tolerant elite and an intolerant majority: "On every issue where orbits of experience matter, education (whatever may be bound up with it as an index: social class, energy, exposure to diverse or proper views, etc.) is crucial" (Bredemeier, p. 52). Riesman described an interesting antitheoretical convergence in public opinion between the educated elite and popular (less educated) opinion:

> Since World War II, the lower classes' perennial distrust of Russia (as of other foreigners) has grown somewhat, but the educated classes, less immune to the news and its interpretation, have moved much more—from relative friendliness to a position much closer to that of the uneducated. (Bredemeier, p. 53)

An important conclusion for international communication can be drawn from this research finding: Without increased cultural understanding accompanying increased education, intercultural exposure may worsen rather than improve international relations between and among nations.

Riesman's lengthy analysis of "the greater political intolerance of women" was an interesting depiction of the schizophrenic attitude about the position of women in communication research of the 1950s. The tone was one of not knowing exactly how to pigeonhole women, because they do not respond on the same indices as men. Consequently, women are viewed as behaviorally deviant. For example, women are termed "mood-engineers" (Bredemeier, p. 58) rather than decision makers in the family because of their cooperative, consensus-oriented communication style in settling disagreements. "Suspicious" and "presumptive" political intolerance was assumed from the fact that the housewives in the study generally preferred to bring their husbands to the telephone to answer political survey questions. It also was considered remarkable (therefore evidence of political intolerance) that working women preferred to discuss domestic concerns rather than politics at their place of work:

> I would suggest that this finding be interpreted in terms of the only partial widening of orbits that work brings to the average woman in factory and office. She is ordinarily at work not because of an occupational commitment but because of a domestic one, or waiting for one: The job is a way of filling and refilling the hope chest, and the woman's eye is on a home freezer or the costs of a baby rather than on rising in a career or through a union-powered escalator for the group. (Bredemeier, p. 61)

Riesman's assumption undoubtedly was true for some women in the above social and economic grouping, but he failed to qualify his statements by identifying the problem as rooted in the organizational power structure rather than in some feminine failing. He was much closer to an objective, although condescending, research index of the problem when he said, "Undoubtedly, for women to take their work and the big political world more seriously, and thus expand their orbits, men will have to fear and patronize them less" (Bredemeier, p. 63). Certainly, it can be said that communication literature of the 1990s demonstrates greater balance in gender research. International communication, however, in its relative newness, provides areas for much needed further study of the role of women in all aspects of international affairs.

Riesman forecast a dichotomy in the future international communication environment. The "expanding orbits of tolerance and acculturation" fostered by the prosperous and mobile American social structure will forever be accompanied by "nativist" reactions—"back to the home, the parish, the region, the ethnic group, and the nation" (Bredemeier, p. 73).

International Media Flows

Two research contributions in this category were of particular importance, "Shifts in the Balance of Communication Flows: A Problem of Measurement in International Relations," by Karl W. Deutsch, and "The Influence of Foreign Travel on Political Attitudes of American Businessmen," by Ithiel de Sola Pool, Suzanne Keller, and Raymond A. Bauer.

Deutsch's research rejected the notion that there is a positive correlation between the growth occurring in international communication research and growth in the types of international communication. Deutsch showed, through statistical studies of intrastate, intranation, and international flows of mail, "that the world in many respects has moved towards a less integrated, rather than a more integrated, communication net" (Bredemeier, p. 143). He revealed that different media of communication have varying chronologies of maximum integration and that statistics of communication flows thus constitute essential background data for almost any effective analysis of international communication (Bredemeier, p. 154). Deutsch asserted that quantitative measurements of relative proportions, often considered statistically difficult in international communication research, can and must be made.

Dimensions such as volume (per unit of time or as a proportion of some total volume of messages), speed and fidelity of transmission, and distribution of initiatives of senders and responses of receivers are all terms of measurable quantities according to Deutsch. He selected volume (frequency) of communication as "the first dimension of international and domestic communication flows that is likely to be measured with any degree of success" (Bredemeier, p. 145). Deutsch developed statistics for local-nonlocal, domestic-foreign, instate-interstate, or intranation-international flows of communication. Deutsch illustrated how research on the measurement of international communication flows can give a better understanding of some aspects of the integration and consolidation as well as the autonomy and relative self-sufficiency of communities, countries, or other kinds of organizations.

Pool, Keller, and Bauer focused on foreign travel alone as a measurable international communication index, documenting the tremendous growth of travel by American business persons and evaluating its impact on political attitude. Pool et al. found that American business persons made use of two main sources for foreign information—the American mass media coverage of foreign news and their own foreign travel experience. Extensive foreign travel (five or more trips within the previous 5 years) counteracted self-interest, leading to a convergence among different points of view and a resemblance among those who travel.

Extensive travel, however, did not generate a more liberal attitude toward foreign trade. Interestingly, a convergence occurred in which protectionists became less protectionist and liberal traders less liberally extreme (Bredemeier, p. 165). Pool et al. also discovered contrary effects between large and small amounts of travel. "One trip provides ammunition for one's previous views. Time and more experience may shake them" (Bredemeier, p. 167). This finding tended to support the cross-cultural training experience that intercultural contact without acculturation reinforces stereotypical and attributive thinking.

Image and Audience Reactions

Articles by Isaacs, Lerner, Kumata and Schramm, and Zimmerman and Bauer—all products of the 1953 MIT center's international communication research program—addressed theoretically significant factors molding perceptions, images, and stereotypes in international communication.

In "Scratches on Our Minds," Isaacs examined the "vagueness about Asia" which "has been until now the natural condition even of the most educated American" (Bredemeier, p. 197). Isaacs asks what information, conceptions, images and notions, especially of China and India and their peoples, Americans have. The importance of such research, Isaac asserted, was beyond question:

All the world also knows by now that Asia, and particularly China and India, have become formidable problems for American policy-makers and matters of deep feeling and sharp, angry controversy for large and important sections of the American press and public. (Bredemeier, p. 198)

Indeed, Isaac's concern reflected that of the MIT center's orientation in international communication research. The Ford Foundation's willingness to fund such studies underscored the forbidding hugeness of the Asian "issue" in the minds of American business persons and foreign policymakers in the early 1950s. For the layperson, "besides school, home, reading, the movies, church, there was, finally, the discovery of Asia through the impact of events as reported in the press, the newsreels, and by radio" (Bredemeier, p. 204).

Isaac's results indicated that recall of events that forced Asia on American attention was to a high degree relative to age. Older respondents located their first serious awareness of events in Asia in the period of Japan's invasions of China, beginning in 1931. The second group clustered its Asian awareness around the Japanese invasion of Pearl Harbor. Using opinion polls from the period, Isaac determined that between 1937 and 1941, "the initial isolationist majority and interventionist minority changed places in an irreversible transformation of the country's outlook on the world. . . . Asia has come to assume wholly new proportions and significance" (Bredemeier, n 2u5). In a sense, Americans experienced culture shock:

> For some this meant not only the sudden discovery of the hitherto unknown half of the world, but being plunged personally into its midst, into new jobs in strange settings, changing their careers, their preoccupations, their picture of themselves and of their world. For the rest, the swift rush of events in this decade has brought with it confusion, bewilderment, and anger, new and inescapable problems and dangers in a vast part of the globe they could no longer ignore, as much as they might wish to do so. (Bredemeier, p. 205)

In "French Business Leaders Look at EDC: A Preliminary Report," Lerner, using 1,500 interviews and four sets of mail questionnaires among the business leaders of France, sought explanations for the defeat of the European Defense Community (EDC) in France. Lerner's hypothesis was that the EDC sought to pool arms and armies when the world seemed headed toward peace. The profound fear of war, an ever-present French attitude configuration, and surprising moderation of French attitudes toward Germany indicated "the strong inroads which Neutralism has made among the business elite" (Bredemeier, p. 217). Lerner's research revealed that

> the French respondents are caught between the desire to avoid thinking about military power and the incompatible desire for military security. . . . They wish, in short, to counter the conviction that the world today is a dangerous place with the hope that it is becoming safer. (Bredemeier, p. 218)

This modern-sounding assessment of the movement toward pacifism, toward peace paradigms and conflict resolution evident in the communication research of the 1950s, has become part of the evolutionary process of international communication of the 1990s and beyond. Formal academic and governmental programs in conflict resolution have evolved to meet contemporary international pressures for peace research. In support of international communication research, Lerner found that broader perspectives through exposure to "the flow of thought and feeling abroad . . . inevitably include more alternatives of choice, hence more subtly formulated decisions" (Bredemeier, p. 221).

"A Pilot Study of Cross-Cultural Meaning," by Kumata and Schramm, was an exploratory investigation of the problem of meaning (meaningful judgments) cross-culturally. Using Osgood's semantic differential scale, Kumata and Schramm's results produced remarkable correspondence across cultures (American, Japanese, Korean) for concepts such as atomic warfare, communism, nationality, and leadership, suggesting the existence of "a pervasive frame of reference used by humans" (Bredemeier, p. 238). As a technique of communication research in studies of comparative cross-cultural meanings, the use of the semantic differential appeared "promising and hopeful" (Bredermeier, p. 238).

Zimmerman and Bauer's research, in "The Effect of an Audience Upon What Is Remembered," has far-reaching results for the evolutionary process of international communication as a field of study. The role of the audience is a central element in the communication process. Ithiel de Sola Pool and Jerome Bruner also contributed to Zimmerman and Bauer's research design for this study. It was hypothesized that an individual's synthesis of experiences abroad occurred when asked to furnish impressions or to give a speech back home. The audience, real or imagined, influences the individual's presentation, causing him to role-play to the point that "potential prospective audiences may be a significant factor in the way in which he perceives, organizes, and uses new information" (Bredemeier, p. 239).

It followed, and was borne out by Zimmerman and Bauer's research results using journalism students and student teachers, that when the arguments and the audience were incongruent, the speaker's loss of recall was greater. A predisposition toward "audience sensitivity" also was found to be a contending factor in increased loss of recall. Zimmerman and Bauer proposed that this communication effect could have important implications in the process whereby groups influence the attitudes and behavior of their members. As with that of Kumata and Schramm, Zimmerman and Bauer's research furthered the evolution of international communication as a field of research encompassing peace studies and the academic formalization of negotiation and conflict resolution. Concern for images, definitions, and audience reactions are central concerns in contemporary international communication research today.

Communications and Politics
in Pre-Industrial Regions

Pye and Damle contributed articles focusing on communication processes in non-Western societies, specifically the functional value of political information. Pye's interest in Asian, African, and Middle Eastern experiments with representative government "is a question of interest and concern to both the scholar and the policy-maker" (Bredemeier, p. 249). It was a centrally stated purpose of the MIT center's research program in international communication sponsored by the Ford Foundation.

Pye theorized that the general communication process performed a key function in structuring the political process. By considering the communication process common to non-Western societies, therefore, a forecast could be made regarding the prospects for representative government. This communication process involved content and structural means. Basic cleavages exist between urban/elite and village/mass levels. Although news of a dramatic event, such as Ghandi's death, may travel quickly and efficiently through a word-of-mouth process of communication, interpretations giving context to events are less efficiently communicated:

> However, the barrier of illiteracy is great and the frame of reference employed by newspapers in communicating to an urbanized audience is often one that is not meaningful to those in the village. . . . Barriers such as these make it difficult for the rural areas to advance their common interests forcefully and thus become a significant and constant element in the political process. (Bredemeier, p. 251)

Pye contended that the atomized, communal basis of politics eliminated "the clash of interests between city and country, commerce and agriculture, which have been such an important issue in the history of Western politics" (Bredemeier, p. 251). The non-Western communication network "encourages a blurring of what are generally thought of as 'political,' 'social,' and 'private' considerations" (Bredemeier, p. 252). The communication process serves a much broader function than just providing information; it defines a wide range of social relations. Relative social positions of status and personal, face-to-face relationships give significance to what is communicated. Zimmerman and Bauer's effect of audience study results also can be useful to Western communicologists and policymakers in understanding the highly associative, nonabstract communication process characteristic of the many non-American cultures throughout the world.

The expressive component of non-Western politics—characterized by ritual, ceremony, pomp, and display—mobilizes support from an undifferentiated and unstructured public and creates conditions favorable to the charismatic leader. "When seen in this light, many of the particular problems that beset the development of representative institutions in non-Western societies become more intelligible" (Bredemeier, p. 256). Pye hypothesized that in some cases, more efficient mass communication might serve only to strengthen existing communal tendencies by providing "revolutionaries" with more complete ideologies. A contemporary application of this hypothesis might be explored in research centering on the general structure or pattern of the communication process within the Islamic revolution.

In "Communication of Modern Ideas and Knowledge in Indian Villages," Damle analyzed the communication process Pye recommended by examining the content and structural organization inherent in the communication of modern ideas and knowledge into several Indian villages. Damle found that the pull of cities proved "tremendously disruptive of the (rural) system." Migration to and from urban areas generated information but little cultural change. "To bring about change the persons who desire it must enjoy social esteem. Communication is also conditioned by status" (Bredemeier, p. 263). It follows that without this understanding, external agencies inevitably are unable "to register any improvement in the life of a people by tinkering with the problem at a surface level" (Bredemeier, p. 264).

Damle concluded that it is not merely proximity to cities that facilitates communication of ideas and knowledge in Indian villages:

> The social structure also determines the qualitative and quantitative content of the communications that are assimilated. Information relevant to the needs and interests of the people (e.g., the Five Year Plan and changing attitudes toward caste) is more widespread than awareness of less functional matters such as foreign affairs. (Bredemeier, p. 267)

The recognition of the human dimension, so tentatively and cautiously expressed in the 1950s, has become integral to the research process in international communication of the 1990s.

Communication in the Global Conflict

A constant concern throughout the history of international communication since World War II has been the communication processes surrounding the Cold War. U.S.-Soviet relations were a central research concern funded by the Ford Foundation in 1952 at the MIT center and remained at the core of international relations research in the 1980s. Davison and George, although not directly associated with the MIT program, contributed important articles on the topic.

A member of the Social Science Division of The RAND Corporation, W. Phillips Davison examined the extent to which the behavior of victims to intense Communist pressure was conditioned by their awareness of an imaginary supporting but distant audience. Using the Berlin blockade of 1948-1949, Davison explored the influence of Western mass media recognition on the opinions and behaviors of the German victims of the blockade. Davison's results revealed that mass communication played a very minor role in the formation of political attitudes during the blockaded period. "The anticommunist attitudes of the Berliners would have remained strong even in the absence of the press and radio" (Bredemeier, p. 330). The Allied airlift operation was the most important means of providing reassurance to the hard-pressed Berliners.

The mass media, however, performed a number of other functions of great political significance. An important one, as a channel for recognition of "the embattled community" (Bredemeier, p. 331), was found to be a bolstering factor in Berliners' morale. There was a dramatically increased intensity of listening to the radio and reading the newspapers from non-communist sources:

> This attention and recognition constituted one important actor making for resistance, and it was one in which the mass media played a highly significant role. The press and radio, in effect, brought about a state of affairs in which Berliners were concerned with what people elsewhere thought about their behavior. They experienced gratification at the praise they received, and they tended to act in such a way as to maintain this gratification. (Bredemeier p. 332)

Davison's findings emphasized the importance of the human, interpersonal dimension of international communication by illustrating the powerful (military resistance) "need of the individual for recognition and response, and the lengths to which the individual will go to preserve his good name in the community" (Bredemeier, p. 332). This human communication need has important political significance.

In "Prediction of Political Action By Means of Propaganda Analysis," Alexander George examined the relationship of communication and action in the relations between nations. Using content characteristics and propaganda strategies pursued by the Nazis, George traced the "inference method" used by the Federal Communications Commission in interpreting Nazi elite propaganda. U.S. political/military decisions were based on interpretations of intended actions inferred from Nazi propaganda communications. Types of actions, audiences, goals, channels, and context the communication components considered. The successful predictive value at the policy level of propaganda analysis positions this type of communication research as a central concern in international relations. Thus, the 1956 *Public Opinion Quarterly* as a document previewed important vectors in the history of international communication as a academic field. The research program of the MIT center for International Studies, sponsored by the Ford Foundation, was complemented by the work of other prominent social scientists of the period. This research formed a foundation on which international communication has grown into an invaluable field of study in contemporary international relations.

First-Generation
Communication Researchers

The early researchers and schools of international communication, such as those at MIT and elsewhere, came from political science, psychology, sociology, anthropology, and other behavioral sciences. A new stream of scholars, however, interested equally in international communication, was being groomed in the schools of communication and journalism across the United States. These scholars, whose training was mainly in media studies, were the first generation of communication researchers independently pursuing the study of global communication outside the mainstream disciplines of social sciences. As history has related, the research and teaching philosophies of the early journalism and communication schools in the United States, however, were fairly conservative in outlook. In the 1950s and 1960s, the leading journalism and communication departments in the country were those of the Big Ten and traditional midwestern universities such as Missouri, Northwestern, Iowa, Michigan State, Minnesota, and Wisconsin.

Influenced by the tone and themes set by such groups as MIT and other postwar social scientists, the communication and journalism teachers of the 1950s and 1960s tailored their early international communication courses more or less on the ideas, research, models, and ideologies of the mainstream American social sciences. Although there were a few liberals among them, the contributions of American communication and journalism teachers to the study of international communication were mainly in the areas of international and comparative media studies.

It was the establishment of the International Communication Division of the Association for Education in Journalism (AEJ)—later renamed the Association for Education in Journalism and Mass Communication

(AEJMC)—that was to a large degree responsible for the organization of the first symposium on international communication in the United States. The "Wingspread Symposium on Education and Research in International Communication," held in Racine, Wisconsin, in March 1969, was sponsored by the International Communications Division of the Association for Education in Journalism in cooperation with the Johnson Foundation. The publication in 1970 of the reports and papers from this symposium, edited by James W. Markham, was a major document in the growth of international communication as a field of inquiry since World War II. The Markham volume built on the precedents set by the MIT center's 1952 advisory report and the 1956 special issue of *Public Opinion Quarterly*, which showed the trend of research by political scientists. The papers and reports included in the Markham volume indicated the interest and activities of mass communication and journalism scholars in international communication, particularly in training, curriculum building, and research.

The volume, titled *International Communication as a Field of Study,* was divided into five parts, with 22 contributors. Topic areas included graduate and professional education, curriculum for comparative and international communication studies, critiques of theory and application, and general conclusions. The symposium focused on the need to internationalize professional journalism and communication school curricula. It also examined the need to integrate international and comparative communication perspectives into the professional education of every future American journalist-communicator. This group included the communication teacher, researcher, and specialist (Markham, 1969, p. 3).

It was felt that the study of American methods and systems alone no longer prepared professional educators and communicators to meet the new international demands of their professions. New professional education was needed for work abroad as well as at home in today's world. The important composite statement made by the Markham volume about the growth of international communication as a field of inquiry was that political scientists and professional educators-communicators together "have come to realize that domestic and international matters are inextricably linked in the modern world" (Markham, p. 4).

Part I of the Markham document spelled out present and future professional demands in the field for those engaged in the task of reconstructing the education of future specialists. From a governmental perspective, the need was for versatile communication generalists versed in multimedia channels. Education for foreign correspondents stressed developing "understanding, interpreting, and communicating world affairs issues in a comparative cultural context" (Markham, p. 6). Ideal characteristics included university liberal arts graduates with social and behavioral science experience. Communication arts, especially speaking and writing "with grace and fluidity," were considered essential. Also important was the knowledge of American studies, packaged with a working ability in a foreign language, written and broadcast journalism, film, and cultural relations.

As expressed in Part I of the Markham document, the goal was, through the reconstructed education of international communicators, to produce professionals with both a broad background knowledge and understanding of public, national, and international affairs. Markham stated,

> This means a knowledge of how communication works, its relation to society and the political process, its role in life and behavior, its theories and research methods . . . a quest for understanding and the basis for self-discovery, rather than solely the transmission and reception of symbolic stimuli. (Markham, p. 9)

Markham summarized Part I by translating this ideal, all-inclusive "Renaissance man" definition of international communication into the need for courses in comparative, cross-cultural, and international communication along with basic training in mass communication skills and techniques.

Part II focused on internationalizing professional communication curricula. In this category, international communication as well as comparative and cross-cultural communication as fields of inquiry demand definition and delimitation. In addition, the question of how to effectively introduce an international outlook and world perspective into undergraduate education was of critical concern. The need recognized in this section of the Markham volume was to view international communication as a new field of study distinguishable from a combination of disparate fields of study. This distinction required careful definition of the content and boundaries of the combined fields and a general redefinition and reorganization. Arpan stated, "This is important because of the great urgency I find everywhere I go in the world for international communications knowledge and training. It is an exciting challenge to provide expertise and leadership" (Markham, p. 64).

Arpan's comment capsulized the attitudes among mass communication and journalism scholars of the late 1960s. Considerable agreement existed among them that the use of the problem approach, comparative case methods, simulation and gaming, area studies, information retrieval, faculty exchanges, student internships abroad, and involvement of foreign students on U.S. campuses can augment the goal of internationalizing communication programs. There is acknowledgment that inadequate account was taken of "the potential explosive force resulting from the enormous technological development and spread of communications around the world" (Markham, p. 65). Markham, in speaking for his contemporaries, commented, "Perhaps because we are so much a part of it, we took it for granted" (Markham, p. 65).

Markham's comment was ageless in its appeal. Scholars and practitioners of all periods have had the benefit of hindsight such as his. Part III of the volume addressed graduate studies in international and comparative communication. A high degree of specialization within the social, political, and cultural context is characteristic of current international and comparative communication studies. "Probably the most frequently expressed common need felt by symposium members was for a more solid theoretical and conceptual base, for all levels of education and research" (Markham, p. 102). Markham noted the prevalent belief among many of his colleagues that the deplorable "absence of theory" will be remedied without effort, solving all problems for international communication as a growing field of inquiry.

In Part IV, "Research Problems: The Need for Unified Theory, Practical Application," Markham et al. recognized "the need to develop a body of theory with a testable set of propositions which would help to conceptualize and explain the process of international communication" (Markham, p. 128). First, there was an outline of the process order in which the present state of empirical knowledge in the field must be documented. Second, research programs or projects must be developed where theoretical formulations appear lacking. Communication factors in the international system considered important included public and elite opinion; the relation of information levels to public opinion; the impact of international or cultural images and values on international negotiation, policy, and decision; and the relation of communication to image formation and change.

It was suggested that a bibliographic and data collection center be established under the auspices of the International Division of the Association for Education in Journalism. Another recommendation was for the founding of a research journal.

The summary provided in Part V capsulized the Symposium issue areas stated above. Six recommendations were officially adopted:

1. An international communication simulation program was to be investigated and documented.
2. Ways of increasing the foreign experience of students and faculty were to be studied.
3. Short-term exchanges of international communication faculty and students between American universities were to be arranged.
4. A central computerized bibliographical service and data bank was to be established.
5. International communication honors courses and independent study projects were to be encouraged.
6. Cooperation between AEJ's Division of International Communication and the U.S. Information Agency (USIA) was urged to encourage the sharing of mutually beneficial nation-by-nation compilations and the distribution of declassified documents and reports. (Markham, p. 128)

Edelstein stated, "One of the major purposes of this conference was to develop standards for teaching, research, and practice to help guide our field" (Markham, p. 148). Edelstein discussed the "potential for unity amid the seemingly irreconcilable elements of international communication" (Markham, p. 149). Achievement of this unity required scientists and journalists to become more interdisciplinary, and international communication seemed to provide this channel. There was a great need expressed by conference members for "qualified, culturally adaptive teachers of international communication" (Markham, p. 150). The problems of data gathering, storage, and retrieval underscored the necessity of cooperative data sharing with USIA and other governmental agencies. Intercultural and comparative communication studies must be incorporated into international communication curricula. "To be a communication scholar of any 'global location,' one should have an awareness of communication in other cultures" (Markham, p. 152).

The Markham volume recognized the growth of international communication. It also documented the interests and activities of mass communication and journalism scholars of the late 1960s in their important contributions toward defining and refining international communication as a field of inquiry.

Formalization of International Communication Studies

A few years after the publication of the Markham volume, two leading American social science organizations, the American Political Science

Association and the International Studies Association, incorporated international communication studies as part of their annual meetings and scientific conferences.

The American Political Science Association's Sixty-Sixth Annual Meeting in Los Angeles, in 1970, represented an attempt on the part of political scientists under Karl Deutsch to reassess the contribution of international political communication theory to the study of international relations. Headed by Richard L. Merritt, panels and volumes were produced that dealt with specific issues. Panelists included Harry G. Gelber, John D. Montgomery, Charles E. Osgood, Irene Tinker, Ton DeVos, Charles T. Goodsell, Robert J. Lieber, Hamid Mowlana, and Bryant Wedge. The Merritt volume was a collective attempt by these political scientists to bring economists and psychologists into the field. An earlier (1965) publication, edited by Herbert Kelman and sponsored by the Society for Psychological Study of Social Issues (*International Behavior: A Social and Psychological Analysis*), reflected a similar attempt by psychologists to bring political scientists into their field.

From a historical point of view, the Merritt volume represents an effort on the part of the political science community to revive interest once again in international communication. After almost 20 years of less-than-systematic research, Merritt and his colleagues were part of a new generation of scholars trying to apply what they learned from their mentors of the 1950s (MIT projects and the like). Of particular interest in the volume was the inclusion of contributions by a number of psychologists (Kelman and Szalay, for example) as well as, for the first time, critics of international political communication, such as Herbert Schiller.

Richard Merritt and Davis Bobrow's articles described international political communication as a field, giving it a broad framework for analysis. Merritt examined international political communication as a mechanism for the transmission of values across national boundaries. He reviewed the content and political aspects of international communication and the types of communicators (government, nongovernment, cultures). He called for new research and synthesis and integration of existing results to move the field beyond isolated empirical findings and to encourage theory building. Bobrow's article ("Transfer of Meaning Across National Boundaries") showed the application as well as the limitation of international communication in the theories of social psychology. Bobrow claimed that the notions of mediated stimulus response, cognitive balance theory, and cybernetics used by social scientists had "only limited use for explaining the phenomena that interest us in international politics" (Merritt, 1972, p. 18).

Beyond the Cold War

The work of Merritt, Bobrow, and other APSA members contributed significantly to both the development of knowledge about meaning and value-transfer systems in the communication of international politics and the history of international communication as a field of research. The work of these and other pioneers helped to overcome the Cold War emphasis on negative, manipulative misinformation propaganda research and strategies that characterized international political communication of the period. The rise of imperialist powers at "the center"—Germany, France, Britain, the Soviet Union, and especially the United States—with territories and markets to protect, boosted the status of communication as economic power. International communication became a means for carrying news across national boundaries as an instrument of persuasion and "modernization and development." International communication scholars who followed benefited from the contributions of Merritt and his cohorts such that by the late 1970s and early 1980s, the field began to distinguish itself from international relations. The rise of anti-imperialist forces of Third World nationalism and liberation, with accompanying ideologies challenging Western suppositions, served to elevate international communication to new levels of importance and respectability in the international community.

Hellman, Nordenstreng, and Varis in the early 1980s contributed to the growth of the international communication field in Europe. In a conceptual work (Hellman, Nordenstreng, & Varis, 1980), they examined four historical traditions of international communication research and compiled a review of literature and themes that have dominated the different phases of development. In their analysis, the first *idealist* phase dates from the 1910s to World War II. In this phase, international communication research focused on increasing understanding among nations and peoples toward the attainment of world peace and integration. International communication in the form of propaganda was considered divisive. Establishment of the League of Nations and the United Nations ranked among the great achievements of this period.

In the Hellman analysis, the period during and immediately following World War II was the *aggressive* phase of international communication

development, in which scholars largely ignored the inherent ethical benefits of international communication as a phenomenon that lends itself
toward ensuring peace. Instead, the goal for the aggressive phase was to
search for measures to strengthen the political strategic effects of propaganda. This led to the elevation of public opinion measures and the
hardening of U.S. foreign policy around conflicts in national interests over
power, in what came to be called *realism*. In this realist phase, communication growth and development were skewed toward legitimizing the
success of state actions with regard to politically accepted goals.

Hellman described the 1950s as a period of "apology" for international
communication:

> The "new strategy" presented itself as a humanitarian development program,
> with the U.S. as its moving force supported by the prestige of the United
> Nations, but, in reality, it became an apology of the cold war and the
> westernization of developing nations. (Hellman et al., 1980, p. 6)

What followed has been a confrontation of the apologetic stage by a
critical phase, spearheaded by communicologists who were critical of
cultural or media imperialism. Acceptance of the critical theory framework of communication research has been limited in the United States,
largely due to the fact that critical literature in international communication has lacked general theoretical validation.

One important achievement of the critical phase of communication
research, however, has been that criticism has been directed at the total
communication structure, leading to an approach or framework that can
be called holistic or integrative. As a result, it is clear today that international communication as an integrative, multidisciplinary field of research
and inquiry bridges political, economic, technological, and cultural systems. The field now must produce the concepts, models, and methods
capable of explaining the complexity of identified contemporary issues,
thereby defining the relationship between the transnationalization of
communication and international affairs.

Note

1. For further elaboration on the relationship between U.S. centers of postwar communication research and government psychological warfare programs, see Simpson (1994).

2

Technology and Society

If the communications revolution and the explosion of information now are undeniable, their nature and causes are much less certain and, as a result, their consequences more profound. The present world order is not ordinary but extraordinary, and the crises of the post-Cold War era are not merely economic or political maladjustment. Instead, technology, information, and economic growth involve nearly the whole industrialized culture and society—both capitalist and socialist—in all their sectors. The point is that the fundamental form of industrialized culture and society dominant for the past four centuries is now in a stage of transition. What we are witnessing, in fact, may be one of the turning points in human history: where one fundamental form of culture and society—that of industrialized nations and their modes of communication and information—is declining, and a different form is emerging.

In the capitalist, and even socialist, West, it is a crisis of sensate culture and communication in search of a new form and new pattern. Compounding this crisis is the onslaught of ever-increasing new technological and digitary information systems that both amplify and contradict individual human needs and desires. In the less industrialized world, it is a confrontation between a collective sensate culture, economy, and policies and an old ideational and idealistic form of native culture. Even though the new informatics age is heralded as the latest technological achievement, capable of reducing conflict, poverty, and disintegration, some thoughtful consideration should be given to the ramifications of this achievement. This chapter, therefore, considers areas of planning for the future that could benefit a world now virtually inured to the constant assaults of the technological revolution in its best and worst forms.

National Systems and Policies: The Privacy of Information and "Information" Sovereignty

Developments in communication technology over the past two decades, such as satellites, computers, video, teletext, fax, and high-definition

39

television, have far exceeded the ability of both policymakers and the academic community to provide effective frameworks for such innovations. Traditional modes of telecommunications, such as telephony, telegraphy, radio, and cable, defined the limits of the comfort zone for policy formulation in the work of international organizations such as the International Telecommunication Union (ITU), now a century old. Issues of privacy of information, intellectual property rights, and national sovereignty have taken on new dimensions in the face of transborder data flow, satellite remote sensing, and direct broadcast satellite capabilities.

New notions of technology also differ from classic concepts of mass media, which today represent print media, radio, television, and cinema. Technological developments are forging new products with enormous potential for expansion into all aspects of daily life, with significant implications for international trade and economic markets. As developing nations examined the domestic impact of communication technologies such as radio and television, it became apparent that the concept of mass communications and mass media—openly welcomed as necessary components of "progressive" societies—were in fact inappropriate in many Third World nations.

It still has not been an easy process for Third World economies to relinquish the attempt to employ the mass media as a means of organizing their populations into Western-style mass societies. Only in the 1960s, when student revolutions and political upheaval revealed weaknesses in Western societies and their assumptions, did the developing world begin to not only see but also seek alternatives to mass development. Again, in the post-Cold War era of the 1990s, ethnic, religio-political, and regional crises would seem the epitome of this continuing process. Traditional channels of communication were revitalized as viable mechanisms capable of both offsetting and incorporating the effects of the most sophisticated telecommunications networks. The integration of modern communication technology with the mosque in Iran for the purposes of education, dissemination of religious teaching, and political mobilization is a cogent contemporary example.

The decline of conventional mass media in the 1960s and 1970s led to a rise of what might be called *class media*—specialized and individually tailored publications, radio stations, and movie houses. With the exception of possibly television, these media can no longer claim to reach vast portions of the populations, and in that sense the term *mass* no longer truly applies. New institutions have sprung up in the context of new technologies, making free use of equally new terms such as *informatics* (the convergence of computer and telecommunications technologies). One such institution, the Intergovernmental Bureau of Informatics (IBI), defines informatics as the rational and systematic application of information to economic, social, and political problems.

The need for coherent policy making in these areas, therefore, is a consequence of the development of this new field of information technology called informatics—a field driven by the rapid emergence of microelectronics technology in the form of microprocessors coupled with broad-band communications, fiber optics, and other advances. Issues of universal access, ownership, control, and distribution work against a background of financial, labor, and infrastructural limitations, contributing to the formation of development gaps between information haves and have nots. National informatics policy, as outlined by the IBI, contains a number of principal recommendations, much akin to those expounded in the New World Information and Communication Order (NWICO) debates as well as the MacBride Report.[1] It was recommended that informatics be considered in the formulation of strategies and policies for national development, with the designation of special informatics authorities and agencies to coordinate their effects. A renewed emphasis was placed on education and training programs to update workforce capability for utilizing the latest technology. Regional and international cooperation and interaction were stressed, as was the development of policies for appropriate use of computer and telecommunications systems and services.

Technological Applications

The development of policies in the domain of privacy of information and national sovereignty has been tested in such new technological areas as transborder data flow, satellite remote sensing, and direct broadcast satellites.

Transborder Data Flow. The increasing role of data communication in information-intensive industries, such as transnational banking, insurance, airlines, multinational corporations, and international news agencies, is premised on the merger of computer and telecommunications technologies in the form of transborder data flow (TDF). The computerized supply of financial and commercial information has become a major and growing source of profit. As a result, many nations have become concerned about growing international networks of computers facilitating the storage, transmission, manipulation, and retrieval of information both in support of and potentially in conflict with national interests. From the perspective of personal privacy to national sovereignty, information now is viewed as a commodity or strategic resource worthy of control. As a consequence, major participants in the flow of data across national boundaries are nation-states, intergovernmental and nongovernment organizations such as private communications carriers, data processing service bureaus, multinational corporations, and transnational associations. Conflicting interests on the costs and benefits, promotion, and restriction of the flow of information are what is making it so difficult to achieve widespread policy agreement on the management of transborder data flow.

The process of information-intensive production, storage, retrieval, and distribution of data is virtually the same for all entities. These include national communication services such as post, telegraph, and telephone (PTT), intergovernmental organizations such as the International Telecommunications Union (ITU), international organizations such as communications satellites consortiums (International Telecommunications Satellite Organizations/INTELSAT), and private communications carriers such as academic networks, data processing firms, AT&T, or Western Union International. Issues of legal compliance, directionality of flow, openness, disclosure, fairness, and accountability are only a few of many areas now requiring policy and regulatory review in the interests of preserving personal privacy of information. There is a propensity, for example, for uneven distribution of computer communication technologies among nations. The limited data processing capacity available in "computer poor" countries, many located in the Third World, makes it necessary for them to export raw data for processing and to reimport the processed data, exacerbating dependency relationships with the industrialized world. A unique information services reversal is also taking place where data processing labor is more cheaply available in low-wage societies. A major U.S. airline, for example, funnels all of its ticket receipts to the Caribbean for hand processing onto a computer database.

The question of national sovereignty arises when vital information affecting national decision making is processed and stored in foreign databases. Fears of vulnerability now extend beyond military security to economic and information security, causing many nation-states to favor more pronounced restriction and regulation of transborder data flows. In other words, one of the most significant impacts of computer communication technology on national sovereignty is the transformation of the concept of sovereignty, as expressed in geographical terms, to information sovereignty. As the role of information in management expands, it is recognized increasingly as a resource over which a nation-state must exercise control. This is leading to the growing belief that information is a commodity that should be taxed and regulated as it crosses national boundaries.

Satellite Remote Sensing. A particularly sensitive issue in the area of information technology is the relationship between satellite remote sensing and national security and national sovereignty. The term *remote sensing* refers not only to conventional aerial photography operations but also to sophisticated satellite sensing operations performed by organizations such as the U.S. Landsat system. These satellites have the ability to sense and photograph nations from a sun-synchronous orbit of 705 km without the knowledge or permission of the nations being sensed. The U.S. space shuttle system also carries remote sensing capability. Enormous amounts of beneficial information can be produced concerning natural resource management, land use analysis, water quality studies, disaster relief, crop predictions, and protection of the environment. For example, the government of Burkina Faso, working with the World Bank, is using Landsat data to identify areas that can support nomadic tribesmen migrating southward because of drought conditions. As revealed in the recent Persian Gulf war, however, remote sensing also can reveal strategic military information regarding troop movement and armament locations. Not surprisingly, such a technological innovation generates debate and concern regarding regulation and access to information.

The United States traditionally has advocated a policy of open skies and free dissemination of information. In other words, space systems of any nation are national property and have the right of passage through space without interference. The U.S. position on remote sensing advocates free dissemination of the information. There is a dilemma for developing nations, because the high cost of access to the information determines a nation's ability to participate freely in data use. The economic and political implications of the knowledge acquired by remote sensing are obvious. The ability to predict agricultural failures and food dependencies, for instance, can influence political judgments and international market bids. There is also a move toward privatization of remote sensing operations. This leaves unresolved at national, international, and global levels the all-pervasive problem regarding the continual lag of social institutions behind technological progress.

Direct Broadcasting by Satellite. Another area of technological advancement that is posing difficulty in the management of privacy of information and national sovereignty issues is direct broadcasting by satellite (DBS). At issue is a new technique that relays satellite telecasts directly to residences without going through ground receiving stations. Soon, technology may be inexpensive enough for such broadcasts to reach mass audiences around the world. DBS technology is generating debate in the world community over the issue that unregulated DBS poses serious threats to national sovereignty. Between 1975 and 1979, for example, the price for a single commercial receiving station dropped dramatically from $125,000 to less than $4,000. Specifically, these perceived threats fall in the categories of propaganda, commercial domination, and cultural intrusion.

National sovereignty issues relative to DBS center on the major problem of orbital or spectrum spacing. Physically, there is ample space in the synchronous orbit for a large number of satellites. There is, however, a limitation on the proximity of their orbits. As a result of the increased number of communication satellites, a problem related to orbital spacing is *band capacity.* In addition, there is intense competition for orbital spacing over industrialized and newly industrializing regions of the world.

An additional major technological problem regarding DBS is *spillover.* This problem arises when the transmission signal overextends or crosses the boundaries of one country into another. This causes numerous legal, social, and political problems. One area that illustrates this well is the ever-increasing needs for regional and local television programs. Many nations fear that direct broadcast satellite technology will result in unwanted reception of foreign programming, both intentional and unintentional. Underlying the question of intentional spillover is a widespread sense that the form and content of the television system in a country is an aspect of national sovereignty. As is the case with transborder data flow and satellite remote sensing, the traditional notions of sovereignty, previously expressed in geographic or spatial terms, are being redefined in terms of concerns about informational sovereignty. Directionality and balance of flow are additional concerns.

The evolution of the issue of direct broadcast satellites, therefore, illustrates changes in the nature of the debate on questions of international communication since 1970. These changes are, in essence, reflections of larger alterations in the international geopolitical structure. Examples include the United Nations system, the international economic order, and the way traditional identities of national interests evolve. From the beginning of the debate on DBS, many nations have hesitated to accept this new technology without some form of control over its application. The political values these countries attach to such concepts as cultural integrity and national identity have taken precedence over what the United States and several other major powers would consider more pragmatic values.

In this light, the assumption of the free flow of information across national boundaries as beneficial to all is a myth. Even the concepts of copyright and intellectual property rights are going through fundamental changes because of the ability of computers to write, revise, edit, and modify programs and texts without generating paper copies. International agendas increasingly include the development and implementation of international agreements regarding the current status and future directions of information technologies and their applications. These topics have become recurrent themes of such entities as the General Agreement on Tariffs and Trade (GATT), the United Nations, and national ministries of trade and telecommunications.

New forms of information flow, such as transborder data flow, satellite remote sensing, or direct broadcast satellite, raise a wide range of issues to be explored. As the rapid development of new technologies continues to change traditional economic and political perceptions, fundamental changes in the structure of global communication must be expected. A workable remedy demands a fundamental transformation and change in our level of conceptualization of communication and information flow. This change, no matter how technological its channel, must be toward an integrative whole.

Technology Versus Tradition in Old Societies

The post-World War II period has seen nationalism, anti-imperialism, and revolution in many parts of the world. Diverse nationalities are seeking self-determination and a new world order as militarily weak nations confront the major powers with increasing success. In response, the great powers have moved from territorial conquest to establishing, restoring, or maintaining governments that are politically reliable and compatible with their strategic, military, and economic interests. Paralleling this has been the development of new technology and weapon systems and the worldwide spread of modern communications. Foreign policymakers are proceeding cautiously in the face of new norms and institutions in the Third World and a sudden decline in distance favoring the rapid mobilization of power in different parts of the world. Internal and regional instability, a high level of transnational influence, and the frequent resorting to coups and other covert operations have encouraged a moralistic and intellectual approach to foreign policy. This is accompanied by an intense concern with communication and persuasion.

Evolution of Communication
Technologies: The Case of Islamic Society

Islamic society provides a good laboratory for examining the relationship of technology and society, because of its powerful emergence worldwide yet relative resistance or lack of exposure to modern information technologies. In the realm of information and communication, the Islamic culture and civilization over the past 14 centuries have been instrumental in the development of three major pillars of human communication:

1. A high level of oral communication and culture in which information was produced and transmitted on a person-to-person basis
2. An unprecedented degree of written and reproduced books and manuscripts that marked an intellectual era in human history and in all branches of knowledge, resulting in scientific, literary, artistic, and linguistic interaction
3. The first attempt in history to bring oral and written cultures into a unified framework of craftsmanship

These factors lay the groundwork for the scientific revolution that was to follow in Europe in such fields as medicine, astronomy, mathematics, chemistry, and a score of methodological and scientific works in history, demography, and sociology.

Oral Culture and Communication. The art of oral culture and communication in Islamic societies finds its best expression in the holy book, Quran, the *sunnah* (tradition), the *hadith* (a record of action and sayings of the Prophet and his *Ahl-ul-bait,* the family of the Prophet). The memorization of the Quran is a common information and communication act that has a long history in all Islamic societies and continues to be practiced widely in all Muslim countries, an inextricable link between oral and inscriptive modes of communication. Although the Quran is the main source from which Islamic practices and precepts are explained and deduced, the *sunnah* of the Prophet was taken from his deeds and judgments, drawn up and fixed in writing. *Sunna* is the standard of conduct along with the Quran. The word *hadith* means primarily sayings, a communication or narrative transmitted from the Prophet and his companions, *Ahl-ul-bait,* and the Imams. A *hadith* can only be credible when its *isnad* or documentation offers an unbroken series of reliable authorities in oral and written communication. Investigation and study of this whole body of communication is called *ilm-al-hadith,* or the science of transmission of the sayings of the Prophet and his companions. Thus, the Quran, the *sunnah,* and the *hadith* provided the main source of Islamic polity and the state in the form of *ummah* or community. During the later years of Islamic history, when the arts of bookmaking and reproduction of manuscripts were widely developed, the oral mode did not lose its significance. It remained an inseparable part of culture and communication in arts, literature, and poetry.

Print Culture. The invention of the Gutenberg press in the middle of the 15th century saw the birth of the print culture and a tremendous quantitative jump in the output of human information, leading eventually to the so-called electronic communication and information explosion centuries later. This was not exactly the case in the Islamic societies. The bimodal development of oral as well as inscriptive communication in Islamic lands was a sustained growth and was characterized by its qualitative, not quantitative, jumps.

As the Islamic world fell short in adopting the new means of technologies, due to political, economic, and social factors internally and externally, it also was left behind for hundreds of years in creating an infrastructure that would sustain the early acceleration in information and knowledge in the industrial era. Thus, a quantitative as well as qualitative gap developed between the West and the Islamic world.

The crisis in the West, on the other hand, was found not so much in the quantity of information but in the distribution of instruments of information processing as well as their availability in forms of knowledge for individual users in society. The process of industrialization, coupled with the rise of economic classes and the establishment of the nation-state system, elevated the print culture to a new frontier. Here, not only was the oral mode of communication an outcast, but a new division between information producers and knowledge producers was also drawn. Now the economic system treated information as any other commodity that could be processed, packaged, and sold in the form of cultural industries, and as an invisible import-export item in international finance, trade, and the transfer of technology.

Electronic Culture. With the development of electronic technology, and especially computers and other information auxiliaries, the West entered a new era in which the production and distribution of data became the central foci of society. The major characteristic of the so-called post-industrial or information revolution has been its ability to produce and distribute data—and not necessarily information and knowledge—in large quantities in modern societies.

It is as unrealistic to ascribe characteristics of a given society to developments of a single historical period of human civilization or individual technological innovation as it is to ignore that tradition entirely. Rather, one might conceive of the communication system of a given society as a hybrid born of multifarious scientific and technological as well as social traditions. This point is especially crucial if we consider other layers of human infrastructure in the form of culture, religion, government, and bureaucracy without which societal communication cannot take place.

Both capitalism and state-controlled socialism have created scores of information and knowledge producers, with the population remaining largely as consumers of and laborers in the packaged information processing industry. This has transformed the nature of the state and has created a new class of *datacratic intelligentsia* and information population with its own elite pyramid. It is precisely this new datacratic and information class that has transformed the traditional nature of civil society to datacratic society in the West. The new class is neither Kenneth Galbraith's powerful but benign "technocrats," nor Noam Chomsky's weak but maligned "servants of power." It also is not what Alvin Gouldner termed a "flawed universal class" as a cultural bourgeoisie of our time. Instead, these are the datacrats, the sources of power and weakness, development and decay, war and peace. In modern politics, these datacrats are both the rulers and the outcasts.

In the West, the print and electronic cultures helped to both concentrate power in the hands of a few and contribute to the centralization of the state apparatus. The oral mode of communication in Islamic societies helped to decentralize and diffuse the power of the state and also establish a counterbalance of authority in the hands of those who were grounded in oral tradition. The individuals maintained their ability to communicate within their own community and beyond, despite the influence of state propaganda and modern institutions. The resurgence of Islam and the political and revolutionary movements within the Islamic countries led by traditional authorities, such as the Ulama, are only one example of the potential use of oral culture and its confrontation with modernism inherent in mediated electronic cultures.

The nature of civil society was not only grounded in print and electronic culture but also synonymous with such modern concepts as secularism, the nation-state, nationalism, and modern European parliamentary democracy. The replication in Islamic society of civil society based on the European model was not an easy task. It had to confront the centuries-old notion of political and linguistic tradition so peculiar to Islam. The incompatibility not only was evident in the modes of communication and their prevalence in society but was also apparent and more pronounced in the concepts of community, the state, and politics and ethics. There was no demarcation between the polity and ethical concepts in Islam, and no differences between the temporal and the spiritual. The Islamic legal system had its own civil and state dimensions, which were at once interwoven and interrelated. The concept of the nation-state was alien to Islam, as were the notions of modern nationalism and state sovereignty.

Communication and
Tradition: The Case of Iran

A brief review of the Iranian Revolution of 1979 further underscores the differences in notions of nationalism and the state and highlights the importance of an appreciation of the total communication system in another culture. To limit the analysis of technology and mass communication to the conventional Western media models is to ignore traditional organizational and group channels peculiar to a region's culture, through which modern mass media messages are filtered. Islam, for example, is not a religion per se; it is a total view with an ideology and political economy. The battlefield of international politics has shifted from the geographical and the physical to the ideological, cultural, and informational level. The Iranian Revolution in general and the U.S.-Iranian crisis in particular embody the latter type of conflict and, with communication as the new ingredient, foreshadowed conflicts yet to come. Various aspects of the connections between communication and technology and political change demonstrate the international significance of the Iranian Revolution.

The Iranian Revolution was aided to a large degree by so-called small media—cassette tapes, Xerox, tape recorders, and telephone. This relatively low-tech communications hardware was used both to communicate and to escape the control of the Shah's regime. The Ayatollah Khomeini's message of an Islamic Republic became a unifying element in the revolution. Exiled from Iran by the Shah in 1963, he and other leading ayatollahs like Muttahari, Beheshti, and Teleghani were the symbols of cultural integrity. From Paris, in the late 1970s, Khomeini sent his messages through telephone and cassette tapes to Iran, where they were copied by the thousands and distributed through the informal and traditional communication networks to the nation. This method of communication provided both the credibility and excitement of oral messages and the permanence and accessibility of written messages.

The Iranian Revolution, as do many of the ethnic and religious regional conflagrations of today, grew naturally from native soil. The impetus for revolution has been traced to many factors, such as the political and economic conditions, foreign interests in oil economy, and the challenge to traditional social structure. Cumulatively, these factors contributed to what best could be described as a conflict between the official culture of the government and ruling elites, which represented and promoted Western influence, and the traditional culture of the masses rooted in Iranian national and religious traditions.

As part of the backdrop to the revolution, the implicit clash between the rulers and the ruled became most visible as the tremendous income from the sale of oil products made Iran a rich, but not affluent, society. The Iranian elite used its wealth to import Western technology for rapid modernization. This was viewed as inherently good, because of the relative ease of incorporating technology—versus ideological and political institutions—into developmental schemes. For the masses, however, with livelihoods largely dependent on agriculture, such technology and oil wealth had an indirect effect. Lacking resources and arable land, peasants left the countryside for cities at a rate of a half million a year, seeking the promises of industrialization. The result for a great majority of the population was social dislocation and a new urban culture dominated by Western goals and ideals.

From a macrocommunication perspective, the issue of world communication imbalance was crystallized in the Iranian Revolution. Global mass media, and especially American media, were fascinated with revolutionary excesses but little concerned with legitimate Iranian grievances. The sophistication and complexity of Iran's social context was overlooked as the Western media decried the leaders as fundamentalist fanatics. No attention, let alone credibility, was given the Iranian view of justice and vision of society, and modernizing progress was judged primarily by the development, or lack thereof, of American or Western European political institutions. American journalists continued to believe, despite indications to the contrary, that the revolution and the crisis in Iran were inspired by outside Communist forces who were trying to take over the country. In short, the American media conceived the revolution as a black-or-white event, leading Americans to conceive of the Iranian people as a faceless, diabolical, dehumanized menace.

Traditional Channels of Communication. Because conventional mass media were totally controlled by the Shah's regime, imported from foreign countries, or on strike, the revolutionaries and people in general relied on traditional channels of communication. The hub of these channels were primarily public meetings or other meeting places at which messages could be spread and resistance to the regime organized. One of the most visible meeting places in the Iranian cities is the bazaar. Although the importance of the bazaar in metropolitan areas has declined somewhat due to the expansion of modern banking and shopping centers, it still remains one of Iran's most important channels of communication and news. The power of the bazaar is due not only to the economic importance of the merchant class but also to its political and social influence. Not infrequently, by closing its doors in protest and thus threatening to stop the economic life of the country, the bazaar has been able to force Iranian kings and governments to withdraw decrees. The movement against the tobacco concession of 1892, the constitutional revolution of 1904-1911, the nationalization of oil and the Mossadegh era of 1950-1953, and Ayatollah Khomeini's 1963 campaign against Mohammad Reza Shah Pahlavi are some examples. The bazaar is also an important center of news, a place where opinions are formed and from which rumors are spread over wide areas with almost incomprehensible speed.

The importance of the bazaar as an intermediary channel of communication becomes even more pronounced when one considers that it is linked through religious ties to other informal communication channels such as mosques, Islamic schools, and welfare and community organizations. It also provides financial support for religious and political organizations.

Another important crossroad in the traditional and information communication system in Iran is the mosque (*masjid*). Denied the outlets of free newspapers, political parties, labor unions, student organizations, and free speech, opponents of the regime gravitated toward the only forum that remained open to them: the approximately 100,000 mosques and holy shrines under the supervision of some 200,000 *mullahs* or religious leaders. The mosque and Islamic sermon have been important channels of political and social communication in Iran. In contemporary history, theological disagreements have been used to foster revolution or to force unpopular governments out of power. A combination of religious sermons and radio broadcasts also has been used to propagate modern ideas and social change in the context of Islamic and Shi'a philosophy and theology.

Another center of social, religious, and political communication is the *hozeh-e-elmmieh* or college of theological studies. Operated independently from the state and located in such holy cities as Qum and Mashad, these colleges provide a place where the grand ayatollahs and Shi'a scholars may hold their audiences. They are the unofficial capital cities of Islamic Iran. During the revolutionary days, they were the centers of the communication activities of such men as Ayatollah Shariat-madari and many supporters of Ayatollah Khomeini during his exile.

A substantial amount of communication of a religious, social, and political nature takes place in what is known as a *hey'at* or mission. Missions are smaller religious gatherings than those convened in a mosque and may take place in private homes. Most of these missions meet weekly or monthly, though more frequently during the religious months of Ramadan and Moharram. Guests are served food and refreshments, and a *wa'ez* (preacher or orator) serves as narrator or moderator. It is here that interpersonal political and social networks are formed and then extended to other communication channels, such as the bazaar or mosque. *Hey'at* is a local phenomenon, with each residential district usually staging its own gatherings. Attendance is free to the public, but members often come from the neighborhoods in which the missions are formed. Though wealthy merchants are often sponsors of such gatherings, participants also include small shopkeepers, workers, students, and government bureaucrats. There are several hundred organizations of this kind in a city like Teheran, with memberships from 50 to 1,000.

Another traditional form of communication center for the Muslims and members of the community is the *takyeh*, of which there are hundreds in Teheran and the provinces. They usually are used for 40 days, starting with the first of Moharram, the month in which Imam Hussein, the Shi'a leader, was martyred 14 centuries ago. Similar to the *takyeh* is the *husseinieh*, which also is used for incidental religious lectures and gatherings. The most well known *husseinieh* during the 1970s was Husseinieh Ershad, where Dr. Ali Shariati, the most creative and influential young theoretician of Islamic theology and revolution, delivered his lectures on Shi'a thought.

Especially popular among the middle and upper classes is another type of meeting—the *doreh*. In the absence of developed or open systems of mass communication, the *doreh* is one of the most important channels for the transmission of news and ideas. It is through the participation of the same individuals in several different *dorehs,* or circles, that information and rumors are passed along. There are social *dorehs* as well as political and athletic ones. Thus the *doreh* can be termed a cohesive group whose membership may include journalists, professors, merchants, or students.

It is through these networks that ideas, attitudes, and opinions flow upward to elites and government; at the same time *doreh* members learn of "behind doors" policies of government and other institutions. Members then may exchange current news and pass it on to friends and family. Secret societies, which were behind the Iranian constitutional revolution early in this century, sprang from *dorehs* whose participants became active in development of the popular press and *anjumans* (or societies). In later years, unable to form political parties, many of the current revolutionary leaders of Iran were active through their *dorehs,* which became the foundations for later political parties and newspapers.

The Role of the Media
Technology in Secular Society

The cohesion apparent in Islam, however, was lacking in secular life in Iran, partly because of the 25-year-old ban on political parties. Coalitions such as the liberal democratic-oriented National Front and the two urban guerrilla groups—the Marxist-oriented militant Fedaeen Khalq (the Fighters of the People) and the left-wing Muslim Mujahedeed Khalq (the Crusaders of the People)—had some political clout. Their political programs, however, had not yet been solidified.

Paradoxically, high-tech media aided the revolutionaries in an unexpected way: The Shah was a victim of "big media," notably television. His direct entry into the Iranian political scene paralleled the introduction of television into Iran in 1958. Prior to that, his occasional appearances in print and over the radio had not shattered the image he had created for many as the King of Kings, the Shadow of God, and the Lights of the Aryans. His constant appearance on television, however, took away that mystery. He was seen not only by the palace elites who knew him in person but also by 35 million of his countrymen and women. He became in many ways a household property, his tone and his Persian not measuring up to the great expectations fostered by the *Shahnameh,* Ferdowsi's legendary Book of Kings. In short, he was vulnerable.

The case of the deposed shah raises the fundamental question: Are the modern mass media—through greed, incompetence, or even ignorance—led to be manipulated by political leaders? Do the media create sensational news and deliberately heighten the feeling of crisis? Instant access to the masses through electronic communications has created a condition of instantaneous demand for, and supply of, information and has forced a measure of accountability on political leaders as well as perhaps a penchant toward the dramatic on the part of the masses. Mass demonstrations such as Tianenmen Square and terrorist threats to global air transportation systems are both causes and results of the electronic mediation of the news as "instant history."

In sum, as Iran continues to move toward the Islamization of its society, communication and cultural issues will occupy an important place in the agenda of the nation. It is a peculiar characteristic of Iranian history that it always has accepted and even adopted alien cultures, but at the same time has always reacted forcefully once these cultures became too dominant. Iran has accomplished this through cultural and traditional communication channels that have remained intact despite foreign or modern technological influences. Thus, the revolutionary movements in Iran must be understood as having taken place in this historical process and serve as good examples of the tension between technology and tradition in developing societies.

Telecommunications and the Emerging International Regime

At the opposite end of the spectrum from traditional channels of communication, technological advances in telecommunications during the past decade have increased greatly the flow of information and information-based products and services. This has provided a wide variety of products and a high risk. What is occurring is an interlocking of the national and international telecommunications sectors. The international market is shaped by a few major actors, who, in turn, are subject to their domestic political, economic, and institutional mechanisms of control. Thus, the spillover effects of national liberalization policies on the international scene can be found at all levels of the telecommunications system. This means that it will become increasingly difficult, or even impossible, to maintain a separation between the international and domestic sectors.

The international environment clearly is not the regime of the past, in which specific long-term arrangements were seldom negotiated. As liberalizing policies are adopted, the telecommunications-related sectors are moving away from a system characterized by government-to-government negotiations, or one structured by agreements among states, to one characterized by a multitude of transnational investors.

For example, the number of network terminating points, that is, the points of connection between user equipment and telecommunication transmission facilities, increased in Europe from 393,000 in 1979 to 1,620,000 by 1987. The total number of bits sent per average working day grew from 1,310 billion in 1979 to nearly 10,000 billion in 1988. Export of U.S. information services increased by 9% between 1982 and 1983 and is expected to continue to increase by 9% annually throughout the 1980s. Today, all the major industrialized nations explore the possibilities of protecting computer software by drawing analogies between the characteristics of the software and other intellectual properties that are protected by the existing legal regime. Yet the extent of U.S. participation in international intellectual property organizations has declined, partially because of its withdrawal from UNESCO and its abstention from a number of early treaties. It was only in November 1988, that the United States joined the Berne Convention. The International Software Protection Act of 1985 by the United States Congress amends the U.S. copyright law to protect a foreign nation's computer software only to the extent that such a nation protects software, or the so-called rule of the shorter term.

The emerging new global information and communication system, therefore, can be examined best by investigating the developments in the field of international telecommunications.[2] Traditionally, the international telecommunications environment in the industrialized world was characterized by relative stability. A small number of monopoly providers had offered telephone, telex, and telegraph services within a structure of bilateral agreements; however, the convergence of telephony and computer communications, particularly in the past 10 years, has created new opportunities not only for national administrations and monopolies but also for merger and globalization of these facilities and services in the hands of a few. Thus, today, the rapidly changing sectors of telecommunications and telecommunications-based services are at the center of competition both among and between the economies and politics of the major financial powers. The pace of change at the national level, especially in the United States, Japan, and a number of West European countries that overlap at the international level, has destabilized the traditional arrangements by which international telecommunication services under the old regime had been provided.

Information Economy

These changes are related to the advent of what has been called the information economy. Indeed, the telecommunications and related information industries are the most significant sectors of the economy today, representing a $600 billion global market. It is precisely on this point that the new global order had to play its role; that is, to prevent the arrangements of the old order, new arrangements had to be organized among the industrial powers. The magnitude of the economic importance of the telecommunications sectors of the industrialized countries lies not merely in quantitative overall economic output but also in the technical properties of telecommunications, in its rapid development and proliferation, and in its significant impact on other economic sectors, such as banking, finance, retailing, and transportation. Adding to this list the strategic, security, and military aspects, the emerging new arrangements are designed once again to maintain intact the information hegemony and its wide range of applications.

Reflecting on that point, the Commission of the European Communities (1988) commented recently that

> information, exchange of knowledge, and communication are of vital importance in economic activity and in the balance of power in the world today. Telecommunications is the most critical area for influencing the "nerves system" of modern society. . . . Telecommunications must now be seen as the major component of a conglomerate global sector comprising the management and transportation of information.

Until recently, it was only deregulation in the United States that was disturbing the once stable international telecommunication environment. Deregulation became a signal for U.S. industry to win the world market. In addition, pressure to enhance international competitiveness has entailed efforts to export the U.S. model; deregulation without reciprocity impairs the position of the national industry. Liberalization in the United Kingdom is having a similar impact on France. The international regime now is accommodating the new regulatory concepts embedded in Japanese law, and national policy shifts in France, Germany, and elsewhere are having similar international consequences.

Thus, the system or process by which international telecommunications are provided has become part of the new order. It comprises an intermeshing of a number of industrialized systems, each one of which by itself is a web of interrelationships. National policy in other countries and economic pressures flow outward into the regional and international arena and are, in turn, influenced by this emerging new information order. Moreover, technological change continues to outpace the policy and regulatory arrangements that accommodate it.

Discussions of *liberalizing* telecommunications markets usually focus on *deregulation* in the United States and on *privatization* in most other industrialized countries. A proper understanding of these terms requires an explanation of their past and current applications in each of the contexts in which they are used; however, the term often carries a connotation implying a "free market" approach that suggests the end of government control over telecommunications services in exchange for a fully private market. For example, privatization has no significant relevance in the U.S. context because of the absence of state enterprise in the telecommunications industry. State enterprise in Europe has traditionally taken several forms. What is clear is that the final outcome is toward a global free market economy in which the major producers and users will play the dominant role.

For example, as the plans for Integrated Service Digital Networks (ISDN)[3] are implemented on a more widespread basis, services provided by multiple suppliers or a single supplier become more of a reality. The development of ISDN during the 1980s is but one indication of the growth of modern technologies in the hands of a few countries and suppliers who are to benefit from the new technological mode. This is because telecommunication policy today is fundamentally concerned not only with the provisions of service but also with movement from traditional industry or institutional arrangements toward a sector responsive to emerging technological and economic pressures. In short, the new order has given totally new meanings and concepts to telecommunications and to its major players. Under this order, new telecommunication companies are engaged in what might be called the movement and management of information worldwide.

These new technological developments have created the potential for new services that cannot easily fit into old regulatory schemes, forcing the review of both industry and institutional structures globally. Giant transnationals and firms are gradually leaving the telephone companies and building their own privately based global data and voice networks.

For example, General Motors (GM), International Business Machine (IBM), and General Electric (GE) all now have private data systems that operate worldwide independently of the common carriers. The same problems face the international satellite industry and international organizations such as Intelsat. Not only can major companies on a global scale operate on their own profitable routes, but fiber optic cable has also been laid and brought into operation by the dominant carriers, such as AT&T, British Telecom International, and France Telecom (DGT) across the Atlantic, and the Japanese KDD, and AT&T and a consortium with Cable and Wireless across the Pacific.

In this context, Susan Strange's *Casino Capitalism* (1986) amply applies to the world of high communication and information technology, which offers the players a choice of games. In place of poker or blackjack games, there are a variety of telecommunications equipment, digital networks, and data processing and retrieval systems in the market with which the players might gamble—with the variety and sophistication increasing daily.

In sum, within the span of 10 years, the world of information and communication has changed considerably. It has been characterized first by the fierce competitive climate among the industrialized economies of Europe, the United States, and Japan, and second by a series of technological and financial agreements creating the foundation for the emerging new global information and communication order that has at its center the Western economic powers. Aside from institutional adjustments, one of the crucial threads of recent telecommunications developments worldwide has been the reappraisal of price and policies for telecommunications services. The parallels among the various national pricing policies are quite striking; cumulatively, they point toward a global trend of reducing the price of interchanged services while making offsetting adjustments in the rates of local services. These pressures on pricing structures are not confined by national boundary lines. These economic interactions, combined with issues of production, distribution, ownership, and access to new communications networks and systems, describe a global matrix for which telecommunications forms the core.

Application of Technology in Development

Few areas of international communication reflect the impact of the Information Age more dramatically than the application of technology to development. Any approach to the study of development necessarily involves a conceptualization of culture and society in relation to communication. Several important concepts, problems, and processes of communication and culture received overwhelming attention in the world of mass media theorists during the 1980s. These included such designations as mass culture, mass media and society, development and society, cultural integrity, communication and cultural domination, cultural dependency, and cultural pluralism. Because these phenomena are highly complex and cover a wide spectrum of social reality, any attempt at a global interpretation necessarily transcends the limits of a given discipline. As a result, interdisciplinary approaches have become more frequent. The study of technology and development, in particular, must involve cross-disciplinary frontiers, making a holistic, as opposed to a specialized, compartmentalized approach to social science imperative.

Technology, Policy, and Planning

Communication is a crucial and pervasive part of society's life support system, and the opportunities for applying improved technology to both stimulate development and mitigate problems appear substantial. Though questions of effective implementation remain largely unexplored, communication policy, strategy, and planning as applied to developing countries have emerged as a significant area of study. At the national level, both developed and developing countries, in fact, have implemented studies on long-term communication policy and, more recently, the impact of modern technology on culture and society. Of a number of approaches taken, several strategies emerge as integral to an understanding of the relationship of technology in development. These include the following:

- Long-range planning with policy goals toward equitable distribution of communication power in a society's future
- Comprehensive planning examining all aspects of a communication system within the broader sociopolitical framework of society
- Technology transfer and assessment, especially innovations in such areas as satellite communications, cable television, and telecomputer link-ups
- Control and regulations and their legal and institutional consequences
- Information economics, determining the information sector of the economy's contribution to overall economic growth

These strategies often must combat major problems at institutional, national, and international levels. For example, although freedom of communication is a highly desirable social goal, the realities of national security and commercial and political interests too often influence and even control communication policy and planning at the level of applied technologies. Furthermore, the application of communication technology without regard for its effects on a people often occurs, because of a lack of coordination of national communication policy and planning as well as its manipulation by commercial and political interest groups.

As evident in early communication research history, most communication policy and planning efforts emphasize the notion that the role of communications technology in national development is to change the audience's attitudes and behaviors. Communication is critical to the process of national integration, socioeconomic mobilization, and political participation. However, communication policies and their implementation, especially at the technical level, basically are derivatives of the political and economic environments and institutions under which they operate; thus, they tend to legitimize the existing power relations, which are not necessarily working for the best interests of the developing country.

A technology-mediated focus on development takes the position that international telecommunication is vital to progress in the developing countries. For example, as advanced countries increasingly transfer their reference materials from hard copy libraries to computerized retrieval systems, the developing nations are faced with a dilemma: tap into these new information stores or fall further behind in information capacity. Because the modern world's technical and scientific culture is global, there is a high cost attached to being cut off from such a flow of knowledge. Information and technology policy choices must be a different mix of technologies for different countries.

In many nations, information technology is an extremely powerful resource, one not depleted with use and one that also aids in the organization and allocation of other resources. Policy making, particularly in the Third World, is influenced unavoidably by extranational forces, such as the political-economic and diplomatic influences of private corporations. Multinational giants, such as IBM, very often are the bearers of technology and innovation and, therefore, have technology agendas that differ from those of developing nations. National policies and the application of technology to development must converge at the point of implementation to avoid the very dilemma at the core of participation: that is, that development cannot be participatory if it ignores the worldview, values, belief systems, and priorities of the societies it is designed to develop.

Viewing the communication process as an integrated whole challenges the *technological determinist* view, which states that the application and acceptance of modern technological innovation determine progress in development objectives. In addition, through technology, the distribution of political, cultural, and economic benefits to society takes place. From the perspective of an integrated approach, however, the connection of different societies and countries or systems to different aspects of communication technology is diffuse rather than direct. Thus, a given society or country on both individual and national levels may reflect features of any combination of traditions of communication systems and technology. Some may be stronger and more dominant than others at different periods and levels, depending on social, cultural, political, and economic conditions.

From folk and traditional media such as leaflets to radio, film, audiocassettes and videocassettes, and telephone, conventional uses of mass media and telecommunications technologies in the development of nations and people are by no means new phenomena. In understanding the development process, theory often falls short of practice. Knowledge about the practical use of modern technology in development remains incomplete. Preliminary research and field studies in the late 1960s and 1970s raised questions about the cost of technology and its various applications in education, health, nutrition, agriculture, family planning, development planning, and rural economics. Researchers soon became aware of information as a resource and its unequal distribution to those already in more socially and economically beneficial positions. The myth of information and associated technologies as great equalizers was exposed as studies on international flow of information and news pointed to patterns that reinforced those of economic disadvantage. Beyond mere exposure were the issues of impact and influence on non-Western cultures. New considerations of the complexity of the change process were important conclusions of the research and pilot studies of communication in development.

Development projects involving communication are implemented at two related levels—macrolevel development programs, established on a national or regional level by central government or provincial authorities, and micro-level projects, targeted more specifically at a smaller group of people, usually in rural areas. Because the micro- and macrolevel projects are so closely related, the former often serving as a pretest or proving ground for the latter, it is difficult to separate the roles and purposes of each. In fact, closer examination reveals the roles to be essentially the same, with the primary differences being degree or scope and media application. An examination of development projects employing particular types of media is a useful way in which to glean beneficial practical information from previous projects. These include journalism and print media, telephonic media, and mobile audiovisual media.

Journalism and Print Media

Most communication and development efforts rely heavily on printed material to supplement or reinforce messages delivered by broadcasts, experts visiting an area, or leaders of small group discussions. Leaflets, graphics, and printed material as well as news media are examples of this category. For instance, in an effort to combat high rates of infant and child mortality resulting from a high incidence of diarrhea among that age group, a mass media and health campaign was launched in Honduras, using printed material and village health care workers, whose message was confirmed by radio broadcast. Infant mortality rates in project areas declined by nearly half in one year's time.

In recognition of the fact that visual messages are much more effective than those unaccompanied by such stimuli, development planners have implemented a wide spectrum of visual and participatory aids. Reinforcing graphic and printed material is commonplace in nearly all development projects and, as visual reminders, represents an inexpensive method of disseminating a message to a diverse and sometimes scattered population.

In terms of the news media's relationship to development, the tradition of the Western world, and particularly the United States, has been to view journalism primarily as an instrument for news dissemination and current affairs coverage. For this reason, the development of news media and journalistic communication in the developing nations of the world generally has not been supported through the agencies or channels of bilateral aid. Journalistic communication has not normally been considered an integral component of development projects. The outcome of such a separation has been that developers themselves attempt to organize and produce the communication aspects of development projects (such as television and radio training programs), rather than relying on those media personnel whose business is the assimilation, production, and distribution of information. Because government ministries contain few specialists as skilled in the art of disseminating information as those in the mass media, such projects often reduce even further the quality of the crucial communication aspects of development.

Telephonic and Related Technologies

In the area of telephonic service provision in developing nations, the central difficulty has been the establishment of adequate infrastructure, especially in rural areas. Furthermore, in developing regions, demand for such services has increased far more rapidly than the technology can accommodate. The telephone medium has been an important tool in development projects for decades, resulting in special emphasis on large investments in telecommunications. With the advent of satellite technology, telephonic services have become even more sophisticated, expandable, and reliable and are increasingly available in rural areas. International agencies involved in supporting such infrastructural projects include the Inter-American Development Bank (IDB) and the Economic Support Fund of USAID. The IDB began its funding for rural telephone projects in 1976. Since that time, the IDB has funded rural telecommunications projects throughout Latin America, in such countries as Argentina, Panama, Costa Rica, Guatemala, Colombia, and Ecuador. USAID has provided concessional loans and grants to establish a microwave link between Nigeria and Chad and to develop a telephone plant in Liberia. Over a 5-year period, for instance, USAID provided $400 million to Egypt for telephone equipment, and Lebanon received $11.7 million to reconstruct a telephone plant.

Although the number of telephones in Africa, Asia, and Latin America has more than doubled between 1968 and 1978 and is continuing to grow, the urban bias for telecommunications investments still is evident. Even within the Third World there are inequities. For example, in 1982, Argentina had 8.1 telephones for every 100 inhabitants, whereas Burkina Faso had .03 per 100 inhabitants.

The advent of computer technologies, especially in the late 1970s and 1980s, provided a powerful mechanism in development efforts, especially as a planning and management tool. The advances in computer and communication technology are staggering and extend beyond conventional media and development. Computer applications in the business community have had enormous success. In the People's Republic of China, for example, some 3,000 programmers and users have been trained under the 5-year plan. The Computer Information Centre in Beijing was established to expand the nation's economic data processing capabilities. Another example is the contribution made by the computer-driven business management information system for the Beijing Municipal Auto Spare Parts

Company that has enabled computerized inventory management to reduce stock on hand by $6 million.

Computer applications in education, electronic mail, instruction in math and languages, as well as engineering, government, industry, health care, and personal use expand the utility of applied technology to development issues. In Tunisia, Indonesia, and Thailand, computers are used to process and store data on court cases and on family planning and have tremendous potential in the planning, implementation, and evaluation of development projects.

Mobile Audiovisual Media

Mobile audiovisual media, such as cassettes and film, are being used increasingly in development projects because of their versatility, mobility, and adaptability. Ease of production and distribution as well as the ability to target specific local situations further endear such media to developing contexts. In Tanzania, for example, audiocassette listening fora were used to train women in family living skills and were found to be effective in securing high participation rates (up to 73%) and in changing attitudes of both literate and illiterate participants. The Village Video Network is a nonprofit organization consisting of several developing nations, including Mali, Zimbabwe, Egypt, Antigua, China, India, Jamaica, Nigeria, Guyana, Japan, Indonesia, and Gambia. Through videos produced primarily for women audiences within specific countries for their own development purposes, the cross-national organization facilitates an exchange of ideas and cultures.

Audiocassettes are more effectively integrated into development projects than video, partially due to smaller, less expensive equipment requirements and to videocassettes' reputation as an entertainment medium in most nations. Film, on the other hand, has the advantage of mobility, flexibility, and participation. The recruitment of local residents as actors increases the participation and information retention levels substantially. Lack of electrical infrastructure is film's one great limitation in an applied development context.

Traditional or Folk Media

With research and increased awareness of the importance and sensitivity of cultural and traditional structures, more attention is being given to the role of folk and traditional media in development. As discussed earlier, the Islamic revolution in Iran drew world attention to the marriage of traditional communication channels and technology. The successful use of these channels in mobilizing an enormous population, through the traditional structures of the mosque and the bazaar, drew attention to the strength and resilience of traditional media in developing countries. Thus, since 1979, the Islamic Republic of Iran has successfully used the traditional systems of social communication in its community and national development projects, especially in the areas of social mobilization and as a system for delivery. Traditional ceremonies, feasts, and gatherings in Egypt, for example, have been incorporated into the Danfa Comprehensive Rural Health and Family Planning project, which recruits local health aides and trains midwives in modern childbirth techniques. The success of the clinics is partially attributed to observance and incorporation of local customs and traditions.

Radio, Television, and Satellites

Radio. Virtually all development efforts at some point involve the use of the global, national, regional, and local infrastructure established for broadcast media. Radio is by far the most diversified and dispersed of such media, with 100 radios per capita in developing countries far greater than any other. The advantages of radio are wide access, low production and broadcast cost, and adaptability to a number of formats, from technical programming of moderate length to short public service or persuasive messages. Radio broadcasting is used on national and regional levels in a number of social development projects to educate and disseminate information. Programming featuring traditional and cultural music or national sports events, for example, can stimulate promotion of national integration of language and national identity.

In the realm of formal education, projects in a number of countries apply radio to teaching, particularly in primary grades. In a project supported by UNESCO, in 1968, rural radio programming was broadcast to organized listening groups in Senegal to motivate farmers to apply improved agricultural practices. In Nicaragua, radio has been used in a program to improve instruction of mathematics in primary schools by supporting teachers' efforts in the classroom. The programs were designed to hold the interest of the children and were followed by another 30 minutes of student-teacher interaction in activities designed to supplement the radio programming.

In short, the versatility of radio is demonstrated by its use for a multiplicity of purposes, including development, entertainment, commercials, longer topical education programs, religious programming, formal education projects, and news and information programs. These are not exhaustive categories for the medium. Instead, they indicate that the capabilities and diversity of radio are great, with numerous creative applications.

Television. More recently, television has been applied in development projects, particularly in education, health, and community development. An advantage over radio is television's capability to show actual scenes of events and places that can transcend language barriers. Expense of production, infrastructure, and maintenance are serious drawbacks. As technologies such as direct broadcast satellites improve, larger numbers of people and wider areas can be covered at lower prices, enhancing the effectiveness and versatility of the television medium.

The role of television as a cultural industry has become particularly controversial. The cost of producing educational and entertainment programming is far greater than that of importing it from the West. Criticism of Western programming that dominates Third World viewing is directed at both entertainment and educational applications. The effects of television programming on violent behavior are of increasing concern, especially as the relationship between viewing violence on television and violent behavior, for example, is correlated through research.

Television in Traditional Societies. A particularly salient example of television's role in developing societies is that of Iran (see Mowlana, 1989). Television has acquired a prominent role in Iran's geopolitical, socioeconomic, and religious milieus. In its three decades of volatile history, the Iranian television system has gone through many cycles. Beginning as a commercial and privately owned operation, it passed through the paternalistic apparatus of Shah Mahammad Reza Pahlavi's royal dictatorship. Then, after the monarchy was overthrown in one of the most popular uprisings of contemporary history, television in Iran became subsumed under Islamic tenets. Consequently, the Islamization of popular culture and communication is particularly obvious in the Iranian television system. Completely reorganized in the past 10 years, Iranian television, with an estimated audience of 20 million (in a country of 55 million), in addition to its more usual role in information and education, has also established itself as a potent Islamic propagation medium.

The technological determinist point of view, often cited in Western scholarly literature, which puts a high premium on television as a most powerful and pervasive means of modern communication affecting popular culture, does not hold much validity in Iran. Contrary to traditional concepts of development, television is a potent medium in Iran not because of the technology itself but because of long-standing cultural factors that give it legitimacy. In the West, particularly in the United States, television has been said to have a ritualistic function—comparable to religion. If television is religion in the United States or Europe, in Iran it is religion that provides television. This viewpoint does not minimize the importance of the conventional mass media, including Iranian television, but serves to point out that as a whole, it is the legitimacy of the media that depends on, and is subordinated to, the traditional channels, not the other way around.

Because it is under the complete control of the state, Iranian television's major function today is the propagation of Islamic culture. Sovereignty belongs to Allah (God) and not to the state or people; the Islamic state, therefore, is a God-fearing not political state. Nationalism is subordinated to the interests of the Islamic community, which recognizes no racial, geographical, or cultural boundaries. The powers of control in the media are exercised through a careful selection of material by the editors and producers to make sure that media content does not violate Islam's traditional ethical and legal codes. Serious educational and current affairs programs get a large segment of television time. Because Japanese dress, conduct, and film content codes are compatible with Iranian customs and do not offend the Islamic tradition, Japanese features and films dubbed in Farsi are among the most prominently placed foreign products on Iranian television. Creating a completely Islamic television model, therefore, is Iran's future challenge.

As the Islamic Iran enters its second decade of revolution, there is no doubt that it has succeeded in the Islamization and institutionalization of many of its political, economic, military, educational, cultural, and media sectors. In the full-scale implementation of Islamic policies, there is no doubt that communication infrastructures, especially telecommunications and television and radio broadcasting, will be given high priority.

Thus, in the larger terms of developing communication technologies, the full potential of television is yet to be realized. Limitations in production, distribution, and utilization of television in projects in developing nations are being overcome through technological advances such as satellite transmission, interactive cable capabilities, and teletext or video

text that allows the transmission of text and graphics. As these technological advances become increasingly applied to diverse developmental
projects for a broad range of purposes, their potential may become reality.

Satellites and Teleconferencing. Today, technological advances represent the management system generally considered responsible for the high
standard of living in many nations. To a great extent, technology provides
the methods for using energy to communicate information and shape our
environment to meet physical and psychological needs. Telecommunications alone, however, does not guarantee socioeconomic development.
Communication satellites, for example, have been studied in political,
economic, commercial, and social contexts. The appropriateness of technology and the ability to build infrastructure remain central issues. A
telecommunications infrastructure is essential, but the economic benefits
are likely to be far greater than providing telephone service alone. It will
facilitate the flow of information about innovations, new products, and
improved techniques, and for coordinating large-scale development projects. Rural areas are particularly in need of a telecommunications infrastructure to facilitate their inclusion in development efforts. In the 1980s,
much attention was paid to the problem of urban bias and the concentration of telecommunications services in the cities. Recent development
efforts have focused on extending the infrastructure and services into rural
areas. Satellite technology has made television broadcasting a much more
viable, effective, and economical method for reaching rural populations.
It simplifies infrastructural requirements and provides the facility for
teleconferencing and rural telephony.

Telecommunications transmission applied to development has been
predominantly one-way, from urban source to rural receiver, without
feedback. Interactive, two-way programming is on the increase. Teleconferencing promises to be beneficial in development efforts through its
establishment of interactive communication links among several locations simultaneously. This newest innovation is applicable in business,
education, training, health care, and numerous other sectors of crucial
importance to developing countries, particularly in community development, resource management, and national integration.

In sum, enormous potential exists for the use of conventional media
technology in development efforts. Backing up this potential, however,
must be truly consistent and effective training, research, and evaluation
processes as integral parts of planning and implementation. Furthermore,
projects that incorporate training, research, and evaluation not only meet

immediate needs and goals but also contribute to the unending processes that constitute the positive growth and change in individuals and their physical, social, and spiritual lives. The critical nature of the development process is that it is an ongoing process for all societies. What we learn from today's efforts will help to ensure fewer mistakes and more effective application in tomorrow's endeavors.

Technology and the Ongoing Communication Revolution

In summary, a definition of international communication must combine national, international, and intercultural dimensions. It is a term today that must describe a complex field of inquiry and research, which consists of the transfer of values, attitudes, and technologies as well as the study of the structure of institutions responsible for promoting or inhibiting such messages among and between nations and cultures. The increasing prominence of international communication as a field and of its related telecommunications technologies is not at all surprising in the face of the changing nature of international relations and world order. Not unlike the relationship of technology to development, the rapid expansion of international communication itself is no guarantee of achieving greater international understanding. More emphasis than perhaps ever before in history is needed on the concept of mutual human involvement in the communication process. There is, in fact, a polemic between enhancing levels of and quests for human *communication* in the sense of "software" made possible by advancing levels of *communications* technologies, or "hardware," of all the myriad types explored in this chapter.

Modern communication technologies may not guarantee improved international understanding, but, used effectively, they can provide an increased possibility for it. The more the world scope of the media and communication is viewed as a whole, the more likely the ultimate establishment of what might be termed a global ethical framework. Communication no longer functions on interpersonal, local and national levels alone. Inevitably, it transcends national boundaries to blanket other countries' operations and gain insight into new and different cultural schemes. It also creates an international or global symbolic environment in which the conduct of international political and economic behavior must take place.

If what is needed now is indeed a shift from a manipulative, technology-oriented communication to more interactive, human dialogue and exchange of ideas, how is this transformation achieved? It requires placing basic human principles on the main agenda of the day, as we normally do with political, military, technological, economic, and business issues. These basic principles include the prevention of war and the promotion of peace; respect for culture, tradition, and values; promotion of human rights and dignity; and finally, preservation of the home, human association, family, and community. What is needed is the merging of human communication and technological processes in such areas as policy, planning, development, health care, and education. This can provide the hope that a social, ethical, and moral ecological balance can be created and a genuine learning process can take place in the international system.

Notes

1. The New World Information and Communication Order (NWICO) originated in the 1970s and represents a call for an examination and critique of the structure of the information communication system on both international and national levels. The report of the International Commission for the Study of Communication Problems (The MacBride Commission) calls for structural changes to equalize and balance the communication structure. Such balance is necessary, according to the proponents of the new order, if development—economically, politically, socially, and culturally—is to be effectively promoted. This approach sees communication as the infrastructure of and precondition for economic growth, and thus, development.

2. Writing on this area has been growing during the past decade. See, for example, Aronson and Cowhey (1988); Bruce, Cunard, and Director (1986); Edelstein, Bowes, and Hersel (1978); Feketekuty (1988); Feldstein (1988); Hills (1986); Tunstall (1986); Gerbner and Siefert (1983); and Mosco and Waski (1988).

3. Integrated Service Digital Network (ISDN) is an evolving set of standards for a digital, public service telephone network.

3

Communication and Power

Conventional ways of looking at power have been challenged tremendously since the late 1980s. In fact, most of the uncertainties and problems arising from our inability to predict world events stem from the fact that power has been and continues to be defined largely in orthodox and conventional frameworks. For example, the concept of power, from Niccolo Machiavelli to Hans Morgenthau and Karl Deutsch, was typically defined from the standpoint of tangible resources. For Machiavelli, power in its simplest connotation is a cost-benefit equation arising out of "the nature of men to be as much bound by the benefits they confer as by those they receive." Although power contains a dynamic quality—a range within which nations can navigate between active and passive roles—at root, for Morgenthau, power is the immediate aim of international politics. The political realist approach dominant in international relations since World War II is based on this concept of the struggle for power measurable in tangible, visible, that is, real terms. Deutsch, too, defined power, in its narrow sense, as "the ability to talk instead of listen . . . the ability not to learn" (see Deutsch, 1966, p. 111; Machiavelli, 1980, p. 68; Morgenthau, 1985, p. 31).

Of these three, only Deutsch, decades ago, tried to place power on a more interactive level by defining it as a currency in politics that can lead political theory toward the development of some form of dynamic interchange model. The concept of power as a currency in interactions between political systems builds on the measurability of more traditional, tangible resources, such as countable voters, soldiers, military hardware, and manpower budgets. Deutsch proposed that, to estimate power in more intangible terms, appropriate weighting also can be given, for example, to morale, skills and resourcefulness, and intensity of support. The effectiveness of sanctions, for example, can be explained in this light. Much like the power of banks in lending out many times the amount of money currently held in deposits, governments can issue effective sanctions against many more nations and people than they could possibly control in the face of generalized disobedience to such intangible power.

The political system, therefore, like the socioeconomic system, can be seen to depend on what Deutsch (p. 122) calls "a fabric of coordinated expectations." In other words, coordinated habits, not threats, are what keep things moving and bestow political power. This by no means eliminates the use of power or force "when the more normal machinery of social control is broken down" (Deutsch, p. 122). This concept, however, removes power from the center of politics among nations and transforms the perception of its utility into that of a currency or mechanism for accelerating control, especially where voluntary coordination may have failed.

Today, the realist model, or nation-state centered paradigm proposed by Morgenthau and others, has lost durability in the rapidly changing environment of world politics and global economy. It has become problematic in that it no longer fully explains contemporary international interactions, such as the demise of the Soviet Union and the emergence of new nation-states in Eastern Europe and Central Asia. Nor does it explain the turmoil of ethnicity, religious and cultural fervor, economic regionalism, and resurgent nationalism. It is becoming increasingly profitable, therefore, to look at the notion of power as less a problem of governing and more a problem of cooperation, learning, and growth.

Power as an Integrated Whole

Elsewhere, a unified strategy of research in this area can be found through the application of a more general notion of power (see Mowlana, 1986, pp. 177-179). Such an approach proposes that the dimensions of power in both national and international systems can be viewed in two distinct but integrated and related categories of tangible and intangible resources available to participants. Traditional tangible resources of power and their allocations include economics, technology, politics, cultural products,[1] educational products, and military hardware. Intangible sources of power are belief and value systems, ideology, knowledge, and religion.

Using an integrated approach facilitates conceiving of power in terms of control over particular base values and the flow of interchanges between the main sectors of society. In other words, power reflects the ability to act and to affect something. It is composed of two dimensions: the *access* to necessary resources to act and the *ability and will* to act. Perhaps it is only in this context that the real process of international relations and information flow as one of dynamic change can be understood adequately, and it is this less tangible aspect of political power that has been ignored until recently.

In the face of rapidly changing international affairs, international relations and international communication models offering alternative perspectives to the realist paradigm gain in utility. Scholars have elaborated on the notion of intangible, sometimes called "soft"[2] sources of power. This concept posits that, although American preeminence in the 21st century may continue, U.S. sources of power are likely to broaden beyond military and scientific resources to new and even renewed concern with economic, cultural, educational, information technology, and ideological bases. Control of the political environment in the face of a general diffusion of power is the key factor for great and emerging powers today. As a result, the power of all major nation-states over goal attainment is diminishing in the face of the increasing complexity in world politics.

Resources of Power

Information-based economies of major nations today are emphasizing less tangible elements of power resources. Employee education and training, for instance, have become crucial components at the policy level in the international tourism industry as sectors compete for volume advantages in what are often areas of slim profit margins. Customer loyalty to tourism destinations, hotels, or frequently traveled airlines are intangible resources that can be parlayed into powerful economic indices in the balance of trade and exports-to-imports at the national level.

Traditional concern for the maintenance of the military balance of power, however, is not being totally supplanted. The military involvement of U.S. and coalition forces in the Persian Gulf war spoke directly to this issue. The limitations and impracticality of a purely military model, however, is self-evident. This is especially true in the face of the growing complexity and interdependence of world events, and the increasing role of such new participants as transnational corporations, newly industrializing and democratizing nations, and the global distribution of communication technologies forming a new basis of what might be called information economics.

New strategies must be devised by nations and regions to accommodate changes in the instruments and resources of power. Traditional analyses of international relations are seeking more alignment with features of integrative communication models.[3] Concepts of interdependence among previously segregated areas, such as security, trade, finance, and even more intangible economic and ecological factors, are drawing attention to communication frameworks outlining power-unified strategies of research

(Mowlana, 1986, pp. 10-11). The power of banks, ocean resources, capital, outer space, shipping, social mobility, and air travel are providing different distributions of intangible power, which are augmenting the significance of participation by other than nation-states in international affairs.

Soft power in this context includes the modern concept of information as an intangible resource, with the prognosis that power now passes from the capital-rich to the information-rich in the international system and heightens the importance to international relations of culture, ideology, and international institutions. In other words, the intangible power perspective gaining credence in traditional international relations analysis states that power is becoming less convertible or transferable to other, especially military, forms, less coercive, less tangible, but at the same time more co-optive. For example, alternative perspectives to traditional models point out that institutions such as the General Agreement on Tariffs and Trade (GATT), though instrumental in the international economy at large, in fact promote American societal and ideological concepts.

National Security

Traditional concepts of national security and power are now plagued with different and increased vulnerabilities, both tangible and intangible in nature (see Nye, 1990a, p. 179). An example of tangible factors is energy security for the United States. The key question centers around whether energy security should be secured domestically, through enforced conservation of oil products, or through costly repeated, extrapolated military involvement in the politics of oil-producing regions such as the Persian Gulf.

Another example is information security. In international tourism, for instance, there is a free flow of both capital and information across national boundaries that defies the very concept of national security (see Smith, 1992). This international flow of information occurs through the globalization of electronic credit card transactions, airline and hotel computerized reservation systems, private networks of financial institutions, as well as educational and diplomatic exchanges. Developing nations in particular are vulnerable to lack of access to and control over such technologies and the informational resources they bear. In response, less developed nations often set not only policies limiting credit card use by foreign visitors to their countries but also travel stipend maximums for their own citizens traveling abroad (Smith, 1992, Ch. 3).

Clearly, the need to address continuity and change in international relations makes it impossible to separate some of the world's most distinguished activities that are not in simple feedback relationships to politics, work, and production. Economic interdependence and changing technologies of communications and transportation are directly correlated. This is occurring to the extent that instantaneous modern telecommunications are revolutionizing and globalizing financial and foreign exchange markets, air transportation, world trade, and especially international banking. Interdependence among these various sectors increases the fragility and vulnerability of world economies as integrative systems during political crises, terrorist attacks, and civil and religious wars.

Economic Power

Information in the international context as economic power in the form of development projects, business ventures, marketing, trade, and technology transfer, has historically resulted in the domination or "Westoxification" of weaker, peripheral nations (Mowlana, 1986, pp. 180-190). Newly developing nations are creating sophisticated international service industries in the areas of transnational banking and finance and information and data processing (e.g., the Pacific Rim countries). As a consequence, information as political-economic power is rapidly accruing to these regions. The diffusion of power from government to the private sector, especially through the spread of modern telecommunications technologies, is strengthening what in traditional international relations terms are "weak" states. The proliferation of nuclear capability in what, heretofore, were regarded as less developed, less industrialized regions of the world appears to follow the path of high technology, leaping over decades of traditional development policy and planning efforts.

At the policy level, therefore, increased focus on nongovernment institutions and organizations and links among issue areas are challenging traditional mechanisms and concepts of power. One result is an increased level of distinction between actual and perceived power. Another is the advent of critical questions aimed at power and peace in international relations. These include power for what and over whom—and whose ideal of international peace and world community is being invoked. Actual power is historically achieved through a spectrum of tangible instruments, including economic sanctions and military coercion. Perceived power is less tangible in format and tends to derive from resources such as belief and value systems, ideology, religion, and knowledge.

**Intangible Resources of
Power and Their Allocations**

Belief and Value Systems

Value and belief systems are at the core of power structures in international relations and are constantly being changed or altered over time. Values and beliefs describe the nature of man, society, and the universe in a manner that transcends association with individuals, families, tribes, and even nations. In an international relations context, values and beliefs define the difference between nationalism and globalism. Within the context of nationalism, for instance, tribal configurations of the past are reinforced and used as sources of power that dominate and define the quality of life.

Belief systems relate to power through the shifting of values on a collective basis. This, in turn, provides the source for mobilization and assimilation of individuals into different arrangements, requiring new relationships among groups, institutions, and even nations. Here, central recognition is given to belief and value systems, or worldviews. These help determine the nature and parameters of action within and by each system.

By means of such a framework, one could specify what kinds of participants possess what kinds of resources for defining, comprehending, and acting on certain important issues of the day. Ecological movements are a good example. In increasing frequency, concerns for the environment are pervading political and economic agendas. "Fast track" approval, requiring only a yes or no vote, was used by the U.S. Congress at the initiation of negotiations for the North American Free Trade Agreement (NAFTA) between the United States, Mexico, and Canada. This process was delayed by powerful interest groups lobbying for the inclusion of text imposing environmental controls on rampant industrial pollution in Mexico. Thus, power in national and international systems involves more than just the reallocation of economic, political, and technological values and bases. It involves multidimensional factors with authority, legitimacy, and will playing crucial roles.

Values and belief systems also define the nature of conflict. For the past 50 years, individuals have tended to value the notion of the nation-state as the primary participant in international affairs. With the collapse of the Soviet Union and the end of the Cold War have come new political values. These, in many cases, are no longer associated with the concept of larger superpower nation-state systems as paramount in international relations. In other words, the concept of the nation-state, from Georg Hegel until recently, promoted and supported the concept of individuals' receipt of social goods and welfare from the state. Nation-state systems began to falter and fail in the delivery of these goods, such as in the former Czechoslovakia, Romania, Poland, the Baltic nations, and the beleaguered Yugoslavia. People, as a consequence, began to withdraw their loyalties to larger political units and to reclaim their heritage in religious, cultural, and ethnic origins outside the domain of the primarily Western, industrialized nation-state system.

Ideology

As a central element in values and belief systems, ideology has proved important as a source of power, beginning in the late 19th century and continuing to the present. Despite continuing rhetoric about the end of ideology and the end of history, our need to better understand what is happening in world affairs would be better served by a different interpretation. Rather than ideological termination, what we are witnessing is the dissolution of one dominant ideology and its replacement by another. Although Marx considered ideology to be false consciousness, a different, more basic interpretation of the word better serves the modern era: "ideo" as idea; "logy" as study.

The rise of Islamic ideology and values and belief systems based on sociopolitical and religio-political frameworks in the non-Western world parallels the rise of both new liberalism and new conservatism in the West itself. Ideology, therefore, is a collective belief system that is nurtured to operate in the service of not only social and cultural but also economic and political objectives. Interpretations vary, and unless there is a consensus of an ideal world, it is impossible for the currently dominant ideas to escape the opposing camp's accusation of ideological imperialism. In addition, there is an inherent fallacy in equating universal agreement with universal good. Human progress springs from individuals who disagree with the norm, who initiate new lines of thought—creative ideas that are tangential to prevailing opinion. In this sense, it can be said that all great truths begin as heresy.

When a particular worldview or ideological system is proposed as an ideal system, it becomes fossilized as the status quo and resists progressive innovations. This can ultimately result in war, for war is not the extension of dispute but rather the refusal to dispute. In addition, the rational pursuit of human good through a universally applicable ideology is an unrealistic expectation from human beings whose rational faculty is often overwhelmed by irrationality and emotion. The "war of ideas" often manifest in contemporary international affairs has been charged with ideological rivalry and fueled by intolerance among nations and hatred among peoples. International relations in its traditional forms only aids and abets international tensions by not promoting peaceful solutions and by not conferring legitimacy on the peacemakers.

The Islamization of Iran and other non-Western regions of the world is an example of the power embedded in ideological renewal. As discussed earlier, the Iranian Revolution of 1978-1979, in light of its unforeseen success, in some regards astounded the Western world. Its success confounded political experts and analysts and compromised the legitimacy of two decades of Western international relations policy and planning.

Religion

The effect of religion, too, is obvious in its relationship to ideology and power. Since World War II, the importance of religion, especially the major ones, has been both diverse and at times politically controversial in national, regional, and international affairs. Judaism's transformation into Zionism, leading subsequently to the establishment of the nation-state of Israel, is only one example. The fate of the Palestinians and the interactions between both Israel and the United States and Israel and the Arab nations of the Persian Gulf region have influenced the direction of political, military, social, and especially ideological involvement of major powers with renewed religious value and belief structures.

Solidarity movements in Poland, Latvia, Lithuania, and Estonia, for example, were not just political in nature but must be viewed as political-religious, religio-cultural movements with dramatic effects on the mobilization of populations toward traditional values, home rule, and nationalism. In addition, religion combined with charismatic leadership is another major base of power.

Knowledge and Education

Knowledge is an important consideration in any framework of power and represents a major product of the late 20th century. The production of knowledge covers many bases, from philosophy to the sciences. In the last decades of the 20th century, knowledge is inextricably entwined with communication and its associated technologies as well as with education. The growth of educational institutions in a given country, for instance, provides an expansion of research and international communication through educational exchange of students, faculty, and information. This inevitably has led to fears of "brain drain" in education for some countries and has been true to some degree, especially for less developed countries. Demographic studies show that a great number of students from developing nations are educated at universities in developed and industrialized countries, such as the United States, France, Germany, and the United Kingdom. To staunch this flow, some countries have instituted precautions ensuring that their students, scholars, doctors, and other professionals return home on completion of their studies.

The United States has gradually become the major center of study for foreign students, following World War II, as it gained in importance as a world power. In 1981, considerably more than 300,000 foreign students attended American universities and colleges; by 1990, this figure had more than doubled. In 1982 alone, the largest single group of foreign students in the United States, about 47,000, came from Iran. The Southeast Asian regions, led by Taiwan with 19,400 students, followed this pattern. More than 30% of the foreign students in the United States came from OPEC countries, especially Nigeria, Venezuela, Iran, and Saudi Arabia. Overseas sources, families, governments, and private sponsors paid 83% of the bill for these foreign students, adding approximately $1.5 billion to the U.S. economy.

In the case of Iran, the one-way flow of knowledge in educational exchange patterns became problematic to Iranian leaders concerned with preserving the traditional values and belief system of Islam. Just prior to the Iranian Revolution, it was estimated that 66,000 Iranian students were enrolled in various colleges and universities in the United States alone, but the total number of college students in Iran itself did not exceed 120,000. In other words, thousands of Iranian students, scholars, and scientists abroad, as well as their American and foreign counterparts residing in Iran, had become a significant aspect of not only the U.S.-Iranian but also the worldwide information flow.

Had the direction, content, and intensity of this type of information flow been taken into account in the analysis of the development in Iran and the region, the Western analysts and the students of politics who were surprised by the revolution in Iran and its outcome would have had a better picture and understanding as the events unfolded. In fact, the two dominant views of what was "really" happening in Iran prior to the downfall of the Shah both proved inaccurate. The first viewed Iranian culture and society under the complete domination of the West, and the second proclaimed the path of development in Iran as an inevitable and irreversible trend toward secular modernization under the Shah. The analysts of both of these views based their evaluations on official information, media content, and economic data. Both dismissed as less significant the power of Islam and of the information generated and circulated through not only the traditional religious and national centers but also the students and academic institutions. Similar misperceptions about the Iranian climate stemmed from a number of otherwise expert and credible sources in the academic field in both the United States and Europe. The study of the Iranian Revolution thus underlined the significance of understanding both the flow of information through educational, cultural, and traditional channels and the total communication system in another culture.

The scramble by Western nations to claim Soviet scientific knowledge and expertise following the collapse of the Soviet Union also illustrates the power of knowledge. Similarly, the transfer of technology in Japan parallels Japan's rise to great-nation status following World War II. Japan's rise to power was premised on its establishment and enactment of a national policy identifying its objectives as knowledge-based and especially technology-based global supremacy, rather than military dominance. In many technological areas, such as the development of television, VCRs, and microchips, the United States had similar opportunities to establish dominance. Through lack of industrial policy and laissez-faire philosophies of the U.S. government, leakage has occurred in many areas, denying American corporations and the economy at large certain technological advantages.

History has visible cycles. What became the Golden Age of the Islamic world were the Dark Ages for Europe. This in its simplest form can be attributed to different levels of knowledge. At the present time, the West has the leading edge in this realm. Tangible and intangible resources and their allocations are no longer separate but, instead, are interconnected. Military hardware is not enough to command power and control in the international system. How nations manage power resources will dictate the leaders of the future. Use of tangible, what might be called "hardware," resources now must be accompanied by shrewd management of intangible "software" resources.

Geopolitical and Strategic
Power and the Persian Gulf Region

Communication and information as less tangible resources are becoming major sources of power in international relations and international politics. Indeed, the process of globalization often can be best understood if examined within the context of intangible sources of power. The international political world is different today from the decades immediately following World War II. Before, peoples and nations could enforce respect for power through military invasion. Now it is possible to win a war militarily and at the same time lose it politically.

An examination of the power resources of the Persian Gulf region prior to the Persian Gulf war helps to delineate this modern day paradox. An understanding of these resources can illuminate what has happened in the Balkans and other regions that exhibited crises over intangible values and belief structures and systems. A crucial yet unexplored area in the study of the Persian Gulf is the geopolitical and strategic aspects of communication and information flow in the region. Modern telecommunications, especially space age technology, has changed traditional notions and strategies of international conflict and cooperation.

It is now possible that these technologies, if desired, could form the core of an alternative security system. Historically, extensive transportation, navigation, and communication services have been the indispensable nerve system of the strategic aspects of the Persian Gulf. In recent times, with the development of modern communication/information worldwide, the region has acquired an even more vital role. In the past, the volume of commodity productions, such as oil and other minerals, was the index of the area's trade and military communication flow. Today the trend is toward information systems as they become more central to the socioeconomic, military, and political infrastructures of the Persian Gulf states. This development is accelerated by the growing desires of external powers to exert influence and intervene in the region's geopolitics to protect their worldwide interests.

Prior to the outbreak of the war, information and communication in the Persian Gulf could be observed in three distinct areas:

- The expansion of military and security alliances accompanied by the growing hardware and software of communication technologies
- The expansion of international trade and services in connection with banking and international finance competing for the existing and potential markets

- The efforts of national governments to implement domestic developmental projects and to expand their internal infrastructure for national and regional integration

These areas, not mutually exclusive, have characterized the region's development from World War II to the present.

Geopolitics of Information and Military Alliances

The geography of the Persian Gulf had not changed much over the century, but the ecological dimensions of the area in the struggle for military, security, economic, and ideological dominance were altered by technological shifts in human ability to build, destroy, transport, and communicate. Geopolitics of information ecology wrapped in modern communication technology had become a crucial and decisive element in the international relations of the area, elevating this region to one of the most sophisticated centers of telecommunication in world politics.

In the arena of economic, military, political, and cultural power, information had assumed its place beside petroleum, natural gas, and strategic metals as an international resource to be bartered, boycotted, and blackmailed. Megabyte streams of digitized data had become the perceived source of power in the Persian Gulf, with far-reaching effects on economic, social, and political development. In short, the geopolitics of information was now a new dimension in the strategic balance of intangible power in the area. The old features of Persian Gulf geopolitics endured but had been supplemented by an even more fateful information and communication geopolitics.

In the first place, the development of satellite technology had dwarfed the traditional land, sea, and air battlefields, as was demonstrated in the 8-year Iran-Iraq war. Not surprising then, an important military use of space in this region was for information-producing satellites, ranging from surveillance, navigation, and communication to danger assessment and early warning.

The great powers, especially the Unites States, benefited most from this technology in the region, because satellites provided the U.S. military with otherwise unavailable information about activities in the Persian Gulf. The satellite technology now carried two thirds of the U.S. military's long-distance communications. At the same time, these increasingly sophisticated communication systems between human operators and "smarter" and more versatile weapons systems had provided the illusion, not the reality, of control. This was demonstrated in the downing of the Iran civilian airline flight 655 by U.S. military ship *Vincennes* on July 8, 1988, which killed 290 passengers. Thus, with each successive stage of the so-called technological progress, the differences between *offensive, aggressive* and *defensive, warning* activities were shrinking to a minimum, with potential regional and global consequences.

Because information and communications systems were perceived as alternative security shields in the Persian Gulf, more than $47 billion of telecommunications and data gathering equipment have been shipped and installed in such countries as Saudi Arabia, Kuwait, and Bahrain. Today, the geopolitics of communication has made the Persian Gulf region the fifth-largest and most complex center of telecommunications and digital networks in the world after the United States, the Soviet Union, Western Europe, and the Pacific basin.

Expansion of International Trade and Services

The Case of Bahrain. Bahrain, for example, is a laboratory for this complex historical, geopolitical, military, and financial picture of intangible power resources that has been in the making in the region. Bahrain's growth of telecommunications infrastructure from 1892 to 1985 underlined the importance of the first telephonic lines in this region, which preceded the development of school, hospital, and transit systems.

Sophisticated satellite systems developed since 1968, combined with Bahrain's economic and military ties to Europe and the United States and its geographical proximity and close ties with Saudi Arabia (both as a communication post and as a place with easy access to Western-style luxuries and entertainment), have caused this island to become one of the most well developed centers of telecommunications and financial transactions in the Middle East. Its three Intelsat earth stations, installed between 1968 and 1984, at Ras Abu Jarjur on the southeast coast, support an international database service of tremendous financial and strategic value, with computer links to more than 20 countries in North America, Europe, and the Far East. The networks in the United States that access Bahrain via this system include Tymnet, Telenet, Uninet, Autonet, and Compuserve. This is supplemented by coaxial cable to the United Arab Emirates and Qatar, and a microwave link to Saudi Arabia. Bahrain Telecommunication Company (Batelco), established in 1981, is a joint venture with Cable and Wireless PLC of Britain, in which foreigners have 40% of shares. Batelco provides private lease lines and terminals, private packet switched network, and intelligent terminals, as advertised in its international promotional material.

Air transport alone has grown 1,000% in the Persian Gulf area, and Bahrain, with its airport and communication system, supports a good share of this traffic, amounting to 35,000 aircraft a year including British and French Concordes; however, it is international banking and the American military facilities in the Gulf with close connection to this island that make Bahrain a strategically important information and communication system. Since the war in Lebanon, Bahrain has become a major center of banking, replacing Beirut's prewar environment in many respects. Many U.S. banks have selected Bahrain as their regional headquarters. With Bahrain's newly established foreign exchange market, the bank's Funds Transfer, PC service (FT/PC), originally designed for the Persian Gulf accounts, had 380 installations in 48 countries in 1988, allowing for the transfer of capital 7 days a week. It is estimated that an accumulation of greater capital could make the Middle East, including the Persian Gulf region, the fourth-largest economic market after North America, Europe, and the Asia-Pacific region.

The military-industrial complex of Bahrain is illustrated in the complex operation of Ali Bin Ebrahim Abdul Aal (ABE), named after its founder Ali Bin Ebrahim. The work of this company has grown from simple construction contracts to information and data services. The company represents U.S.-owned Kraft and Mars Chocolate companies in Bahrain, installs and maintains computer sites and related security systems. It serves Batelco through a British firm providing spare parts for video and other electronic equipment. Another client of ABE is the Bahrain Defense Force, which is equipped with U.S.-built jet fighters. According to Jemil Ebrahim, ABE group managing director, weaponry is not a priority, but it is envisaged as a need in the near future. During the Iraq-Iran war, Bahrain had 25 to 30 American warships apart from other battleships in the region.

The Case of Kuwait. In 1988, American warships were escorting Kuwaiti tankers, protecting an important part of what has come to be known as "Kuwait, Inc." in the U.S. media: "an expanding overseas empire built around oil with a Western investment portfolio worth perhaps $100 billion, including massive real estate holdings and a wholly integrated petroleum industry that is challenging the power of multinational oil giants."[4] What gave Kuwait high importance in the United States and the West was not the geographical position it held in the area but the amount of capital it exported to the United States and other industrialized countries in the

West. In the 1980s, Kuwait set up two investment funds worth $40 billion each. Prior to the Persian Gulf war, Kuwait's investment in the United States and Western Europe was estimated to be $100 billion, $80 billion of which was in government holdings, with the remaining invested by the rich and upper class of Kuwaiti society. Half of Kuwait's investment portfolio is with American corporations, including virtually every company on the *Fortune* 500 list of industrial firms.

With the Saudis' high investment in economic, military, and strategic sectors and their close relationship with the United States in military and intelligence matters (Saudi Arabia is the sixth-most important overseas market for the United States and one of the few where the balance of trade is in U.S. favor), the three countries of Kuwait, Bahrain, and Saudi Arabia alone have established enough dependencies with the West to make the information and communication infrastructure of this region, at least technologically, vulnerable to the existing and future policies of external powers. The downside for the Persian Gulf region is the fact that the Persian Gulf countries have more communication networks with a few power centers of the world than among themselves. This, in part, prevents them from concentrating their resources for regional integration in such fields as economics, social, political, and cultural spheres.

Communication, Integration,
and National Development

The efforts of the Persian Gulf countries to implement domestic developmental projects for the purposes of national integration, political unity, and social and cultural cohesion provided another major factor in the rise of communication and information as crucial intangible elements in the region's geopolitics and strategic map. This could be seen by examining the development of mass communication facilities and conventional telecommunication infrastructures (such as postal service, telephone, and telegraph, radio and television, and scores of other cultural industries) in relation to educational, cultural, social, and political sectors.

Among the technological changes that have been sweeping through the Persian Gulf since the end of World War II, the development of communications has been the most fundamental and pervasive of all in its effects on the region's diverse societies. The dramatic upheavals in the cultural, economic, political, and social structures of the Persian Gulf region have their origin in radical change in the outlook of individuals on the world in which they live; thus, the study of communication agencies—both technological and human, old or new—and of the political behavior, public opinion, and mass media of the Persian Gulf countries has accelerated rapidly in the past several decades.

A major factor responsible for this renewed emphasis has been the postwar interest in the developmental processes of the region, with an accompanying concern for both understanding and promoting social change. The rise of the Islamic movement as a major revolutionary social and political force, the use of traditional channels of communication as a major vehicle for mobilization, and the integration of modern means of communication technologies into the old social networks—all these have further accelerated the interest in the analysis of communication systems in the area. It can be said that the early arrival of modern mass media in the Persian Gulf region was an import from the West, an aspect of the impact of the West on the Middle East. Importation of mass media usually occurred on two levels: via communication technology—through introduction of the printing press, telegraph, telephone, radio and television—and via their content, various forms of nationalism, ideology, news and entertainment material. Each level stimulated growth of the other, and although communication content at times came to reflect indigenous cultures, the influence of Western technology and ideology remained unabated.

The Power of Mass Media

Since the demise of Western-style development in Iran and the Islamic revolution of 1978-1979, the mass media in the region have developed a new awareness of the outside world and at the same time a great degree of Islamic self-consciousness. If the substance and strategy of the revolution in Iran were new, so too was the realization that, in Islamic societies of the Persian Gulf such as Iran, control of modern communication media does not guarantee political control. Modern media must achieve the power and penetration of traditional channels of communication if they are to be useful as social, political, and economic tools.

Being on the crossroads between Europe and Asia, the Persian Gulf region receives a significant amount of international broadcasting. Stations in Europe, India, Pakistan, and the Newly Independent States can be clearly heard. The Voice of America and the British Broadcasting Corporation (BBC) are among the many international sources that for years have beamed programs in Arabic, Persian, and other languages to the region.

Political developments in the Persian Gulf have had considerable influence on the interstate broadcasting in the area. With the exception of the Islamic Republic of Iran, most states in the region import from 40% to 60% of their television programs—most of which consist of entertainment—from the United States and Europe. There has been a good deal of criticism of these programs in the media, on the grounds that they not only convey values foreign to the region's cultures but also create an alien world with their commercialism and consumerism; however, more imaginative cultural programs and documentaries, coupled with greater discrimination among audiences, have been on the increase in several countries of the region.

The indiscriminate importation of foreign and Western values through media products since World War II had a dysfunctional and negative impact on the region's population. This was because such imported values undermined traditional national and religious values without providing new sources of community cohesion. As many Middle Easterners saw it, such cultural imperialism of the lifestyle and socialization of urban and younger peoples set the stage for inevitable confrontation of the old ruling elites and the new generation. This conflict clearly manifested itself in the Islamic Revolution in Iran and in the continuing protests against the cultural domination of the West elsewhere in the region.

The Private Industry of Information

The relationship of power, information, communication, and culture is a relatively new multitiered concept of intangible resources in the international system. The recasting of this relationship in the form of an equation, outlining tangible and intangible aspects of what might be termed a general consciousness industry, is presented in an effective manner in the work of Herbert Schiller (1989). In his view, the effort to take over public (largely government) information for commercial advantage has spearheaded the entirely new private industry of information.

One example of this co-optation is the transformation of historical and cultural entities, such as museums, from appearance as public resources and sites of public creative expression to enlistment as instruments of corporate sponsorship. Another is the mass-mediated political propaganda and commercial exploitation of national celebrations, such as Independence Day and the centennial of the Statue of Liberty. Such seizure of public events and celebrations for corporate commercial advantage divorces the public from its connection to public life and history. In other words, much of the nation's physical space, according to Schiller, is now a private preserve, carrying the messages and culture of the corporations that dominate economic and political life. The extension of this intangible form of control to the domain of the airwaves provides "access to the most personal places of daily life: the living room, the bedroom, and the kitchen" (Schiller, 1989, p. 106).

Television's role as a substitute for formal education is becoming well documented. The near-total utilization of television, since its inception in the late 1940s, for corporate marketing is less well understood. An incessant identification of consumerism with democracy has developed to the point where "marketing has become so much a part of the political process that it is increasingly difficult to determine where it leaves off and politics begins" (Schiller, p. 107). Presidential debates are an example in which corporate sponsors receive as much advertising airtime as candidates. In addition, the major divisions characterizing American society are avoided in television broadcasting. Rather than present serious social criticism on the air, television airways feature personal crises and conflicts. Inquiries into the nature of children's television and possible noncommercial television system alternatives are frequent but are rarely borne out in policy or regulation.

Conclusion

In the past, the trends in production of such commodities as oil, coal, and steel were the backbone of the nation's military might. Today, the trend is shifting toward information and communications systems. Nations and regions having a high stake in international system maintenance must maintain a posture to satisfy their domestic political, military, and economic elites. A war between the major powers would most likely mean global destruction because of the development and proliferation of sophisticated atomic weapons. A total victory is no longer possible for any one power. As a result, access to domestic and international communication channels has become the major goal for advancing the perceptions of military, economic, and cultural superiority.

In short, communications hardware and increasingly important intangible forms of communication software have become instruments in the globalization of power. The effect has been to correlate and equate low, middle, and high-level nations as near-equal participants in domestic and international affairs, especially those concerning nationalism, regionalism, revolution, ethnicity, and religio-political movements around the world. Thus, control over intangible measures of information flow and communication now must accompany access to material and natural resources to obtain power in the international system.

Notes

1. The notion of cultural industries includes such entities as the postal service, telephone and telegraph, and radio and television.

2. For an elaboration of the "soft power" concept, see Nye (1990b).

3. See "Two Stage of Information Flow and International Flow of Information Models," (Mowlana, 1986, pp. 10-11).

4. For further detail, see "Geopolitics of Communication and the Strategic Aspect of the Persian Gulf," Mowlana (1989, p. 96).

4

The Making of Community

One of the major questions in the modern world is how societies organize and define themselves over time. As humans, we have witnessed a historical series of sociocultural organization as well as community formation ranging from nomadic life, the Greek city-state, St. Augustine's City of God, Rousseau's political community, Marx's proletarian community, De Tocqueville's democracy, to the European Community and the United States and the former Soviet Union's superstate communities. What formerly was best known as a military community, from ancient Rome to the North American Treaty Organization (NATO), has emerged in the post-Cold War era as an international political community based on the increasing prominence of economics and world trade.

What Is Community?

In the United States we use *community* to mean different things. A group of people is one concept of community. There are residential communities—and even ruined communities in many cases. Another concept of community has to do with a group of a particular size or description. In the United States, when we refer to community, we more often mean small groups than large. For the purposes of this chapter, however, community is defined as a network of information flow or communication grids that can exist within and outside national boundaries. Even beyond this, a community must be based on values or a belief system of a much higher level, and therefore it can transcend national boundaries.

The quest for community has been a continuous one involving individuals and their relationship to information, without which the establishment of community cannot take place. As it did for both ancient and modern societies, community formation is paralleled by the growth of information of an increasingly technical nature. The question becomes, What is the relationship of communications—in the sense of the technologies of information—and community?

Community and National
and Global Development

One item closely related to traditional concepts of community is that of national development. Although emerging Third World views and approaches have generated considerable controversy over the meaning of development, it has nevertheless been explained largely in terms of plans and strategies, rather than in terms of community building in the context of culture and prevailing worldviews. Thus, static and asymmetrical notions of people and society have been the core of developmental policies and planning. The overall field of development, in fact, continues to be plagued with a number of epistemological and practical difficulties. Consequently, the question of how it can relate to specific technological, economic, political, and especially cultural factors is a complex one and needs to be addressed as such. This is necessary if we are to understand completely the development process and its relationship to community and related technologies.

Studies of economic development and the use of modern communication technologies, on both local and national levels, are revealing a slow but sustained and systematic drive toward the processes of human and societal evolution. This trend is evidenced by the emergence or resurgence of religio-political movements in a number of geographical areas and by nations that have isolated themselves to pursue development within their traditional cultural and philosophical perspectives. These movements typically include increasing reliance on traditional channels of communication rooted in renewed concepts of community and community building. This trend is not limited to less industrialized societies and to Third World nations and has become evident in the industrialized world as well as in such campaigns as the ecological and environmental movements.

To better understand these processes of evolution and social change, and to appreciate and overcome the complexities and shortcomings of the term *development,* we propose a framework of analysis with its focus on the central worldview that underpins culture as an integrating element in the process of change. We specifically emphasize values and belief systems that permeate the process and help us proceed to the parameters of both individual and societal change in a more systematic and coherent way. Communication and development are no longer separable; they are different but interrelated terms. Development, in all its complexity, is communication, and communication is development. Therefore, communication development, if fused as an area of inquiry and research, should be referred to as a single term. It should encourage the construction of development programs to fit the society, rather than orienting society to fit development programs.

For example, since the 1950s the notion of development, both implicitly and explicitly, has been connected, exploited, used, and abused in regard to the concept of nationalism. Both the decline of nationalism and secular national ideologies patterned on European and Western schools of thought and the concurrent discourse and revival of notions of community along sociocultural lines open an entirely new area of inquiry and research that needs to be studied by those interested in societal change and evolution. Development and developmental projects must, therefore, be discussed in more comparative ways so that the study of any given phenomenon related to social change can examine the problem, not only in the Third World or less developed world's laboratory but also in the industrialized world. The functions and dysfunctions of developmental projects are not unique to the Third World but are also experienced in some form in the rest of the world. It is the discourse of development that has determined that the East needs development and not the West; these propositions must be tested in both worlds.

Implicit in both the literature and the evaluation of development projects is the notion that there is indeed a communications revolution and that the phenomena under consideration are in the realm of the information society. This notion demands more critical examination and analysis. What is termed an *information* society can at best be described only as a *data* society. Information is knowledge, but the abundance and increase in the quantity of data and their utility and relevance to different societies do no necessarily indicate information and knowledge as a unique phenomenon of this age.

The concept of an information society in the postindustrial age has been associated with the division of labor and the increase of services. It is necessary now to depict society as neither an information nor a services society, for if the prevalence of services is the predominant aspect of the economics of this newest society, Third World nations would be the leading candidates for such a designation.

The Media as a Forum
for Community Building

Several important concepts, problems, and processes of communication and culture have been receiving overwhelming attention from mass media theorists, especially during the 1990s. As with development, the role of the media as a forum for community building is central to such discussions and necessitates further elaboration of what community building is. It is possible, for example, to use media within a community without using it for community building. It is necessary to redefine and reconstruct the definition of the media to understand this dichotomy. Mass media no longer constitute the classic definition of mass communication. When we refer to mass communication, we do not necessarily refer to modern technology and mass audiences, or even group audiences. Indeed, radio, television, computers, and fax are all part of mass communication, but mass communication is possible without mass media. Consequently, the study of mass media and culture must involve cross-disciplinary frontiers, making imperative a holistic, as opposed to a specialized and compartmentalized, approach to social science.

In older societies, for example, the traditional means of communication have ritualistic functions. In the Muslim world, each mosque is like the subscription of 10,000 newspapers based on the ritualistic function of participation. Association with those ritual functions provides legitimacy, and for this reason, the ritualistic function of a medium ought to be taken into account above and beyond the communication function.

Based on this, when asked which comes first—the media or the community—the response must be the community. The media will never be able to create a community, although they play an important role. A community is created when people get together and communicate, when they act together. The media contribute to this as organizers, mobilizers, crystallizers, and legitimizers. The media also perform as an educator, a source of information, an advocate for policy or ideology, and a forum in which to transmit culture. This, however, is not community building but rather helping the community come to some action, providing integration and identity, or transmitting values and facilitating communication among members. The community itself, however, preexists the media and their influence.

The role of community media when conflict occurs within the community can have a valuable and positive, rather than negative, effect. The community media are not meant to be neutral but to represent community interest. Conflict itself, though almost always perceived as necessarily negative and to be avoided in Western society, can in fact be a very positive component in the building of community. Unfortunately, in Western culture, we associate conflict with violence. In many other cultures, conflicts are basically disagreements, and disagreements can be constructive. Looking at the positive side of conflict within a culture, the media can provide crucial fora for conflict resolution.

The question of economics and the costs of mass media for the community is another important area. One of the major problems in the area of communications and development is that accompanying the introduction of modern information technologies is the burden of carrying costs to the local community. It becomes crucial to ensure that the economy of the communications infrastructure being built takes into account the community's ability to bear the cost of expensive new technologies. In most cases, the introduction of new methods is strongly associated with the expansion of trade and the diffusion of technology by multinationals. For this reason, introduction of a given technology in a given community, be it small or large, will have profound implications as far as the burden that will fall on that community.

Integrative Model of
Community and Culture

What conceptual framework can house, in the sense of describe or explain, the role of the media in culture and community building? There has been a quest for cultural integrity around the world and with it a development of political, social, and economic subcultures in both the Western and non-Western worlds. This is revealing the emergence of pluralist societies in which an increasing variety of solidarities has been developing. Most discussions of the mass media and culture are historically biased in the direction of preserving the standards of the past. What is needed is a dynamic and integrative paradigm that can take the social, economic, political, and structural variables into account and make a distinction between production and distribution of cultural messages.

There is a need for a shift in emphasis in the analysis of communication systems, especially mass communication systems, from an exclusive concern with the source and content of the messages toward analysis of the message distribution system. Increasingly today, control of the distribution process is the most important index of the way in which power and values are distributed in a communication system, which may be the global community, a country, or some smaller cultural unit.

The distribution sequence of the mass media has been one of the most neglected areas of communication research; yet this very distribution sequence has become the most critical, vital, and controversial aspect of the total mass media system today. Our traditional preoccupation with the rights of individuals and groups to *produce* and *formulate* their desired messages rather than the right to *distribute* and *receive* them has been one reason for this neglect. The growth of communication technology, the expanding national and international market, and the creation of institutional policies and regulations have made distribution the most important sequence in the chain of mass communication.

Cultural Content. In analyzing the mass media and culture, the structural changes occurring in the media must be taken into account, for they produce expansion, differentiation, domination, and cultural pluralism. One major consequence of national development, therefore, is the expansion of and accessibility to cultural content by a large segment of the population. In the new societies, and especially in the Third World countries, the most conspicuous example has been the expansion of education.

Differentiation. The second aspect of change is that of differentiation. The term *mass media* itself is misleading, suggesting undifferentiated content and audiences. Few if any mass media are directed at or used by the entire population. Instead, the preponderance of mass media is explicitly directed at differentiated segments of the population in the form of specialized or class media.

Domination. The third aspect of change is domination. With differentiation and specialization come domination. Not only can one medium become dominant over another, but such dominance also can lead to changes in content. That is, one system's method and content can become dominant over the other. The consequence of this interaction will determine the cultural level of that community, society, or system.

Cultural Pluralism. Another key aspect of what is called the integrative model of culture and community is the concept and phenomenon of cultural pluralism. Although the notions of cultural pluralism and multiculturalism are recent, the phenomenon they express is not. The birth of nations from the 1950s through the 1990s, and the upheavals and changes occurring in the old nations, are not simply the result of drastic changes in demographic or economic sectors. They also indicate an important development on the intellectual level. Advances in communication technologies and transportation, for example, have helped to lessen cultural isolationism and to increase the cultural awareness of minorities by making them more conscious of the distinctions between themselves and other groups. Communication and mass media, therefore, play a pervasive role not only in social mobility and nation building but also in strengthening ethnic consciousness.

The mass media system, therefore, is viewed here as a complex social system, consisting of actions carried out within the context of the external social conditions of the community and the society in which it operates. No part of the mass media system stands alone, but each part is related to both the formation (production) and distribution processes of its messages.

Community Through Dialogue

Western theories of human development, both Marxist and liberal democratic, proceed from a shared assumption that the development of societies requires that modern economic and social organization replace traditional structures. Widely accepted in the West and diffused among the elites of the less industrialized countries, this assumption encompasses, among other things, industrialization in the economy; secularization in thought, personality, and communication; the development of a cosmopolitan attitude; integration into the world culture; and rejection of traditional thoughts and technologies simply because they dominated the past and thus are not "modern." But contemporary movements around the world, whether in groups, communities, or nations, all share an alternative vision of human and societal development. It has its roots in more humane, ethical, traditionalist, antibloc, self-reliance theories of societal development. It seeks to promote not itself or its ideology but instead dignity through dialogue. It is the quest for dialogue that underlies the current revolutionary movements around the world.

The French Revolution, for example, for all its noble ideas and promises, in the end did not further this quest for dialogue among individuals. On the contrary, it marked the watershed in the rise of the individual vis-à-vis the nation-state. The concepts of freedom, equality, and fraternity that came to the forefront—in terms of political and economic aspirations by the individual making demands on the state—have played a major role in revolutions ever since and led to the rise of modern nationalism.

It is this juncture that can be identified as the point of departure of individuals from their communities. No longer was interpersonal communication the main mode of communication. Bureaucracies arose to take care of human needs. Humans communicated with each other more as roles than as individuals. Mass media began to mediate government-citizen communication. People became alienated from one another as cultures moved inexorably away from those based on associative processes toward more abstracted levels of interaction. The growth of *instrumental* and *functional* communication became paramount in the decline of genuine interpersonal dialogue.

The detrimental effect of modern technological society and its institutions on the capacity for interpersonal and intrapersonal communication has been well documented, analyzed, and basically accepted as a fait accompli by countless sociologists, anthropologists, and psychologists. Missing from these analyses is the possibility of reversing this trend, of reviving the capacity for human communication among already alienated individuals. To accomplish this, a reorientation in communication studies is required, moving from a sole concern with the roles, effects, and impacts of communication media to the study and discovery of a communication theory of society. Second, an environment must be created in the form of a restraining influence that can protect humanity from self-destructive behaviors and eventually direct the machinery of communication to explore human growth and potential.

Communication Theory of Society

A communication theory of society would be based on the premise that the mode of communication—not in its technical and instrumental forms but in its human-interactive form—determines the outcome of social processes. In such a communication theory, cultural traditions are the basis of the rationalization of action. They are the organizational principles of communication that determine the range of possibilities in which economic, political, and technological development might evolve.

In terms of international relations and world society, a communication theory would justify and encourage new approaches to cross-cultural relations. The discontent and revolutions in many parts of the world have been efforts by individuals and communities to articulate their needs for dialogue—and for respect and dignity. More is at stake in these recent conflagrations than traditional struggles for nationalism and material goods. Transcending these limits would benefit not only those individuals and institutions interested in the humanistic sharing of values but also those with political, economic, and technological concerns. International relations cast in this new intercultural light will emphasize more than relations among nation-states or transnational actors; they will emphasize relations among individuals along social and psychological channels.

International communication entails an analysis of channels and institutions of communication, but more important, the mutually shared meanings that make communication possible. This involves refutation of the notion that the numerical multiplication of communication channels and international interactions will automatically generate greater international understanding and mutually shared images and meanings. Instead, value systems of the communicators are the single most important element in determining the effect of the message on images; therefore, for communication to have meaning, it requires a change in the image of the recipient of a message. The ultimate ethical power of communication institutions within this context is to serve the public, and the zenith of serving that public is reached when a communication entity succeeds in raising a group, a community, a public, or a world to a higher level of understanding and insight.

Community and World Order

The traditional concepts of community and development as ones concerned primarily with what is happening in the Third World are changing. Development is now a global issue. Its roots in community and community building cannot be overlooked. It is no longer just a question of technology transfer, foreign direct investment, or even free-market economies. Instead, development has become a universal concept. Today, there is hardly a major political, social, or economic problem in the developing world that cannot be observed to some degree in both the capitalist and the socialist industrialized regions. Societal decline, hunger, violence, poverty, homelessness, and human hopelessness have come to roost in the most sophisticated, technologically advanced citadels of the modern industrialized world.

Modernization, or the Western style of development, as we have come to know it, is not an inevitable culminating stage in the evolution of societies. Some societies are choosing to leave modernity behind or to go beyond it. Former systems of implicit legitimation have been eroding for some time, and the search for *lebensraum*—space for growth and life—in those societies dominated by impersonal bureaucratic organization now is self-evident in current events, with nation states increasingly unable to control the flow.

Since World War II, development theorists and historians have usually sought their models for social, political, and economic structures in

Western history, primarily in the history of the modernity syndrome. In contrast, social behavior and societal transformations in any system must today be understood and planned on their own terms. To understand these transformations, we should give primary attention to the worldviews of these societies, to their own accounts of their inner and outer worlds, and to the terms in which individuals, groups, and nations explain their choices. Today, cultural and ecological issues are extending the political and economic frontiers to information and communication as the foci of analysis.

A new appraisal and review of the global shift in development and communication are indeed needed and long overdue. The so-called developing world, or the South, is in transition, with problems of personal identity, of revolutionary ideology, and of struggle for everyday life. The Western world has different—but not milder—problems. The demand for a New International Economic Order and the quest for a New World Information and Communication Order of the 1970s have been transformed into a new global economic competitiveness. The North-South issues have been crystallized but not resolved, and the East-West and West-West relationships have entered a new political, economic, and technological era. The result is characterized by a good deal of human uncertainty and insecurity. In short, if the explosion of the current unrest is undeniable, its nature, its causes, and its consequences are much less certain.

War and Peace

Western theories of human development, both Marxist and liberal democratic, proceed from a shared assumption that the development of societies requires that modern economic and social organization replace traditional structures. This same paradigm has permeated the agenda for international peace. Whereas international security, balance of power, levels of military hardware, and issues of armament and disarmament previously consumed the attention of those striving for international peace, a different notion of world peace must be sought today. In the past, the preservation of the status quo among great powers necessitated tremendous expenditures in global capital to keep the major adversaries from fighting each other in a devastating nuclear encounter. Though successful in preventing world war, preservation of the status quo among the great powers meant that other nations and regions, called on to support the system of deterrence and containment in the interests of peace, have been the ones constantly at war. What was a Cold War for some has been a hot war for many others.

The post-Cold War euphoria over possibilities for peace dividends from reduced militarism subsided quickly in the face of renewed struggles for new world orders. These struggles are increasingly caused by conflicting religio-political ideologies, scarcity of economic resources, and the loss of legitimacy of fundamental political and economic institutions. Events such as the recent Persian Gulf war, the wrenching ethno-political strife in Europe, the breakup of the former Soviet Union, and the erosion of legitimacy of transnational financial institutions and markets, symbolized by the increasing number of corruptions and scandal in the West (or the North), are compelling evidence of the need for redefinition of the concept of peace and security. Today, the road to a stable peace in the world requires a learning process not only on the part of the national decision makers but also on the part of the public as a whole. International media are in a major part responsible for the perpetuation of the so-called threat and arms gap notions through the long history of media coverage of the arms race. Prevention of war, respect for human dignity, and recognition of diverse cultural values, religions, and traditions different from our own are the areas that must be promoted and publicized internationally to shift this attitude. The world scope of the media and communication ultimately must be viewed as a whole.

In addition, the utility and value of international communication fora must not be underestimated, especially in view of the recurrent scenarios in world history, in which comparatively small countries can set in motion chains of events that climax in catastrophic conflagrations. The United Nations and many other intergovernmental and nongovernmental organizations and institutions must serve as peacekeeping theaters where nation-state actors play out their roles, communicating frustrations that, if left unexpressed, might lead to violence. It must be recalled that there is hardly a single international treaty concluded since World War I that has not been violated or deliberately scrapped by one or all of the signatories. It is no wonder, then, that the international system as a contractual community is crumbling.

The Meaning of Justice

Such a redefinition of what is meant by global peace in itself supports the argument that what is needed now is a shift from a manipulative, technology-oriented communication to more human interaction and exchange of ideas. To achieve this, we must move to create and promote a set of principles or considerations in the notion of justice and human rights that is not culture bound but universal, that strives for the dignity and potential of human beings, and that protects the world from catastrophic war and destruction. Today, as the West moves toward the so-called information society, the concepts of justice, derived from civil society by the international elites of the 19th and 20th centuries, have run into trouble. On the international level, the conventional argument was popularized that if one wants peace, one should prepare for war.

Present narrowly defined "ethical" or professional codes of ethics are irrelevant, inconsistent, and ineffective as tools in creating such an atmosphere of understanding simply because they do not challenge the technological determinist view of global interactions, are acquiescent to the centralized system of management, and put too much hope in the hands of the nation-states and other participants to deliver the goods. A confluence of historical factors has produced this disorder in the moral and ethical dimensions of the international system. The utilitarianism that pervades the world and marks various political economies generates a stream of dissenters who consider social dictums, presented as social choices, as unjust and intolerable. Until some synthesis of the moral and justice systems is achieved, our conduct at home and abroad will continue to be indecisive. But before we can begin to suggest a better future, we have to engage in a dialogue and national debate about the cycle of desire in our own institutions.

In other words, like the concepts of community, development, and peace, the notion of justice has changed. It no longer necessarily derives from agreed-on social values but now also emanates from questions of cultural heritage, religion, traditions, and the environment. As the concept of justice increases in prominence in international relations, it can be seen to move from narrow parochial definitions into a much broader universe of meaning.

If we argue that the notions of community, development, peace, and justice are all changing, then we must contend as well with the concept of social political transformation and its manifestations in both tangible and intangible processes. If information and communication underlie all the processes of development, peace, and justice, we have indeed entered a new era that was not feasible in the past. What makes possible this new era of information and communication we have entered? By speaking of a *communication era,* we must not limit our thinking to the role of conventional media or even to the dramatic extension of telecommunications in the form of modern satellite, video, or fax. Instead, the question of freedom of the press and communication is not just technological or even simply philosophical and theoretical. The central question in the new information and communication era is one of production, distribution, ownership, and manipulation of information and communication technologies and media. Who owns and controls the channels of communication—and for what purpose and intent—is the critical issue in the transformation of development, peace, and justice in the modern era.

In short, the profound global social, political, and economic changes witnessed over the past two decades have been the struggle on the part of individuals and communities to move from communications (as a means) to communication (as sharing and trust), from the alienation of impersonal, mechanistic social and political authorities and structures to social transcendence through traditional forms of human communication and interaction.

5

Language and International Communication

All communication is conducted in some form of language—spoken language, body language, sign language, binary-machine language. In the widest sense, all are ways of structuring meanings in signs that are mutually understandable and transferable. Language is the "basic stuff" of human (and machine) interactions. Language is employed in theater and literature, transmitted over radio waves, relayed via satellites, and translated into digital form to be carried along cables and between computers. When nations communicate, they do so in a language. The economic and political transactions that take place between different peoples and different societies employ language as their basic agent or instrument of interaction. Nations use language when they exchange radio programs, send news wires or sell television programming.

Despite (or perhaps because of) language's consummate centrality, it is usually ignored in the field of international communications except for specialized studies in the field. Research and policy focuses on the *media* that carry language: television, radio, newspapers, magazines; the *subject matter*: health care, sex, education, violence, advertising; and the *institutional structures, technologies,* and *finances* that make international communication possible. Another branch of international communications looks at the attitudes and behaviors of publics as sources and receivers of communication. Rarely, however, does international communication examine language itself as an issue.

Two main reasons account for the relative disregard of language issues in the study of international communications. One we will call language's invisibility, which has to do with questions of language as the language peculiar to a people—French, English, Russian, Malay, Uzbek. The other is language's transparency, which has to do with questions of language's role in structuring reality. Both dimensions concern language as power. The combined systematic methodological and epistemological omissions of invisibility and transparency have resulted in the relative neglect of language in the field of international communications and the lack of concern with language and power in international relations.

The invisibility of language comes from the state and ethnocentricism of most international communications research. Transparency comes from the positivist methodologies that are employed in this research. Language issues are invisible in most international communication research, because this research is carried out by scholars and institutions from one of the main linguistic groups internationally and from the dominant linguistic groups nationally. Language is not a problem for these societies and has become invisible. The relevant questions asked of international communications are questions of content, technology, cost and benefits. They are not questions of using one language or another or of providing various language alternatives to different groups within society.

Language is transparent in most international communication research because the positivist underpinnings of its epistemological foundations regard language as by and large unambiguous and unproblematic in the search for empirical verification. Language is not seen as an active agent in structuring meaning and relationships. Even critical studies of ideology usually ignore language itself and focus on the content and interests behind the messages.

Let us look more closely at the implications of the invisibility and transparency of language in international communications.

Invisibility

Depending on the definition of a language and the cutoff point for the number of its speakers, there are between 2,500 and 7,000 languages spoken in the world today. Of the total number of languages, between 1% and 3%, about 82 languages, are spoken by 96% of the world's population. The largest number of speakers belong to Chinese—more than 1 billion. A second tier of speakers are those of English, Hindi/Urdu, and Russian. A third group contains Spanish, Arabic, Bengali, Portuguese, and Malay/Indonesian (Laponce, 1987). Most of the world's languages are unwritten—only about 300 are in regular use in written form, and fewer than 100 of these have a written literature of any size (" Giving Power to the People," 1992, p. 1).

Mainly as a result of how the modern nation-state has crystallized, this extraordinary variety of languages is mostly absent from the concerns of the fields of international communication and international relations. With the formation of the modern nation-state system, language usually became synonymous with nationality. The English, French, German, Spanish, Danish, Dutch, Italian, Portuguese, Chinese, and Japanese were simultaneously languages, nationalities, and nation-states. This convergence changed with colonization and the imperial expansion of the European powers. The new countries of Latin America spoke Spanish but were neither Spanish nationalities nor Spanish states. The same held true for the French, English, German, and Portuguese colonies of Africa. The English colonies of America spoke English, but fought to become an independent state. When new nation-states were formed, they embraced a national language in the same way that they chose a national anthem and designed a national flag. The devaluation of native languages through colonization usually accompanied the devaluation of the other social institutions of that colonized society.

In both colonies and colonizers, national languages invariably blanketed considerable internal linguistic diversity.[1] The linguistic unification of Spain, for example, took centuries and is problematic even today. The linguistic unification of France was faster.[2] Today, in Western Europe and North America, national boundaries are roughly coincident with linguistic boundaries, and universal education has largely eliminated illiteracy. Language problems are mostly confined to ethnic minorities. In other parts of the world, however, national boundaries and linguistic boundaries have little in common, and linguistic fragmentation is the norm. Sometimes linguistic fragmentation is functional to the ruling powers. In apartheid South Africa, for example, language differences were encouraged and formalized in the nine "black languages" of the "homelands," although South Africa can probably best be divided into three main languages. The apartheid language policy followed the divide-and-rule needs of the South African government rather than any linguistic criteria (Louw, 1992). In other countries, a high percentage of the total population is unable to participate directly in the political life of the country because it is excluded by language. Language is no minor communication problem; it is utterly central to the future of the nation.[3]

Likewise, language is central to the future of the individual:

> The native speaker of a major language enjoys an important advantage in the world today. The international community is open to him; the economic benefits of high technology are potentially his for the asking, and his ability to articulate his needs in international debate is inherently superior to that of the linguistically deprived. The native speaker of a local or regional language may find his communication rights abridged not because he has no physical access to the technology or political institutions needed to express himself but because he has insufficient command of the prevailing language. The right to communicate is bound up with linguistic status. Conversely, to

deprive an individual of linguistic expression (by manipulating or changing the linguistic rules, for example) is to deprive that individual of access to the economy and the political system. (Universal Esperanto Association, 1978, p. 20)

With few exceptions like Canada, Cameroon, Belgium, and Switzerland, very few bilingual or multilingual states give equal footing to more than one national language. Only 15% of the world's independent states officially recognize more than one language as the language of their central government. Fewer states allow minority languages to enjoy secure geographical niches protected by boundaries, as in Switzerland and Belgium.

Analysts of international language issues have observed that the policies of states strongly influence the survival of languages within their borders, the modern state being typically one that assimilates its peripheral languages. This is seen to be a function of the survival of the state:

The main purpose derives from the state's goals vis-à-vis its international environment. States that project their power beyond their borders and beyond their immediate neighbors have sought, through unilingualism, to strengthen their internal system of communication, hence giving themselves a secure home base. They see linguistic fragmentation as an obstacle to mobility and/ or communication. They may even see it as a threat to the state's territorial integrity if educated minorities are concentrated at the periphery of that state and if the leaders of these minorities resent being controlled by central authorities. (Laponce, 1987, p. 193)

Most international communication research rarely takes language per se into consideration—witness the spread of the English language through the transnationalization of television. The cultural dependency literature from Latin America examined the flow of television programs, films, and magazines to the region in terms of their nationality, content, ownership, and financing. The fact that they were in English, Spanish, Quechua, or Portuguese; dubbed or original; native speakers or neutral regionwide Spanish did not enter the analysis. Similarly, communication research in the former Soviet Union did not examine the role of the Russian and "minority" languages in domestic communication interactions and their relationship to wider social movements.

There are many international communication phenomena that are primarily language-based and should be included in the field. Language is not invisible but constitutes an active force in international relations. Some of these phenomena are explored below.

Nationalism and Regionalism:
Language-Based Regional Broadcasters in Europe

As momentum in Europe built toward 1992 and a pan-European market, a regionalism of smaller culturally defined communities—the regions of Italy, the Länder of Germany, the national regions of Great Britain, the autonomous communities of Spain—was also noticeable. Regionalism as a defensive ideology is often directed against what is perceived as excessive centralization of national broadcasting rather than against non-European programming, traditionally from the United States and increasingly from Japan (EEC, 1990).[4] Partly out of economic necessity and partly out of regional nationalism, some regional channels use larger amounts of non-European programming dubbed into regional languages than do their national counterparts. As pan-European satellite channels jump national borders and reinforce English, French, and German, the strongest of the official EEC languages, regional television systems, often based on minority languages,[5] exert a countervailing force.[6]

The efforts of European regions, communities, nationalities and "nations without states"[7] to create their own media have resulted in a wide variety of television systems that are hard to place in neat categories. Some regional television services, especially those transmitting in minority languages, seem premised on a vision of European evolution that would advocate the weakening of the sovereignty of the national state (Schlesinger, 1990), as in the case of the Basque Country and Catalonia in Spain. In France, the premise is providing better local and community services through regional and local television, but the regional televisions of Belgium and Switzerland are premised on the rights of groups within multilingual states. Regional television broadcasting in the United Kingdom, Italy, and Germany is based on combinations of regional languages, commercial interest, and strong regional structures.

International Security and Conflict:
International Radio Broadcasters

International radio broadcasting has been around since World War I. States employing shortwave radio technologies have broadcast outside their boundaries to citizens of other countries and to their own nationals living abroad. These broadcasts usually employ multilingual services. The British Broadcasting Corporation (BBC), Radio Moscow, The Voice of

America (VOA), Radio Peking, Radio Iran, and Deutsche Welle are only a few examples of international radio broadcasters, many of which broadcast in more than 40 languages. Many of the broadcasts and the selection of languages they use are based on strategic political and economic interests of the sender country. The use of language by foreign powers to reach ethnic minorities within national boundaries has become an accepted part of international diplomacy and conflict.

International Commerce
and Trade: Language Quotas

On October 3, 1991, the European Broadcasting Directive went into effect. The directive was created to forge a unified market for production and distribution of TV programs and establish standards for advertising and sponsorship. Under the new rules, broadcasters must try to reserve a majority of airtime for European programs. This European TV quota has been the source of discord between the EC countries and their non-European trading partners, especially the United States and Japan (both major exporters to the European television market).

On April 1, 1992, new rules went into effect in France, requiring that 60% of all drama, scripted documentaries, and animation broadcasts by a network be European in origin and 40% be French language. The new rules on French-language programming are a result of the European Commission's decision the previous year to make the French government change its regulations concerning French quotas on drama and film. The EC ruled that national quotas are against Common Market principles and should be based on *language* rather than *nationality*.

According to the French rules, a production—feature or television program—must satisfy 14 out of 18 points to be designated as European. For example, if the director of the program is European, the production gets three points; if the screen writer is European, the production gets another two points. The production company must be headed by a European national or resident, and a majority of its board of directors must be actively responsible for not only the financing but also the technical and artistic aspects of the production.

Forty percent of all drama, scripted documentaries, and animation must be shot *principally in French* and not just redubbed or translated from an original English-language script. Feature films are governed by the same rules, but they are counted separately rather than grouped together with telefilms, soap operas, and the other program types subject to the quotas. Game and variety shows, news, and sports are exempt from quotas.

Transparency

Most research in the field of international communication regards language as a neutral tool of communication. This is the case in the communication-modernization paradigm as well as in the Marxist paradigm of class struggle and dependency. In the former, language is a neutral medium that carries prodevelopment messages and information. In the latter, power, domination, exploitation, and influence are first and foremost economic and political phenomena. Language and culture are usually a result rather than a primary cause. Although cultural domination can be the result of foreign ownership of broadcasting facilities, the impact of international broadcasters, or the flow of foreign wire services, these phenomena are studied by using categories of economic or political analysis—percentage of foreign content, capital, or technology—rather than categories of language or linguistic analysis.

Anthropological linguists and linguistic philosophers were the main contributors to the understanding of the nontransparency of language. The school of anthropological linguistics associated with the writings of Edward Sapir and Benjamin Whorf posits a close relationship between the structure of a language and the conceptual categories that govern the behavior of native speakers of that language. They claim that the world of language and the world of categories are to a great degree coterminus and that there is no way in which one can get outside the perceptual set a language enforces on its speaker except by speaking another language (Strong, 1984, p. 82).

Linguistic philosophers and the schools of philosophy associated with ordinary language

> have contributed to a new universe of discourse where we are much more profoundly aware of the complex ways in which linguistic practices, concepts and institutions shape political and social reality. The new universe of discourse and sensibility that is emerging requires that we become increasingly aware that human beings are self-interpreting creators and that these interpretations are constitutive of what we are as human beings. (Bernstein, 1976, p. 113)

From the philosophy of language, Bernstein observes, we have learned to appreciate how language is embedded in practices and shaped by intersubjective constitutive rules and distinctions.

The thoughts of Friedrich Nietzsche on language are a combination of both these approaches:

> For Nietzsche, it is not that we are bound be our language, but that we are in effect defined by our chains. Without the fetter of our language, so to speak, there would be nothing and no one at all. The choice of Nietzsche is not prison or freedom, but limitation of the chaos or not being there. (Strong, 1984, p. 82)

In the positivist tradition in which much of international communication research has been conducted, language is treated as a "symbolic structure that is external to existence and is to be used to represent or stand in place of things" (Shapiro, 1981, p. 14). However, other schools of inquiry, such as hermeneutics, rather than understanding conduct by constructing concepts and establishing their meaning externally as observational or measurement rules to get on with the task of explaining by producing and testing hypotheses, suggest that "human conduct be understood by investigating the way of life or system of norms that underlies and gives meaning to what is said and done" (Shapiro, p. 14). For the hermeneutic tradition, as well as the writings of Husserl and Heidegger and the English linguistic tradition of Wittgenstein and others, language is an expression of human existence. It is the primary medium through which conduct achieves meaning. It is part of the data of analysis for inquiry rather than simply a tool for speaking about an extralinguistic reality.

Analysts following this tradition affirm that language is not transparent. It is not about objects and experience, it is constitutive of objects and experience. The research and policy implications of this line of inquiry are that of developing an approach to language that delves into questions about the status of political inquiry—political inquiry that uncovers the political presuppositions inherent in languages and in alternative speech patterns. This means that rather than regarding language as a tool of political analysis, and the role of language as methods of organizing and dissecting a subject matter, one can regard language as the bearer of subject matter in itself.

In this context, Foucault's emphasis on language is illuminating:

> If, following Foucault, we view discourses as domains within which power and authority are conferred on some and denied to others, as political analysts and theorists our approach to language must shift. Rather than regard-

ing language and speech practices as denotational tools for discovering aspects of experience, we can regard them as representations, in themselves of political relations. (Shapiro, 1981, p. 140)

According to Foucault, in every society the production of discourse is at once controlled, selected, organized, and redistributed according to a certain number of procedures. Language operates with rules of exclusion, providing boundaries invested with institutional supports and correlated with a variety of social, political, and administrative practices.

In sum, language is only one cultural system of communication. It is always influenced by other systems and does not take place in a vacuum. It is said that the internal structure of the mind is the major influence on language. Others have argued that language is a product of cultural and environmental factors and that the mind is therefore influenced by the resulting language. Both of these ideas have validity and have been given much thought by scholars in a variety of fields, ranging from anthropology and psychology to biology and linguistics. What is clear is that we are human by virtue of the kind of interaction that goes on through human communication systems, and language is the most sophisticated of such systems. Today, the English language, with American popular culture, has become the closest thing to a global lingua franca.

In a very general sense, one could consider language to be almost identical to the mind—and to culture. In this sense, language is both a significant system in the creation and distribution of power and a pivotal medium in global communication.

Notes

1. Almost two thirds of all independent states (65% in 1984) have linguistic minorities accounting for at least one tenth of their population. Laponce (1987, p. 193).

2. "Centralization and the imposition of French over the regional languages has been a government policy since the Revolution of 1789. The Revolution found other-than-national identities threatening and politically incorrect. For Talleyrand and his contemporaries, linguistic unity was necessary for political unity. Speaking regional languages implied disloyalty to the new form of the French nation state." Astroff (1992, p. 3).

3. "Language Problems: Communication Problems," document submitted to the International Commission for the Study of Communication Problems. Universal Esperanto Association (1978).

4. The Japanese program presence is surprisingly large and is mainly in the field of cartoons. Many are violent and are closely linked with lines of toys. In 1989, 60% of the 11,000 hours of animated programs transmitted on the television stations of the countries of

the European Community were imported from Japan; only 350 hours were produced by member countries. See EEC (1990).

5. The 56 or so minority and regional languages are spoken by about 40 million of Europe's 340 million people. Although German is spoken by about 100 million, the Welsh or Basque languages are spoken by less than a half million (Garitaonandia, 1990).

6. Circom, an association of international cooperation of regional television channels in Europe, founded in 1983, has more than 200 members from more than 20 countries, including Poland, Czechoslovakia, and Hungary.

7. A term used to denote population groups within countries who, although they culturally and ethnically comprise a nation, do not possess a state.

6

The Remaking of
Community: The Case of Islam

Cultures are challenging the dominant paradigm. If we are to improve our knowledge in the face of change, we must understand alternative versions. For this reason, the phenomenon of communication and culture has been the subject of many heated discussions and debates during the past several decades. Although numerous studies have been carried out in this somewhat general and prolific area, the comparative aspect of this concern has remained fairly underdeveloped, particularly by the students of communication theories. There are a number of distinct reasons for this neglect, among them, conceptual unclarity, epistemological rigidity, insufficient skill in language and area studies, a high level of ethnocentrism and parochialism, and many ideological biases. Consequently, our knowledge of communication, culture, and social systems is provincial rather than universal. Suffice it to say that if human communication as a discipline remains our focus of attention, we must strive to understand and study cultural and social systems in a comparative and universal context, paying particular attention to those cultural and geosocial areas with which we are less familiar.

One of the cultures challenging the Western paradigm is Islam. The following discussion examines social and value systems within an Islamic context as a contemporary laboratory for studying community building. A social system is a process of interaction of individuals within a larger unit called society, which exhibits the property that Ibn Khaldun, an Islamic thinker, called solidarity (*assabieh*), a term also employed later by Durkheim in his works. As Kroeber and Parsons have noted, a social system is not the value itself, but a system of values and actions of individuals that are associated in terms of symbolic meaning. On the other hand, values are instruments of maintaining the cultural integrity and cohesion of society, serving to legitimize the modes of more concrete actions. Here, we are concerned with the question of cultural systems and how they interact with problems of conceptualization, theorization, and practices of information and communication. What impact do cultural settings have on the studies of communication? What communication theories and practices do they foster?

The Islamic World

The Islamic world consists of a vast and diverse geopolitical area, stretching from Indonesia and the Pacific Ocean in the east to Morocco and the Atlantic coast in the west, from central Asia and the Himalayas in the north to the southern African nations and the Indian Ocean. As one of the major religions of the world, Islam encompasses one quarter of the world's population—more than 1 billion people. From the death of the prophet Mohammad (572-632 A.D.) and the period of the first four Caliphs (632-661 A.D.), to the end of World War I and the demise of the Ottoman Empire, the Islamic community has been a major world power. In the context of decolonization and increasing numbers of sovereign nation-states, the Islamic world politically, economically, and often culturally began to integrate into the existing sphere of the Western-dominated modern world system. The contacts between the Islamic world and the West in the 19th and 20th centuries increased the absorption of many Islamic countries into quasi-secular political entities ranging from hereditary monarchies to modern Western and military-style republics. This also resulted in pronounced conflicts between modern secularism and the Islamic tradition of *al shari'a,* the canonical law of Islam.

To understand the current social communication processes in the Islamic world and to assess their future directions, it is necessary to examine not only a number of the fundamental principles on which the Islamic *tabligh* (propagation) framework has been built but also how the Islamic societies have come under constraints as a result of global political, economic, and cultural developments over the past century. The central foci of analysis will be on the fundamental principles of Islamic ethical methods in communication and on the objectives and aims of *tabligh.* This understanding should help clarify the function of some of the modern institutions of communication in contemporary Islamic societies.

Definition of Terms

A distinction should be made between the Islamic term *tabligh* (propagation) and the general concepts of communication, propaganda, and agitation commonly used in contemporary literature. The word *communication* comes from the Latin *communico*, meaning share, and it is essentially a social process referring to the act of imparting, conveying, or exchanging ideas, knowledge, or information. It is a process of access or means of access between two or more persons or places. Also implicit and explicit in this definition is a notion of some degree of trust, without which communication cannot take place. In its reductive approach (mathematical, technical, and some scientific analysis), communication is associated with the concept of information linking the process with chance events and various possible outcomes. This so-called atomic view gives emphasis to quantitative and linear aspects of the process and not to its cultural and cognitive meanings (see Cherry, 1961; Kirschenmann, 1970; Shannon & Weaver, 1961; Wiener, 1961, 1967).

The term *propaganda* is a Western concept and was used for the first time by a committee of Cardinals (founded in 1622 by Pope Gregory) of the Roman Catholic Church having the care and oversight of foreign missions. Propaganda comes from the Latin word *propagare* and originally meant propagating the gospel and establishing the Church in non-Christian countries. The contemporary usage of the term *propaganda* in its political, sociological, and commercial contexts, however, dates back to the beginning of the 20th century. Since World War I, its definition has evolved to connote an instrument of persuasion and manipulation of individuals and collective behavior in national and international scenes.[1]

Thus, according to French sociologist Jacques Ellul, "propaganda is a set of methods employed by an organized group that wants to bring about the active or passive participation in its action of a mass of individuals psychologically unified through psychological manipulations and incorporated in an organization" (Ellul, 1965, p. 61). In a somewhat similar fashion, Harold D. Lasswell (1942) has defined propaganda as "the manipulation of symbols as a means of influencing attitudes on controversial matters" (p. 42). This follows the common definition of propaganda as spreading ideology, doctrine, or ideas, and of agitation as an instrument for arousing people to spontaneous action. The Communist position on propaganda and agitation differs methodologically from that of Lasswell. As defined by Vladimir I. Lenin, "A propagandist presents many ideas to one or a few persons; an agitator presents only one or a few ideas, but he presents them to a mass of people" (1935-1939, p. 85).

Note that contemporary propagandists do not need to be believers in an ideology or a doctrine. Here, propagandists are people in the service of the state, the party, the political or commercial campaign, or any other organization that is ready to use their expertise. Propagandists are technicians, bureaucrats, and specialists who may eventually come to despise the ideology itself.

Propagation, on the other hand, is dissemination and diffusion of some principle, belief, or practice. The Islamic word for propagation, *tabligh,* means the increase or spread of a belief by natural reproduction; it is an extension in space and time. It is the action of branching out. *Tabligh,* in an Islamic context, has an ethical boundary and a set of guiding principles. In a broader sense, *tabligh* is a theory of communication and ethics. This theory of communication and global community integration is well stated by Ibn Khaldun (1967) in *The Muqaddimah (An Introduction to History).* Here he cites "truthful propagation" *(tabligh)* and group cohesion *(assabieh)* as two fundamental factors in the rise of world powers as states and large communities (pp. 123-127).

Communication and Ethics:
Their Boundaries and Frontiers

A study of *tabligh* in Islamic society in the early days—and certainly before the rise of the modern nation-state system—has a unique element to it (Mutahhari, 1977, 1982). This was because it was rooted in oral and social traditions and the notion of *ummah* or greater Islamic community. Also, the geographical entities now called Islamic countries were not heavily influenced by Western methods, conduct, and regimes in conflict with the major tenets of Islam. With the exception of the Islamic Republic of Iran, which is founded on the Islamic notion of the state, the remaining Islamic countries have state systems that are a mixture of the modern and traditional monarchical or republican systems. Thus, their legal and ethical codes are heavily influenced by non-Islamic frames of reference. In many current analyses, great confusion arises from the failure to make a distinction between a nation-state and an Islamic state. It should be emphasized that although the nation-state is a *political* state, the Islamic state is a *muttaqi* or religio-political and God-fearing community or state. The ecological terrain of *tabligh* in an Islamic community empha-sizes intrapersonal-interpersonal communication over impersonal types, social communication over atomistic communication, and intercultural communication over nationalism.

Moving from the process of *tabligh* to the definition of ethics, it must be emphasized that the boundaries of the study called "ethics" vary from culture to culture. For the purposes of the present study, a method of ethics is defined to mean any rational procedure by which we determine what an individual human being as a person and as a member of a community ought to do as a right action by voluntary means. By using the word *individual* as a member of a community, this definition does not make a distinction between ethics and politics. From an Islamic perspective, the study and conduct of politics cannot be separated from the methods of ethics; the need is to determine what ought to be and not to analyze what merely is. Consequently, the concept of ethics here essentially deals with the Islamic perceptions of conduct as an inquiry into the nature of the unity of God, humankind, and nature, and the method of attaining it (Mutahhari, 1985).

Beginning with the Enlightenment, the West gradually divorced religion from secular life. Ethical conduct of the everyday life was left to an individual's conscience as long as such actions did not conflict with the perceived public morality. In Islam, this separation of the religious from the secular sphere did not materialize, and if attempts were made by the late modernizers to do this, the process was never completed. Thus, throughout the Islamic societies, religion not only encompassed a person wholly but also shaped the conduct of the individuals in general through application of Islamic socioreligious ethics. In short, whereas modern ethics in the West became predominately social in nature, in Islamic societies that power remained social as well as religious. As the Quran says, "The noblest of you in the sight of Allah is the best of you in conduct" (49:13). In the Islamic tradition, the word *adab* means discipline of the mind or every praiseworthy conduct by which a person is excelled.

Until the 19th century, Islamic canonical law, *al shari'a,* provided the main if not the complete legal underpinnings of social and economic conduct in Muslim societies. The intimate contact between Islam and modern Western industrial countries, coupled with the process of colonization of substantial parts of Asia and Africa, introduced a number of Western standards and values to these societies. Thus, at the beginning of the 20th century and with the introduction of modern means of communication, transportation, and technologies, the fields of civil and commercial transactions proved particularly prominent for change and new methods of conduct.

The first foothold of European law, both criminal and commercial, in the Islamic countries (particularly in the Ottoman Empire) was advanced as a result of the systems of Capitulations, which ensured that the European citizens residing in the Middle East and a large part of Africa would not be governed by the Islamic laws and conduct of ethics but by their own laws and traditions. Furthermore, the reform movements, such as the Tanzimat in the Ottoman (1839-1876) and the Constitutional reform in

Iran (1906-1911), were indeed direct translations of French and other European codes, which tended to establish secularism and injected the kinds of rules of conduct that were particularly European. In Egypt, from 1875 onward, that process went even further in the adaptation of European laws in such fields as commerce and maritime and included the enactment of civil codes that were basically modeled on French laws and contained only a few provisions drawn from *shari'a.*

Tabligh and Ethical Thinking
and Practices in Islamic Societies

The current ethical thinking and practices in Islamic societies, especially as they might relate to *tabligh,* community, communication, and social interactions, are usually based on two different but important dimensions:

- Normative religious ethics, as explained in the primary source of Islam, the Quran and the traditions (*al-sunna*) of the Prophet and the Imams
- Normative secular ethics, ranging from Greek tradition of popular Platonism, to the Persian tradition of giving advice to sultans and wazirs about government and politics, to the more contemporary ethical frameworks introduced by the West through modernization, development, industrialization, and secular humanism

In the first category, the study of ethical principles in the religious tradition dates back to the 8th and 9th centuries, during which two lines of argument were developed: the rationalist and the traditionalist. The rationalists, those who subscribed to rational opinion, *ra'y,* argued that where there is no clear guidance from the Quran or tradition, the Islamic judges and lawyers might make their own rational judgments on moral and ethical questions. The traditionalists insisted that ethical and moral judgments can be based only on the Quran and tradition. This led to major debates among the various groups, which are well known in the study of the Mu'tazilites, the Asharis, the Shafi'is, and the Hanbalis, who took different positions on the questions of ethics in classical Islam.

In addition to these varied schools of thought, there is also a strong tradition in the mainstream of Islamic philosophy. This is seen mainly as the contribution of Islamic philosophers on *akhlaq* (character) in the works of such philosophers as Farabi (870-950), Ibn Sina or Avicenna (980-1037), and Ibn Rushd or Averroes (1126-1198), all of whom have contributed significantly to our knowledge about the sources of mystical as well as Sufi and Hellenic traditions in the classical Islamic system of ethics.

However, it was Ibn Khaldun, the father of sociology, who theorized about *tabligh* as a social institution that grew according to the need of the community. *Tabligh* provided, for a vast number of people from diverse races, languages, and histories, a common forum for participation in a shared culture, which was Islam. According to Ibn Khaldun, the states, governments, and political systems of broad power and great authority have their origin in religious principles based either on prophethood and propagation or on a truthful *tabligh* carried out by *khatibis* (orators/ communicators) (Ibn Khaldun, 1957, pp. 310-316; 1967, pp. 125-127). Ibn Khaldun was one of the first thinkers to point out that communication based on ethics is the web of human society, and the flow of such communication determines the direction and pace of dynamic social development. To him, combinations of the *assabieh* feelings and *tabligh* approach provided a more dynamic view of organizational behavior than can be readily derived from the more conventional concepts of states, of hierarchical position, and of role that had usually been used in the discussion of politics, government, and large social organization. He thus concluded that propagation cannot materialize without group feeling. The relationship of *tabligh* and Islam, therefore, emerges from the very nature of these two institutions. One is the source of society's values; the other propagates, disseminates, and maintains the value system of society, the *ummah* or community.

In the Islamic tradition of epistemology, the sustained discussion on ethics in Islam has been discussed in the *kalam* literature, the theologian's discussion and debate on the sources of right. Following is an outline of a number of fundamental Islamic concepts that have been the basis of Islamic *tabligh,* ethics, and sense of community. These concepts are the sources of many of the contemporary social, political, and economic debates in the Muslim world, especially in regard to normative secular ethics and in relation to the influences and values coming from the West and the non-Islamic traditions.

The Theory of Tawhid

The first and most fundamental outlook regarding man and universe in Islam is the theory of *tawhid,* which implies the unity, coherence, and harmony among all parts of the universe. Thus, one of the most basic ethical pillars of the Islamic world is born: the existence of purpose in the creation and the liberation and freedom of humankind from bondage and servitude to multiple varieties of non-Gods. It stands for the necessity of exclusive servitude to God, and it negates any communication and messages—intellectual, cultural, economic, or political—that subjugate humankind to creatures. The principle of *tawhid* also negates any right of sovereignty and guardianship over human society of anyone except God. Society can be expected to be free from all deviations and excesses only when the affairs of society are delegated by a Power Transcendental to an individual or a council of rulers, with a power commensurate with responsibilities within the Islamic legal framework.

Thus, all man-made laws and ethical codes that arrogate judgment to themselves, or to any authority or institution other than in obedience or enforcement of "Allah's Own Judgment," are void. Therefore, all man-made laws, communication contents, mass media, and public fora that attempt to put restraints on Allah's sovereignty must be void. The concept of *tawhid,* if exercised, provides the principal guide in drawing the boundaries of political, social, and cultural legitimation by a given communication system. The content of *tabligh* must not be directed toward creating and perpetuating political, social, economic, and cultural idols; nor are they allowed under this principle to promote the cult of personality.

Under the principle of *tawhid,* another fundamental ethical consideration in *tabligh* becomes clear: the destruction of thought structures based on dualism, racism, tribalism, and familial superiority. The function of communication order in Islamic society, according to the principle, is to break idols, to break the dependence on the outsiders, and to set the *ummah* or community in motion toward the future. Thus, one of the important functions of *tabligh* is to destroy myths. In our contemporary world, these myths may include power, progress, and modernization. Personalities, as they represent these, must not be superhumanized and superdefined. One of these dualisms, according to this principle, is the secular notion of the separation of religion and politics.

The principle of *tawhid* also requires the absence of any economic, political, intellectual, or other centers, including the media, in which power can be amassed. The freedom of expression, assembly, and that of the media of communication do not have meaning when there is no social accountability on the part of the individual and institutions. The fight against the cult of personality, and that of any social institutions associated with it, is the fight against the communication system that attempts to propagate it.

Additional consideration under the ethical framework of *tawhid* is to campaign against the material foundations of dualism. Because among the characteristics of dualism is a desire for superiority through wealth, the content of *tabligh* must not stress the value of wealth over spiritual growth and the elimination of dividing lines and forms.

The Doctrine of Responsibility, Guidance, and Action

A second principle guiding the ethical boundaries of *tabligh* in Islam is the doctrine of *amr bi al-ma'ruf wa nahy'an al munkar* or "commanding to the right and prohibiting from the wrong." Implicit and explicit in this principle is the notion of individual and group responsibility for preparing the succeeding generation to accept the Islamic precepts and make use of them. Muslims have the responsibility of guiding one another, and each generation has the responsibility of guiding the next. The Quranic verse explains this: "Call people to the path of your Lord with wisdom and mild exhortation. Reason with them in the most courteous manner. Your Lord best knows those who stray from His path and best knows those who are rightly guided" (16:125). This points out the responsibilities of Muslims in guiding each other, especially those individuals and institutions who are charged with the responsibilities of leadership and propagation of Islamic ideals. This includes all the institutions of social communication, such as the press, radio, television, and cinema, as well as the individual citizens of each community.

Thus, a special concept of social responsibility theory is designed around the ethical doctrine of "commanding to the right and prohibiting from the wrong." This concept has taken on an extra dimension of its own in the Islamic communities and societies throughout history, because Islam, as an all-inclusive systematic religion, is an interrelated set of ideas and realities covering the entire area of human notion and action, beliefs and practices, thought, word, and deed. This is particularly important in light of the fact that Islam is not only a set of theological propositions, as are many other religions, but also a set of comprehensive legal frameworks that govern every action of the individual in society and in the world at large.

For example, on the social and collective level, the doctrine has been practiced systematically in the mosque in the Islamic societies. The mosque, as a major channel of social and public communication, has always been a pivot of spiritual and cultural movements since the days of the Prophet. It has fulfilled not only the role of purification of the soul but also the acquisition of knowledge and public affairs information. Mosques and major universities existed either side by side or within one another for many years in Egypt, Iran, Spain, and many parts of central Asia and other Islamic areas. In fact, many mosques were the centers of higher education in the Islamic tradition. Today, in a number of Islamic societies, the systems of mass communication have been well integrated within the classical and traditional systems of social communication of the mosque, especially the Friday prayers.[2] The result has been a high level of organization and mobilization, making the process of political, cultural, economic, and military participation extremely effective.

It is here that the concept of martyrdom (*shahadat*) in Islam and the concept of Holy Struggle (*jihad*) may be understood only if the doctrine of enjoying good and forbidding evil is properly appreciated. The term *Islam* is derived from the Arabic root *salama,* meaning surrender and peace or peaceful submission to the Will of Allah. Thus, the concept of martyrdom, like all other Islamic concepts, is fully related to the concept of *tawhid,* or the absolute unity of God, humankind, and universe. In this sense, under the social responsibility theory of "commanding to the right and prohibiting from the wrong," the concept of *jihad* is no exception. Thus, from an Islamic perspective and ethical framework, martyrdom and struggle cannot be explained purely in terms of intercession and mediation; they should be understood within the framework of the principle of causality and not solely as spiritual mediation. In short, according to Islam, there is no martyrdom without struggle and *tabligh* in the course of Allah.

Tabligh and the Concept of Community

A third fundamental concept in determining the nature and boundaries of *tabligh* and that of social ethics, particularly as they might relate to the political life of the individual and Islamic society, is *ummah* or community. The concept of *ummah* transcends national borders and political boundaries. Islamic community transcends the notion of the modern nation-state system: An Islamic community is a religio-economic concept and is only present when it is nourished and governed by Islam. The notion of community in Islam makes no sharp distinction between public and private; therefore, what is required of the community at large is likewise required of every individual member. Accordingly, the *ummah* must be exemplary, setting the highest standards of performance and the reference point for others. It must avoid excesses and extravagances, be steadfast and consistent, know what to accept and what to reject, have principles and at the same time remain adaptable to the changing aspect of human life.

Under the concept of *ummah,* race is not accepted as a foundation of the state. Values follow piety, and the social system of Islam is based on equity, justice, and ownership of the people. There is no individual or class of individuals to dominate, exploit, or corrupt the state. Intercultural and international communication (the emphasis here is on nationality and not the nation-state) are the necessary ingredients of Islamic *ummah.* The Quran says, "We created you from a single (pair) of a male and a female, and made you into nations and tribes, that you may know each other (not that you may despise each other). Verily the most honored of you in the sight of God is (he who is) the most righteous of you" (Sura 49:13).

In the Islamic *ummah,* the sovereignty of the state belongs to God, not to the ruler nor even to the people themselves. The ruler or leaders are only acting executives chosen by the people to serve them according to the Law of Islam and the concept of *tawhid.* Every citizen in the Islamic state is required to offer his best advice on common matters and must be entitled to do so. Thus, consultative methods in politics are not only recognized but are a moral and ethical duty of the people and the ruler. Furthermore, man, according to Islam, possesses liberty and free will, so that by intervening in the operation of the norms of society, and by manipulating them creatively in accordance with the Quran and tradition, he may plan and lay foundations for a better future for both the individual and society.

Under the *ummah,* Islam has a new concept of community. One of the most important aspects of *ummah* is that Islam does not differentiate between the individuals as members of its community. Race, ethnicity, tribalism, and nationalism have no place in distinguishing one member of the community from the rest. Nationalities, cultural differences, and geographical factors are recognized, but domination based on nationality is rejected. It is the individual and his or her relations to the community that are valued; however, this relationship alone is not the sole purpose in itself. Both the individual and society must make their relationship clear to God: Are the individuals in society against God or under God? *Ummah,* as a social organization, emphasizes communality and collectivity based on Islamic tenets and not interindividualism. The social contract that becomes the basis of *ummah* is not based on free will of undefined choice but subject to higher norms: the will of Allah. Communal cohesion is based on divine rights and not on natural rights. Thus, the term *theocracy,* often cited in the West, cannot apply to the Islamic community, because the notion of church as an institution is foreign to Islam, which as a religion combines both spiritual and temporal powers. It is an ideology possessing no centralized body, yet its monotheism implies a single global order advocating the universality of moral principles. The *ummah* is beyond the nation-state in that the notion of community in Islam cannot be compared to the stages of societal development found in Western community histories—principally that of an independent and an incorporated political community or military community.

Modernization movements in Islamic societies over the past 100 years failed in part because they were unable to elaborate a coherent doctrine based on the unity of spiritual and temporal powers, the interconnection of what is known as civil society and the state. Islamic reformism, despite its idealistic unity, failed to take into account the multidimensional aspects of the society that was the *ummah.* Instead, its political culture, its mode of mobilization, and its administrative framework became ingrained in the concept of the modern nation-state system and its bureaucracy. Attempts were made to shift the models but not the dominant paradigm, which stood in contrast to the meaning of the *ummah* (see Chay, 1990; Mattelart, 1990; Mowlana & Wilson, 1990; Schiller, 1989; Shari-ati, 1980; Smythe, 1981; Van Dinh, 1987; Walker, 1984).

It is in this political, spiritual, and ethical framework that *tabligh* must play a pervasive role in the preservation and maintenance of the unity of the Islamic community. Thus, *tabligh,* on both interpersonal and social levels, becomes both basic and vital to the functioning of the *ummah,* for it sustains and encourages the integral and harmonious relationship between God, the individual, and society.

The Principle of Taqwa

A fourth and a final principle outlined here to explain the ethical framework of *tabligh* in Islamic societies is the concept of *taqwa* or, roughly translated, piety. In Islamic societies, *taqwa* is commonly used in reference to the individual's fear of God and the ability to guard oneself against the unethical forces that might surrender the environment; however, the concept of *taqwa* goes beyond this common notion of piety. It is the individual, spiritual, moral, ethical, and psychological capacity to raise oneself to that higher level which makes a person almost immune to the excessive material desires of the world, elevating the individual to a higher level of prophetic self-consciousness.

The assumption is that human beings possess in their nature a set of divine elements that are other than the material constituents that exist in animals, plants, and inanimate objects. Human beings are endowed with innate greatness and dignity. Recognizing that freedom of choice is a condition for the fulfillment of obligation, the person is held responsible to perform his or her obligations within the Islamic framework of ethics. In short, it is recognized that human beings perform some of their actions only under the influence of a series of ethical emotions, rather than with the intention of gaining a benefit or of repelling a harm. Thus, as a virtue and as an important element in the ethical framework of Islamic *tabligh,* both on the individual and community levels, *taqwa* should be the underlying ingredient in almost every action of a Muslim.

For example, fasting is an institution that has been practiced by various peoples in different times and places. In modern times, fasting has taken the two extreme forms of either ritualism and hunger strikes or dieting. Islamic fasting, however, is different in the sense that if it does not emanate from and lead to *taqwa,* it cannot be regarded as fasting. The Quran says, "O, you believers and faithful, fasting is prescribed for you as it was prescribed for those before you in order that you may develop *taqwa* (piety)" (2:183). On the leadership level of the *ummah* and community, it is the high level of *taqwa* that must be valued and counted the most. Technical knowledge, managerial ability, scientific know-how, communication skills, and so on, if not associated with *taqwa,* cannot and should not be the sole criteria for promotion in an Islamic context. In the Islamic tradition, the conduct of politics and journalism is associated with *taqwa,* and those who do not possess a degree of *taqwa* have faced the crisis of legitimacy.

This represents an attempt to evaluate the Islamic implications of our knowledge of the dynamics of communication ecology. A number of concepts have been introduced and examined to understand the phenomenon of communication and ethics in an Islamic context. It was shown that Muslim thinkers and philosophers throughout history not only recognized the importance of *tabligh* and ethics in determining the cultural profile of the Islamic civilization but also regarded the propitious equilibrium of spatial and temporal biases in Islam as an established fact. Over the past century, however, and especially during the past four decades, a dualism and contradiction have been created within the Islamic countries as a result of the introduction of the secular nationalist framework and the accompanying new concepts and methods of *tabligh* and ethics. A crisis of legitimacy has been created because of a conflict between the "official culture" of the ruling elites, which in many cases now represents and promotes Western influence, and the "traditional Islamic culture" of the masses, rooted in centuries of religio-political and socioethical experience.

Nowhere is this communication and ethical conflict better illustrated than in the structure and use of the means of communication at the disposal of both cultures. The overwhelming evidence suggests that Muslim societies have, by and large, not responded positively to modern communication ethics coming from outside their own culture; nor in the postcolonial Muslim world, has the political and communication system acquired from the West gained a broad popular base. On the contrary, such political and communication systems have become increasingly authoritarian, dictatorial, and military. As stated earlier, in Muslim societies today there exist two competing and mutually exclusive ethical methods and frameworks: the imported political culture of the ruling classes, and the indigenous political culture of the Muslim masses.

A look at the premodernist reform movements of the 18th and 19th centuries that swept over a large part of the Muslim world might offer some lessons. These movements were generated from the heart of the Islamic world itself and were directed toward correcting social evils and raising the moral standards of the community. Such movements appealed to the Muslims to awaken and liberate themselves from Western economic, political, military, and cultural domination and carry out the necessary internal reforms that would make for ethical and moral regeneration and strength. It would be a mistake to consider these movements as being primarily the result of Western influence on the Muslim world. All of these movements, without exception, emphasized a return to the tradition and ethics of Islam (Khomeini, 1361-1365). The current movements in the Islamic world are simply a continuation of the premodernist movements that tried to resolve contradictions created by exogenous forces.

Here, the central question is not one of economics but of culture, ethics, and *tabligh*. It is in this context that contemporary movements in the Islamic lands must be studied and understood. The question that Muslims have to answer is how best to devise structural changes and institutional setups that would help to maintain the precious communication and ethical balance that has traditionally been part of the Islamic civilization.

Civil Society and Information
Society: A Quest for Community

For centuries, Western political and social philosophies have been preoccupied with two problems: community and leadership; community lost and community found; leaders appeared and leaders disappeared. If community or the quest for community was the essence of Western social philosophy, anticommunity and social conflict were the other side of the same coin. In this light, the concept of civil society was another attempt in search of community, where the rights of the state and the rights of individuals were supposed to be defined.

The concept of anticommunity does not exist in the dictionary of Islam; nor is there evidence to support such a stream of thought among the Muslims and their history. Although political conflicts existed, social conflict within the meaning of *ummah* was very minimal and it was due primarily to racism, tribalism, and nationalism. This is one of the fundamental differences between the history of Western civilization and Islamic history. From the time of St. Benedict, through the writings of Sir Thomas More, down to the works of such political and social thinkers as Proudhon, Marx, Engels, de Tocqueville, and others, the notion of community stressed the relationship between man and the physical world, groups and the phenomenon of nature. It explored the technological, political, bureaucratic, and even ecological aspects of the community. Its discourse centered around pluralism, but it always fell short in integrating the diverse phenomenon of human activities in a single whole. Military, politics, economics, bureaucracy, and rationality were all departmentalized. Emphasis on one determined the social conflict inherent in the other. Communities were identified and coined when a single phenomenon, such as religion or politics, was emphasized.

For example, the quest for religious community was, in part, a response to the disenchantment of the political community, which we see in the works of such thinkers as Augustine, Aquinas, Luther, and Calvin. If power lies at the core of politics, modern scientific discovery gives prominent plea to economics and commodity production; in the West, the marriage of the two, called political economy, plants the seeds of revolution—that is, the quest for the revolutionary community. The concept of civil society was one of the last chapters written in the collection of communities that was to mark the epoch of industrialization and complement the Hegelian political philosophy.

Information Society and Islamic Society

As discussed earlier, the concept of society in Islam is based on Divine Law, which finds the foundation of world order in the principle and theory of *tawhid* (unity and oneness of God). Accordingly, the concept of society is not sectarian or racial and tribal but universal. Life according to Islam is an organic whole and all components—political, economic, religious, and cultural—are parts of the whole. Society is governed by law, that is the Divine Law, but this law precedes the society and controls it, not the other way around.

The methodological principles of *tawhid* can be summarized briefly as the rejection of all that does not correspond with reality, denial of ultimate contradictions, and openness to new and/or contrary evidence. The responsibility or obligation, known as *taklif* laid down on man exclusively, knows no bounds. The task of Islam is thus global, and the nature of the task is moral and religious, not political or economic. It was based precisely on this theory and action that the early Muslims began to establish a new order that differed from that of the Egyptians, Greeks, Persians, Romans, and even the Indians.

History of Colonialism

To say the least, Muslim societies in general have a rather skeptical picture of the West's information and media expansion. The history of colonialism shows that the West extended its hold on Muslim heritage and resources not only economically and politically but also culturally and through the expansion of their communication media and control of information (Mowlana, 1990). This colonial motivation was couched in at least four distinct but related stages, each reinforcing the other.

Missionaries and Education. In the first instance, during the late 17th century and continuing on until the mid-1920s, Christian missionaries, by establishing some of the first printing, publishing, and educational institutions in the Islamic land, laid the groundwork not only for the dissemination of religious ideas and values but also for the recruitment of corps of educated elites, who had to play a vital role in the process of political development in the later decades.

Early Telecommunications. The second stage included the establishment of some of the early telecommunications. These included telephonic and telegraphic systems in such countries as Iran, Iraq, India, and Egypt— established by the British, French, and Germans—through which the colonial lines of the European empires were linked from the center to the peripheries. This strategic use of information helped to maintain the European grip on power and gave an economic and political advantage to their native friends during the crises and anti-imperialist movements that swept Islamic lands in Asia and the Middle East in the 19th and early 20th centuries.

Rise of Orientalism. The rise of Orientalism for changes in classical Arabic and Persian orthography and bibliographical control of Islamic literature and arts was the third stage in the control and manipulation of information and images for strategic and political purposes. Indeed, the volume of literature on Islamic studies in Western languages, from the beginning of the print culture until the end of the 19th century, has been estimated to be 10,000 titles. This lopsided approach to information control on Islamic history and civilization was multiplied by the expansion of rapid growth in the print industry and by the centers of the so-called Oriental and Islamic studies, from Cambridge to Berlin and then to the New World and the United States.

Modern Mass Media and Information Society. The fourth and current stage of information dissemination and control found its way through the modern mass media, expanded globally by the West since World War II, and became the major source of news and information in the Islamic lands. In the era of cumulative indexing, the utilization of bibliographical information for certain strategic and political purposes was too obvious, because the West used the existing knowledge to cope with the problems faced in the Islamic lands. The writings of the Orientalists in the West colored the images of Islam in the modern world and shaped the agenda of scientific inquiry and discourse in this area. Also, many thousands of manuscripts by Muslim authors were moved, through the process of acquisition and colonial control, to European and American libraries.

With the coming of the so-called information explosion and information society, one of the most crucial questions facing Islamic societies pertains to the ultimate control of information processing and technology. In the face of the contemporary electronic age, there has been a gradual disappearance of the oral or traditional culture that has been a major resistance force in the face of cultural domination. The concept of civil society as a secular society was introduced into the complex life of Islamic lands at the time when the forces of resistance were at a minimum. With the new awareness and the degree of mobilization and cultural resurgence that we have witnessed during the past decades in Islamic communities around the world, introduction of the information revolution and entry into the information society seem to land on rocky soil.

The crucial question for the Islamic societies is whether the emerging global information communication community is a moral and ethical community or just another stage in the unfolding picture of transformation, in which the West is the center and the Islamic world the periphery. Throughout Islamic history, especially in the early centuries, information was not a commodity but a moral and ethical imperative. Thus, from an Islamic perspective, it seems that linguistic and political vocabularies and concepts, now at the center of global politics, both celebrate the arrival of a new communication age and hold the key to ultimate information control.

Ultimate Objective
of Community Building

Is the information society a kind of network community, in which a new rationalism is likely to impose a policy of radical instrumentation whereby social problems will be treated as technical problems and citizens will be replaced by experts? Will the new technologies of information encourage the centralization of decision making and the fragmentation of society, leading to the replacement of forms of community life with an exasperated individualism? Will the progressive replacement of mechanical and energy-based models by more cybernetically oriented models, inspired by information communication paradigms, serve to transform rational self-perception and give individuals a new image of themselves? Is the information society in a position to produce qualitative changes in traditional forms of communication and eventually transform social structures, and will such new structures require new ethics?

These are the central questions of our times. Are we talking about just teaching skills, bringing about some sort of helping infrastructure, or are we talking about community? If we speak of community, community is at a much higher level than just teaching literacy. If we want to build community in the terms discussed in this chapter, we must go beyond just literacy and health issues, beyond mass media and mass communication. Unfortunately, we arrange development projects and respond to mass mediation efforts so that the perceived purpose is to make sure that people get up early in the morning or wash their hands, stand up straight or use clocks. Development in terms of community, for example, can mean statistical reductions in infant mortality and the spread of sexually transmitted diseases. Community and mass media help to convey such messages.

These issues are by no means irrelevant, but they are on the periphery of the type of transformation of community outlined here. In fact, we can have a much greater impact if we pay attention to how community can be built, to its process. Once we pay attention to this, the process of delivery or transfer, access to and distribution of goods and services can take place. Dynamism in community—be it in development per se or in the larger context of values and belief systems surrounding community building—rejects setting goals for the completion of the change processes in societies. Whereas projects and plans may have specific goals and objectives, change in a society is continual movement in time and space and originates largely from transformation within the individual rather than from external sources.

The Information Society Paradigm

This analysis begins by questioning whether the global information community now emerging will facilitate or impede the social use of information and genuinely social aims of the Islamic community. The answer lies in examining the elements of the so-called information society, which is central to the dominant model of economic, political, social, and cultural activities of the United States and a number of other countries. It also calls for an examination of the broader concept of social life that underlines the Islamic model of community and the state.

At the center of the controversy are two visions of society: the Information Society Paradigm and the Islamic Community Paradigm. On the intellectual and philosophical levels, the philosophy and theory of information and communication have replaced transcendental discourse as the prime concern of philosophical reflection in the West. On the practical and policy levels, the Information Society Paradigm in the West has come to portray the ideology of neomodernism, postmodernism, or postindustrialism without abandoning the capitalist economic and social systems that continue to characterize its core. Thus, the Information Society Paradigm is presented as *the realization of society that brings about a general flourishing state of human intellectual creativity, instead of affluent material consumption.* According to this assertion, the relationship among the state, the society, and the individual will be determined by the production of information value, not material value. Thus, the information society, as it is argued, will bring about the transformation of society into a completely new type of human society. Some of the characteristics of the Information Society Paradigm, according to its proponents, are *spirit of globalism, the satisfaction of achieved goals, participatory democracy, realization of time value, voluntary community,* and a *synergetic economy.* Furthermore, we are told that such an information society is based on services; therefore, it is a game between persons. What counts is information. The central person is the professional who is educated and trained to provide the kinds of skills the information society requires. The information society is also supposed to be a supersecular knowledge society based on the nation-state system.

These elements of the Information Society Paradigm, when compared to the Islamic Community Paradigm and its historical experience, pose three fundamental questions:

- Should the Information Society Paradigm dominate the epistemological, theoretical, and practical aspects of the Islamic Community Paradigm, or should the latter control and direct the former? In short, which paradigm must be the basis of the process of social, political, economic, and cultural change?
- Is the Information Society Paradigm truly an information and knowledge paradigm, and whose version of information and knowledge are we talking about?
- What economic and political systems are prerequisites for the Information Society Paradigm, and what are the economic, political, and social implications of this paradigm for the Islamic societies?

The Islamic Community Paradigm

In a number of fundamental ways, the notion of the Information Society Paradigm and the emerging global information community runs counter to the basic concept of Islamic community and a number of principal tenets of Islam. More specifically as it relates to the central questions posed in this chapter, four areas of inquiry are fundamental to understanding the Islamic Community Paradigm and its experience with the West. These are the worldview of *tawhid,* the sociology of knowledge, the integration of personality, and the meaning of society and the state.

The Worldview of Tawhid

The Islamic Community Paradigm is the paradigm of the revelation and not the paradigm of information. It is Islam and the aforementioned theory of *tawhid* (the unity of God, human beings, and universe) that determines the parameters of information, not the other way around. In the world of natural and transcendental orders, it is the latter that a Muslim looks to for the values by which to control the direction of the former; therefore, information and knowledge are not value-free but have normative, ethical, and moral imperatives. The worldview of *tawhid* provides meaning, spirit, and aim to life and commits the individual to an ethic of action. In short, it is the eternal principle of *tawhid* that regulates the Islamic Community Paradigm and does not allow itself to be subservient, in whole or in part, to any other paradigm.

Thus, from the perspective of Islam, the science paradigm, developed largely as a result of the industrial revolution, and the information paradigm, now promoted to depict the postindustrial societies, are both partial and in a state of change. A major dualism and contradiction, created in the Islamic countries over the past 100 years, was precisely the fact that the Western science paradigm was imported and presented as a dominant force to guide the processes of economic and social development. Now, the Information Society Paradigm is being echoed as the realization of society that brings about a general flourishing of human intellectual activity and spiritualism. Why should the Islamic communities wait for the coming of this information paradigm to bring about spiritualism when the worldview of Islam is founded on spiritualism and human activities in the first place, with its elaborate legal, judicial, and ethical principle?

The Sociology of Knowledge

The contemporary information revolution that underlines the Information Society Paradigm should not be portrayed as a unique phenomenon in human civilization nor should it be treated as a separate phenomenon from the Islamic Community Paradigm. As argued elsewhere, in all three stages of technological and societal development—agricultural, industrial, and now postindustrial—information has been the central and most pervasive and common element in their development processes. Information in the form of skill and knowledge preceded capital formation and, in many ways, characterized all three stages. If we accept this assumption, it simply means that information and knowledge are not the exclusive property of industrialized societies, unless information and knowledge are defined in terms of Western epistemological and technological content. An example is the amount of scientific information and knowledge produced in the Islamic world in such fields as medicine, mathematics, geography, history, astronomy, philosophy, literature, architecture, and the arts, not to mention the development of communication, transportation, navigation, the paper industry, and bookmaking.

Indeed, the Islamic Community Paradigm was responsible for the information and scientific revolution that characterized the medieval ages. What is known as a dark age of the medieval period in Western history was a golden age in the Islamic community, which stretched from Indonesia and the Pacific in the East to Spain and the Atlantic coast in the West, from central Asia and the Himalayas in the North to the southern African nations and the Indian Ocean. Islamic community and civilization in Spain were, during the Middle Ages, a source of worldwide progress in information and science. While Europe was passing through a phase of ignorance, the schools of Cordoba and Granada became the centers of light for the continent. When ancient classical thought was buried in the darkness of monasteries, the Islamic scholars, philosophers, and scientists were producing a variety of knowledge in Central Asian cities of Bukhara and Samarkand and in the metropolitan libraries of the Middle East, from Ray in Iran to Baghdad in Iraq. The knowledge acquired was not only exponential in nature but also molded into such technology as mechanics and agriculture.

The orientation of Islam toward temporal life in this period was highly significant, and it left a deep impression on the course of information science and technology. The fundamental difference between the Greek culture of the classical period and the Islamic culture of the medieval time lay in the fact that while the Greek mind was riveted on the study of mankind only, the Islamic culture encouraged its scientists to study the whole universe. Thus, the scientific and information age that marked the development of Islam between 700 and 1300 witnessed not only the spiritual learnings but also the temporal, and with them came the enormous contribution of Islam to such areas as mathematics, astronomy, chemistry, biology, medicine, as well as those in philosophy, literature, history, geography, demography, politics, sociology, and economics. The Muslims developed interests in interstate relations and international problems and, as a consequence, a great appreciation for knowledge and power.

The concept of the unity of God and the brotherhood of mankind—the two fundamental concepts within the theory of *tawhid*—gave sustenance to the knowledge and scientific inquiry of this period. The concept of the unity of man knocked down the geographical barriers and racial and linguistic walls promoted earlier. The Greeks systematized, generalized, and theorized about knowledge, but the systematic investigation and scientific methods, prolonged observation, and measurement belonged to the Islamic era of information and knowledge. What we know as modern science arose in Europe as a result of this new spirit of inquiry, which was introduced by Muslim scientists to Europe before the period of the Renaissance. This is an important point for the appreciation of Islamic culture and characteristic of the information-science era that transferred the static quality of the classical Greek to one of a dynamic universe in terms of the infinite in space and time. Islam underlined reason and experience and put emphasis on nature and history as sources of human knowledge.

Information-Scientific Period

It is not possible here to give a full account of the information-scientific period that gave birth to many original contributions; however, for those unfamiliar with the information-scientific revolutions of this period, a few illustrations are in order. In the realm of information, Islam regards both self and world as sources of knowledge. The method of observation and experiment, the scientific method of induction, emphasis on sense perception as a source of knowledge, all belong to this period of information and scientific revolution in Islamic history. Indeed, had it not been for the fall of Cordoba and the sack of Baghdad and Ray at the hands of foreign invaders in the 12th and 13th centuries, Europe would not have had to wait three centuries to see the dawn of its scientific renaissance.

The Islamic Community Paradigm was also responsible for the production of hundreds of great literary and creative works in poetry, symbolism, and mysticism by such giants of history as Ibn Arabi, Mowlana Rumi, Hafiz, Sa'di, Nizami, and Attar. All of these were important works in the expansion of Islamic weltanschauung, a communication and information worldview that has yet to be examined and explored fully. They are not simply the literary and poetic interpretation of Islamic values but also have significant sociocultural and psychonormative dimensions that characterized the Islamic society.

Contributions of Islamic Scholars

Al Khawarizmi (780-850) was the founder of modern algebra whose contribution moved the theory of a static universe to one of a dynamic universe. His work was used in European universities as the principal mathematical text until the 16th century, with great influence on the works of Leonardo Filionacci of Pisa, Master Jacob of Florence, and even Leonardo da Vinci.

Razi, known to the West as *Rhazes* (865-925), was one of the founding fathers of medicine. His great work on medicine, especially his research on smallpox and measles, were printed at least 40 times between 1498 and 1868 as major texts in European universities.

Ibn Sina, known in the West as *Avicenna* (980-1037), as one of the great thinkers and medical scholars in history, gave both experience and reason a share in the formulation and growth of the data of the scientists. Not only were his medical books the texts in Europe until the modern time but his contributions to logic, philosophy, psychology, and metaphysics also anticipated some of the foremost views of Descartes, Kant, and even those of Bergson.

Al Haitham (965-1039) was a renowned physicist and one of the greatest investigators of optics and communication science of all time. His research and tabulation of corresponding angles of incidence and refraction of light passing from one medium to another laid the foundation for the training of the late scientists of Western Europe.

Al Kindi (803-873), the first Muslim philosopher, brought science and philosophy together. His application of quantitative methods to medicine brought him very close to propounding the Weber-Fechner law and won him praise from Roger Bacon, who, along with Witelo and others five centuries later, was influenced by him in his scientific and methodological works. He was one of the early pioneers in the theory of knowledge.

The scope of this information and scientific revolution has been recognized by many historians in the West and is well summarized in the words of Briffault:

> For although there is not a single aspect of European growth in which the decisive influence of Islamic culture is not traceable, nowhere is it so clear and momentous as in the genesis of that power which constitutes the permanent distinctive force of the modern world, and the supreme source of its victory—natural science and the scientific spirit. (Iqbal, 1982, p. 130)

Information was not neutral but a social and cultural commodity. Its conversion into knowledge, its pursuance and understanding in religion, social, and natural sciences necessitated the study of linguistic, grammatical, and even speculative fields. The speculative aspect of this knowledge, especially in the matter of beliefs, was responsible for the development of the science of *Kalam* (scholastic) and the discipline of *Tasawwuf* (mysticism/ spiritualism). At the same time in its comprehensive character, *Fiqh* (legal science) developed among Muslims.

Al Farabi (870-950), Alpharbius of Latin scholastics, known as the second Socrates, made original contributions to the fields of ontology, cosmology, rational psychology, and political economy. The great Christian scholastics, Albert the Great and St. Thomas Aquinas, acknowledged their indebtedness to him in the development of their own works. His views are extremely close to Spencer and Rousseau in political theory. His treaties on the "Opinion of the People of the Ideal City" and "Political Economy" resemble those of the Hobbesian law of nature, Rousseau's theory of social contract, and the Nietzchean principle of "will to power."

Al Bairuni (973-1014), the father of geodesy, was a great scientist, mathematician, astronomer, and historian who searched into every branch of human knowledge. His theory of the universe; his work on cosmogony, calendar, and chronology; his critique on Aristotle's Theory of Moving Cause in which Bairuni advanced the notion of a dynamic and changing world—all these made the 11th century the "Age of Bairuni." His travel to India and his monumental work on the subcontinent is only one example of the emphasis given to data gathering and information by the Muslim scholars of the medieval period. He emphasized the importance of the *akhbar wa rawayat* (information, news, and traditions) in understanding the international relations of the time and the propagation of knowledge "to speak truth."

Al Ghazali (1058-1111), was one of the greatest and most original thinkers of all time. In reviewing his work, one finds traces of ideas and theories that later became Descartes's method of doubt, Hume's skepticism, Kant's criticism of pure reason, and the spiritual empiricism of a number of philosophers of modern times. He doubted the evidence of sense perception and, for the first time, advanced the notion that there is no necessity to any causal connection. As Hume found out centuries later, Al Ghazali argued extensively that what we call causality is mere "following upon" and repetition, leading us to conclude that a cause is usually followed by its effect. His works began to be translated as early as middle of the 12th century, first in Latin and later in Hebrew.

Ibn Bajjah (1106-1138), known as Avempace or Avenpace in Latin and English, was a celebrated Muslim philosopher from the Iberian Peninsula who traveled in Spain and North Africa. He dealt mainly with the question of ethics and, like the Hegelians, he believed that thought is man's highest function; but, like the Platonists, he added that perceptual experience of the particulars, as opposed to purely conceptual experiences of the universals, are deceptive.

Ibn Tufayl (1110-1185), known as Abubacer, was a Spanish Muslim philosopher, physician, mathematician, and poet whose work was translated into Hebrew as early as 1349 and into most of the European languages. The German philosopher Leibniz (1646-1716) studied Ibn Tufayl's work in the Latin edition and had a very high estimation of him. It is reported that his celebrated philosophical romance, *Hayy Ibn Yaqzan* (*The Living One, Son of the Vigilant*), was borrowed by Daniel Defoe and formed the central idea of the famous novel, *Robinson Crusoe,* written in 1719.

Ibn Rushd, Averroes in Latin (1126-1198), was a great thinker whose work represented the most complete analysis of Aristotle at the time. He has been called the Commentator in Dante's *Divine Comedy* because Ibn Rushd was considered the greatest commentator of Aristotle's work.

Ibn Khaldun (1332-1406) was a Muslim thinker and historian who has been called the father of sociology and demography. His economic analysis of social organization produced the first scientific and theoretical work on population, development, group dynamics; his monumental work, *Mugaddimah* (*The Introduction*), laid the ground for his observation of the role of state, communication, and propaganda in history. According to Arnold Toynbee, Ibn Khaldun "in the *Mugaddamah* to his *Universal History* . . . has conceived and formulated a philosophy of history which is undoubtedly the greatest work of its kind that has ever yet been created by any time or place." The views of sociologists like Spengler, Danilevsky, Sorokin, Kroeber, and Ogburn are in conformity with Ibn Khaldun's work.

Unlike the Roman and Persian empires, which had to rely on military and administrative machineries to hold the various nationalities together, the early Islamic state had the unique advantage of possessing the Divine Book—the *Quar'an*—and the Divine Law—the *Shari'ah*—which eliminated national political boundaries and accelerated the process of physical and social mobility across the vast Islamic land. Communication was needed for the exchange of goods and services and the dissemination of information and science within the Islamic model of community. This led to the establishment of new postal transportation and navigation networks and to the publication of geographical guides and maps detailed in historical-economic descriptions of each place, with the names of cities and towns arranged alphabetically. The time and place of daily postal service in each town was announced in advance by governors so that both official and private letters could be dispatched in time from such destinations as Egypt to Central Asia.

The calendar created by Umar Khyyam outdistanced by far any other scientific calendar, including that of the Gregorian period. Muslim mariners established navigational networks stretching from Basrah in Iraq to the coasts of China. Today, words such as *arsenal, cable, monsoon,* and *tariff,* which are all of Arabic origin, are testimony to the communication and information age that characterized Islamic history during the medieval period.

Acquisition of knowledge is one of the highest values in Islam; however, it was the concept of society as an integrated whole within the Islamic Community Paradigm that directed the course of information and scientific revolutions of the Middle Ages in Islamic civilization, not nationalistic, economic, political, or corporate interests. In Islam, the ideal and the real, that is, the social policy and information, should not be developed separately because they are not irreconcilable opposing forces.

Stagnation in the Islamic world over the past five centuries began precisely when the internal forces, in terms of dynastic disorders and conflict, and external forces, in terms of colonialism, began the process of disintegration. The demarcation between Islamic and modern science on the one hand and a drift toward luxury, materialism, and metaphysics on the other set the Islamic community into decline. Thus, Islamic thought on science and the arts remained practically stationary. The process of dependence on Western science and technology began to take its course. Impressed by the new round of scientific and industrial revolutions in Europe, weakened by the division of the community into smaller units, fearful of the rise of the new order, the rulers of the Islamic world began to embrace the Western models of development, making themselves subservient societies under the rising international economic and political systems. The rise of Orientalism, complicated by dependence established on the Westernized education system, produced a class of intellectuals and modern bureaucrats whose political leadership helped to accelerate and legitimize this process of disintegration and disunity.

The Integration of Personality

The Information Society Paradigm is based on secularism, but the Islamic Community Paradigm is founded on a religio-political, socioeconomic, and cultural system based on an elaborate legal code and jurisprudence. The *ulamas,* as scholars of the Islamic religious sciences and especially jurisprudence, are unlike the information experts and intellectual class of secular societies, whose tasks center around economics, politics, and law alone, and unlike the priesthood class of Christianity, who are preoccupied with theological questions alone. The *ulamas* or scholars of Islam are considered *marja-i-taqlid* (source of practices), whose authoritative guidance is followed in matters of Islamic polity, law, economics, and culture.

Thus, secularism becomes alien to Islamic social and political thought when it attempts to separate religion from politics, ideas from matter, and rationality from cosmic vision. Islam views all these as an integrative whole. Western secularism was not welcomed into the Islamic communities and did not develop into a positive virtue because it symbolized the atheism and materialism of the West—a process of materialism in which technologies, methodologies, and ideologies were imported from Europe and later America. The Islamic concept of secular (versus religious) life is difficult to describe, because there is no demarcation between properly political and other kinds of institutions. Islam encompasses all aspects of social and political life and formulated norms of conduct. Because there is fundamentally no separation between religion and politics in Islam, the Islamic community has never constituted, either in theory or in practice, a theocracy, as was the case with Christianity in Europe. The term *theocracy* is both improper and paradoxical in Islamic history, because the heads of state in Islamic communities have never been religious chiefs alone, as occurs in the Christian tradition. Moreover, a priestly class has never governed Muslim societies, because the concept of church is an institution foreign to Islam. No intermediary exists between the individual and God in Islam, and no person has the authority to modify, amend, or complete the Divine Law, the Quran, and the *Sunnah* (tradition).

The French Revolution gave rise to political and philosophical dimensions of modern secularism when it replaced the regime controlled by the Christian Church. In contrast, the Islamic Revolution in Iran was the end of the secular monarchy, promoting Western models of development and the rise of an Islamic state based on the authority of Revelation and the Quran. Whereas the execution of Louis XVI symbolized the death of sacred monarchy and the rise of secular polity in France, the removal of the Shah marked the death of the secular *taghut* (oppressor) and the reappearance of spiritual and temporal power in Iran. Modernization movements in Islamic societies over the past century have failed because they were unable to elaborate coherent doctrine based on the unity of spiritual and temporal powers. In the Islamic Community Paradigm, these two forces are inseparable.

The Meaning of Society and the State

The Islamic notion of community or *ummah* has no equivalent in either Western thought or historical experience. The concept of *ummah* is conceived in a universal context and is not subject to territorial, linguistic, racial, and nationalistic limitations. Thus, the Islamic Community Paradigm is not based solely on either political economic or communication information foundations. The community is a universal society and polity whose membership includes the widest possible variety of nationalities and ethnic groups, but whose commitment to Islam as a faith and ideology binds them to a specific social order. Sovereignty belongs to God and not to the state, ruler, or people; therefore, the concept of *ummah* is not synonymous with "the people," "the nation," or "the state," which are the vocabulary of modern international relations and are determined by communication grids, information flows, geography, language, and history or a combination of these. It was the concept of *ummah* that for centuries had guided the Islamic state since the time of the Prophet and made it a world power. The border of such a community is determined by Islamic beliefs and values and not by geographical, political, and treaty boundaries. This paradigm supports the notion of nationality but rejects the concept of nationalism. It acknowledges and respects diversity, but it emphasizes the unity. Thus, the Islamic Community Paradigm runs counter to the nation-state system that characterizes the current global political system. This includes the Muslim lands that are divided into small political entities unable and unwilling to mobilize their economic, cultural, natural, and human resources under a unified Islamic state.

There is a misconception in the West and among the general public that Islam is only a religion. The division of the world into sacred and profane, religious and secular, priesthood and laity does not exist in Islam. The separation of politics and ethics and politics and economics is unnatural under the Islamic Community Paradigm. Islam is a total life system and, hence, the Islamic *ummah* provides guidance for the conduct of human activity. Only a small section of the Islamic law deals with rituals and personal ethics; the large part concerns social order. Unlike the West, where religion is a private affair for the citizen, religion is a public affair in Islam. Whereas in liberalism the political and communication sovereignty stands for the sovereignty of persons, the sovereignty in the Islamic community stands for the sovereignty of Islamic principles. Similarly, the notion of fundamentalism or fundamentalists, so often used in Western media discourse, has no place in the Islamic dictionary. Unlike with Christianity, there was no historical separation between religion and the state in Islam—and thus no fundamentalism or reformation—and if attempts were made by the late modernizers to do this, the process never succeeded. Thus, Islamic socio-religious ethics not only encompassed a person wholly but also shaped the conduct of the individual in general. In short, whereas modern ethics in the West became predominately social in nature, that power remained social as well as religious in Islamic societies.

It is precisely here that the Information Society Paradigm and the Islamic Community Paradigm have philosophic and strategic conflict, and this conflict has a cultural base and information cultural consequences. For example, ever since the Islamic Revolution in Iran in 1979, the term *Islamic fundamentalists* has been created and used in the European and American mass media, primarily in reference to the militant resistance of those in the Islamic world, especially the *Shi'a,* who strictly oppose the interventionist policies of the West in their lands in all forms. The Saudis, who are *Sunnie Wahhabies,* are not mentioned as fundamentalists in the Western media, presumably because the Saudis are moderates and have close ties to the West. Appalling as it may seem, the term *Islamic fundamentalism* is being used in the scholarly circles and discourse of the West in parallel with such movements as evangelism in the predominantly Christian worlds of America and Britain. These terms are political, value-loaded, propagandist, unanalytical or even antianalytical, and represent a kind of communication ecology by the dominant media and their intellectual spokespersons. Specifically, the depth of poverty that exists in the communication field in regard to Islamic history, ideology, philosophy, and science has contributed more than its share to the type of cultural ecology that characterizes the current international scene.

In sum, the nation-state system has divided the Islamic *ummah* into smaller parts, a process of disintegration and political frontierism that emerged in the early part of this century. The failure of the ruling elites of the Islamic countries to challenge the dominant political and economic paradigms, which laid the foundation of the existing world order, has slowed down the grassroots polity characterizing the Islamic Community Paradigm. The Islamic state was founded by the Prophet in 622 A.D. in Madinah. The political culture and the constitution that cultivated this state kept Islam as a world power until the end of World War I, despite the internal turmoil and division created within the larger Islamic law. The Islamic *ummah,* now divided into various states, is being confronted with a new order that has its base in modern information and communication technologies. Will the new order bring communities closer together, or will it tend to atomize relationships that are already precarious?

For centuries, the Islamic culture maintained a fine balance between oral and print cultures and between interpersonal and intermedia communication. The print and electronic culture, primarily in the West, helped to both concentrate power in the hands of a few and contribute to the centralization of the state apparatus and corporate monopoly. On the contrary, the oral mode of communication in Islamic societies helped to both decentralize and diffuse the power of the state and economic interests and establish a counterbalance of authority in the hands of those who were grounded in oral tradition. The individuals maintained their ability to communicate within their own community and beyond, despite the influence of state propaganda and modern institutions. The resurgence of Islam and the political and revolutionary movements within the Islamic countries, led by traditional authorities and institutions such as the *ulama,* are only one example of the potential uses of oral culture and its confrontation with modernism inherent in mediated electronic cultures. Today, the information needs of many countries are manipulated primarily by market interests and the media, and by the dominant global powers, and not necessarily by the articulation of the genuine needs of individuals, groups, and societies.

Social justice and economic order are at the heart of the Islamic Community Paradigm, as are the notions of globalization and interdependency. What is presented as a discourse of globalization today is a kind of complex interdependency, a process of networking, which brings interconnectedness in the sphere of economic, financial, natural resources, and technologies without generating a meaningful cultural framework that characterizes the community. In the West, among the early examples of such writers were Hugo Grotius and Immanuel Kant. Grotius is commonly known as the founder of Western International Law and Kant as the first cosmopolitan thinker. Although from different perspectives, and with different aims in mind, both personalities wished to assign a liberal morality to international relations—Grotius on the basis of the natural law of states and Kant on the basis of individual human rights—however, both emphasized their thinking from the perspective of the nation-state system.

From the Marxist and the neo-Marxist points of view, globalization was nothing more than the expansion of capitalism as a world system. Through this process, different national units are assigned different roles in a global division of labor; however, as Wallerstein, one of the proponents of this thesis, explains, although the states are no longer regarded as the units of analysis, they nevertheless keep playing a very crucial role in maintaining the global status quo, which features a privileged core of states against one exploited periphery.

And who are among the periphery side of this equation? The more than 1 billion or one fourth of the world's Muslim population. Who will assume responsibility for maintaining contact with this large population and for establishing communication between individuals and the *ummah*'s larger institutions? In the medieval ages and later, the provisions of the Islamic Law, known as *Shari'ah,* made it possible for industrial and agricultural goods of non-Islamic nations to move freely into and out of the Islamic territories. Globalism was as much a fact of international trade of this early time as it was of cultural, educational, and social consciousness of the Muslim world. Indeed, the Islamic Community Paradigm created the first comprehensive welfare system, abolished frontier customhouses, and encouraged truly free trade. Today, the Islamic countries, with their vast and rich natural resources, capital, and potential geopolitical and strategic locations, are incorporated into a global order that contributes to their fragmentation and not to their integration into a unified community.

Dark Surprises or Lights of Hope

What emerges from these historical developments, in regard to both the Information Society Paradigm and the Islamic Community Paradigm, are the two cultural ecological systems that account for a multitude of economic, political, and social factors. This larger cultural ecological sphere will determine not only the parameter of actions but also the possibility of convergence, or even of dominance, of one paradigm over the other. Furthermore, the lack of comprehension or the neglect of this broad ecological, cultural framework is responsible for much of the inability to understand, explain, or even predict the social and political movements of our time.

Contemporary global events took many American and European international relations experts and social scientists by surprise. In a pattern well established immediately after World War II, millions of dollars were spent on social science research to learn just how the political and communication systems worked in such lands as the then-Soviet Union, Eastern Europe, and the Middle East. Yet, in the spring of 1989, almost no one in the West entertained, let alone predicted, the unraveling of the Communist regimes, the fall of the Berlin Wall, and the unification of Germany. The "experts" in academia, the government, and the media were wrong: The third rise of Germany in this century was heading for a supposedly different ending from its precedents in 1914 and 1939. The Russians, Czechs, Poles, and Rumanians were indeed successful in attempting to challenge their political institutions. Simulation models, game theories, bargaining, and decision-making texts, so dearly memorized by graduate students and admired by their teachers, were of little help to explain these phenomena. A few scholars and observers who had predicted these developments were either ignored or put aside.

A decade earlier, virtually no one in the West foretold the resurgence of Islam and its consequences in the Middle East and around the world. The Islamic Revolution in Iran was perhaps the greatest imbroglio social science research and methodology had suffered in some time. Practically no one in mainstream social science, the government, or the media could have guessed that Mohammad Reza Pahlavi, the Shah of Iran and close friend of the West, would be overthrown by Ayatollah Ruhollah Imam Khomeini, a man then relatively unknown to the West. If the resilience of the Iranian people to withstand the 8 years of imposed war by Iraq surprised the observers, the alignment of the West and the conservative states of the Persian Gulf with Saddam Hussein of Iraq in the 1980s, and their realignment against him following his subsequent invasion of Kuwait in the 1990s, were indeed astonishing.

What went wrong? Why did the observers neither prophesy nor delineate the communication, political, and cultural landscapes that prevail today? Was this because they paid too much heed to those elements in modern life that characterize formal institutions and formal ideologies? Or, did they simply misconstrue the processes of social change taking place in our time? Were they misled by their cultural bias and the pattern of discourse that had dominated their social interactions? How critical were their "critical" methodologies?

Indeed, at the closing decade of the 20th century, there were some reflections among the group called "strategic thinkers" that there must be more to international relations than simple military-diplomatic situations. They were realizing that the world they had known for four decades since World War II could not go on forever. With such global development and its molecular ferment of popular movement and immanent relation between capital and information, we had entered the plane of chaotic digital transformation, in which human, real estate, social relations, and international politics now were converted into a complex and uncertain world. The unpredictability of international events and the insecurity dominating the major powers are one side of the coin; the other is the increasing capacity of smaller nations to mobilize their populations and resources to challenge the old order and demand a new. The implosive collapse of the state machine, in which it becomes sucked into its own black hole rationality through electronic and bureaucratic techniques, is only one symptom of this phenomenon; the erosion of the legitimacy of the nation-state system in all its ideological forms is another.

The political-economic division of this planet into three distinct worlds was never scientific, and its reconceptualization into a single world is proving to be no better. The Third World is divided, as the Persian Gulf war and other events proved; the Second World and the Soviet Union have unraveled, and America and the rest of the First World are becoming increasingly irrelevant for the rest. To appreciate the transformation and the complexity of global politics, a communication and cultural perspective is indeed needed.

Notes

1. Lasswell, Lerner, and Speier (1980), in three volumes. The first volume deals with "The Symbolic Instrument in Early Times," and the second volume concerns the "Emergence of Public Opinion in the West." The third volume deals with the contemporary world situation.

2. Mowlana (1979b, pp. 107-112; Mowlana & Wilson, 1985). For a review of global information and international communication, see Mowlana (1986, 1988).

7

The Future of the State:
An Islamic Perspective

The discourse on the nation-state in the Western industrialized world deals almost exclusively with evolution of a particular kind of state that had its origin and development in Western Europe over the past 200 years in predominantly Christian and capitalist countries. In the Islamic countries of the Middle East, the conception of the state, however, historically offers a radically different version of the relationship of governing bodies to society. Over the past 14 centuries the notion of the state in an Islamic context has undergone the process of articulating its unique identity in the contemporary world. The dividing of different geography, linguistics, and nationalities in this part of the world into a modern nation-state system has created a unique picture and a cultural ecology that now require close scrutiny.

This chapter will explore the concept of the state and communication as practiced in Islamic countries of the Middle East, with an emphasis on features that distinguish the Islamic state from the common conception of the state. The relationship between communication and the nation-state has been an uneasy one in the Islamic countries of the Middle East, for the modern state system has played a major role in only two distinct directions: The institutions of communication, and especially modern technologies, have been used to promote modernization and development as the state sees fit; communication also has been used indiscriminately to preserve and legitimize the state entity and authority over the community at large. Thus, a process of contradiction and a crisis of legitimacy have been engulfed within the region and within these countries, especially in the sphere of communication and the state. These contradictions, and in some cases paradoxes, are a result of a number of historical, philosophical, and cultural factors, both internal and external to the region. To understand the relationships between communication and the state in the Islamic countries of the Middle East, one needs to briefly consider the following historical dimensions:

- Concept of the state in Islam and its relations to *ummah* (Islamic community)
- Concept of communication and its meaning as it is perceived by the community at large
- Development of the nation-state system in the Islamic countries of the region
- Impact of the West and colonialism
- Islamic reform movements in contemporary history

Islamic Concept of the State and Community

Historically, the distinction between a nation-state and an Islamic state has been fraught with misperceptions and lack of understanding. The foundations of the Islamic state are the Quran, the *sunnah* (tradition), and the *shari'ah* (Islamic canonical law). Whereas in a secular nation-state, sovereignty rests in the people, in an Islamic order the sovereignty of the state rests in God and not in thrones, individuals, or groups of people. Where the state does not acknowledge the sovereignty of God, religion becomes a private affair for the citizens. In Islam, religion is not a private affair; it is a public affair. The spiritual and temporal powers are united. When Islam appeared as a world power in the 7th century A.D., the concepts of the nation and the state as we know them today did not exist.

Instead, Islam developed the concept of the *ummah*—the community of the faithful who professed to believe in both the spiritual and temporal dimensions of Islam. The concept of the caliphate as head of the community was formulated after the death of the Prophet to represent the political and spiritual powers of Islam. The political theories of the classical period of Islam identifies the caliph or Imam as the head of the state and community—the *ummah*. In the Islamic context, the power of the caliph or head of the community is limited and can be removed by the community if the caliph fails to exercise the Islamic tenets and exceeds the power identified for him.

From an Islamic perspective, the study and conduct of state affairs cannot be separated from the methods of ethics; the need is to determine what ought to be and not to analyze what merely is. A study of relationships between the state and communication in the early days of Islamic history, and certainly before the rise of the modern nation-state system, has a unique element to it. The concept of *ummah* transcends national borders and political boundaries. Islamic community transcends the notion of the modern nation-state system: An Islamic community is a religio-political concept and is only present when it is nourished and governed by Islam. The notion of community in Islam makes no sharp distinction between public and private; therefore, what is required of the community at large is likewise required of the state and every individual member of society. Both the concept of the state and *ummah* emphasize communality and collectivity based on Islamic tenets and not interindividualism. Communication in society and by the state must have ethical and moral dimensions.

The classical period of the Islamic state, which began with the Prophet himself (572-632 A.D.), and the period of the first four caliphs (632-661 A.D.) exemplify the ideal period in which communication between the state and society was most harmonious. The general political principles in Islam directed the affairs of the state. These principles called for just leadership, provision for the weak, and a critical yet constructive dialogue between government and the members of society.

The Meaning of Communication

It is interesting to note that the word *communication* in its Latin usage does not exist in Islamic literature, and when it is used and translated in its contemporary context in the Middle Eastern countries, the term takes a more technical rather than social connotation. This atomic use of communication in a non-Islamic context emphasizes quantitative and linear aspects of the process, not to its cultural and cognitive meanings. Yet, when one considers the process of communication and interactions in an Islamic context, the term corresponds to such words as *brotherhood, cohesion, unity,* and *understanding.* For example, the term *propaganda,* in its contemporary usage in the West, refers to people in the service of the state, the party, the political or commercial campaign, or any other organization that is ready to use this technique. The aim is the objective of propaganda, and the method is utilitarian.

Propagation in an Islamic context takes a different dimension. It is the spread of a belief by natural reproduction; it is an extension in space and time. In short, communication in an Islamic context has an ethical boundary and a set of guiding principles. In a broader sense, propagation is a theory of communication and ethics under the Islamic concept.

Because in the Islamic *ummah* the sovereignty of the state belongs to God and not to the ruler nor even to the people themselves, the leaders are only acting executives chosen by the people to serve them according to the law of Islam; therefore, communication on both interpersonal and social levels becomes both basic and vital to the functioning of the *ummah,* for it sustains and encourages the integral and harmonious relationship among God, the individual, and society. Thus, the special concept of social responsibility theory, designed around the ethical doctrine of "commanding to the right and prohibiting from the wrong," establishes the boundaries of communication in society and especially in the affairs of the state. For example, on the social and collective level, the doctrine has been practiced systematically in the mosque in Islamic societies. The mosque, as a major channel of social and public communication, has always been a source of spiritual and cultural movements since the days of the Prophet. It has fulfilled not only the role of purification of the soul but also the acquisition of knowledge and public affairs information. In the ideal Islamic system, because the state and community both represent the tenets of Islam, social communication at both levels is not adversarial but complementary.

Separation of the State and Community

A divisive force in Islam sprung out of the ascendancy of Muslim rulers who valued their political authority of the state more than their religious duties. From the 7th century of the Christian era, beginning with the Umayyad and the Abbasid dynasties until the demise of the Ottoman Empire at the end of World War I, the Islamic state gradually became separate from its original concept. Power became divided between the rulers, who issued laws under their jurisdictions, and the *ulama* or religious scholars and leaders, who announced verdicts under the *shari'ah* or Islamic canonical law. Thus, two lines of communication streams were established in the Islamic countries, often in an adversarial position and gradually evolving into conflict. The situation is well captured by an Islamic observer of the 11th century, Abul Malli, who said that "we obey the King in matters of State, but in matters of religion the King must consult us" (Guahar, 1978, p. 306). In time, contradictions between the state and religion ensued. The system of the caliphate as a governing body gradually lost its authority yet attempted to retain its communication dominance, resulting in repressive measures.

The changing nature of the Islamic state during this period resulted in the alienation and separation of the community from the state. In many cases, there existed only the community and its leaders; the state as such had no place in their scheme of things. The rulers were more preoccupied with repressing disorders and reestablishing themselves against rebellion. In short, the state authority was not evenly effective throughout the territory or the communities claimed by it, tending to assert itself forcefully only in the immediate surroundings of the ruler. The separation of the *ummah* and the state toward which the community gravitated, while at the same time insisting on the service functions of the state, characterizes to a considerable degree the current dilemma of the state in Middle Eastern countries.

For example, while the state attempted to centralize the institutions of communication by controlling the traditional channels such as the mosques and traditional schools of education, the community, under the leadership of the religious scholars, the *ulama,* maintained competing channels of communication that challenged the conduct of the state. The 17th- and 18th-century political systems in a number of Middle Eastern countries, including Iran and Egypt, were characterized by this proverb: "If you see the *ulama* at the gates of kings, say there are bad *ulama* and bad kings. If you see the kings at the gates of the *ulama,* say there are good *ulama* and good kings" (Algar, 1969, p. 22). Thus, the contradiction between Islamic domination and secular power spurred further antagonisms within the Islamic world throughout this period. With the public denouncement of the state, the *ulama* were pressured to act independently of the state. This type of conflict is best illustrated by the Constitutional Revolution (1906) and the Islamic Revolution (1979) in Iran. The resistance of the *ulama* to becoming mere instruments of the state, and the correlating division between Islamic and secular leadership, triggered these eventual revolutions.

The emergence of the modern nation-state system in the Middle Eastern countries partly arose out of the shifting of traditional Islamic politics toward secular government that manifested itself in Turkey's abolition of the caliphate in 1924. Turkey's decisive move toward secularism had serious repercussions in the rest of the Muslim world. Although Islamic political thought had been undergoing scrutiny by both religious reformists and traditionalists since the end of the 18th century, Turkey's action compelled the Middle Eastern countries to realize alternatives to the caliphate, which had divorced itself from the original ideas of the Islamic state. Hence, different religious viewpoints surfaced with Turkey's move toward secularization. On the one hand, the reformists or Muslim revisionists perceived the abolition of the caliphate as an auspicious event marking the overthrow of an old and corrupt hierarchy. On the other, for the more orthodox Muslims, the Turkish and modernist trend toward Western thought and secular practice reinforced the traditional view that Islam must be preserved as an all-encompassing way of life guiding moral, political, and communication actions of society. Indeed, as the history showed, the cultural agenda of Kemal Ataturk in Turkey and his contemporary ruler in Iran, Reza Shah, exemplified an effort to diminish the Islamic aspects of Turkish and Iranian peoples.

Communication, Colonialism, and the State

The penetration and intrusion of the major European powers in the affairs of the Islamic lands in the Middle East had a profound impact on the relationship between the state and communication institutions. It must be recalled that this direct incursion of the European powers in the affairs of the Muslim world signaled the beginning of both colonialism and the spread of modern communication technologies, including navigation, telephonic and telegraphic systems, transportation, and railroads. The introduction of the European powers in the Middle East, beginning with the Portuguese attempt at hegemony over the Persian Gulf in the 16th century and continuing later with the Dutch, the British, and the French penetration into vast Islamic land from Egypt to India, had two important consequences. First, it reduced the authority of the state in the Islamic Middle East, subjecting it to the political and economic will of colonial interests. Second, this colonial influence established communication dominance over the affairs of governments in the region and controlled channels of modern communication whenever possible.

The power of the state and the *ulama* was further distinguished by their relationship to foreign actors. The government tended to yield to the influence of outside courtiers and ministers, whereas the *ulama* held a clear concept and practice of authority, despite its restrictions, that resisted outside pressures. The steadfast quality of the *ulama* nurtured a close relationship with the community through the mobilization of traditional communication channels, but the state typically ignored its subjects and used modern communication channels and the emerging mass media systems to maintain its legitimacy, collect taxes, and recruit soldiers. Hence, the *ulama* became an intermediary channel of communication between the people and the state, acting on behalf of the *ummah* as well as the nation; however, it must be noted that the foremost loyalty of the community remained toward Islam rather than the state. Muslim disfavor of both the state and imperialism was proclaimed in an Islamic rather than a nationalistic framework (Mowlana & Wilson, 1990, chaps. 1-9).

Islamic Reform Movements

The contacts between the Islamic world and the West in the 19th and 20th centuries increased the absorption of many Islamic countries into quasi-secular political entities, ranging from hereditary monarchies to modern Western or military-style republics. This also resulted in pronounced conflicts between modern secularism and the Islamic tradition of *shari'ah,* the canonical law of Islam. Until the 19th century, *shari'ah* provided the main if not the complete legal underpinnings of social and economic conduct in Muslim societies. The intimate contact between Islam and modern Western industrial countries, coupled with the process of colonization of substantial parts of Asia and Africa, introduced a number of Western standards and values to these societies. Thus, at the beginning of the 20th century and with the introduction of modern means of communication, transportation, and technologies, the fields of civil and commercial transactions proved particularly prominent for change and new methods of conduct. The first foothold of European law, criminal and commercial, in the Islamic countries (particularly in the Ottoman Empire) was advanced as a result of the systems of Capitulations, which ensured that the European citizens residing in the Middle East and a large part of Africa would not be governed by the Islamic laws and conduct of ethics but by their own laws and traditions. Furthermore, the reform movements, such as the Tanzimat (1938-1876) in the Ottoman period and the Constitutional reform in Iran (1906-1911), were indeed direct translations of French and other European codes, which tended to establish secularism and injected the kinds of rules of conduct that were particularly European. In Egypt from 1875 onward, that process went even further in the adaptation of European laws in such fields as commerce and maritime and included the enactment of civil codes that were basically modeled on French laws and contained only a few provisions drawn from *shari'ah.*

The development of Islamic law and the state can be explained by reviewing briefly the classical period of Islam, during which the general political principles directed the affairs of the state and the manner in which communication took its course. These principles during the first four decades of Islamic history called for just leadership, provisions for the weak, a critical yet conservative dialogue between government and the members of the community, government and individual responsibility in the fight against evil, collective mobilization to defend faith, and government compliance with regard to that which is permitted and prohibited and rules of inheritance, penalties, and retaliation. During this early period, which extended to the fourth caliphate under the leadership of Ali, the Prophet's son-in-law, the state exemplified the enactment of many of these principles. The success of their application can be attributed to strong leadership and piety, cultural homogeneity, and spiritual and moral familiarity with the meaning of the Quran, especially as it is related to the solidarity between the government and the governed.

For 23 years, the Prophet guided many leaders under his spiritual and moral direction and encouraged their political and administrative involvement. At the point when the Prophet needed to be succeeded, a concern arose over who should take on this authority and in what manner. Two perspectives gained attention: the Shi'a and the Sunni schools of thought. A major difference between the two schools is the Shi'a belief that Ali, the Prophet's son-in-law, is the Prophet's rightful successor, the first legitimate leader of the Islamic community as the Imam, who was declared by the Prophet himself to lead the Islamic world. The Sunni branch of Islam, although not rejecting Ali, considered him only fourth in the first group of caliphs or leaders chosen to head the Islamic state after the Prophet's death.

However, the Shi'a school of Islam did not develop only by the question of political succession of the Prophet of Islam, but it related to the functions and qualifications of such a person. According to the Shi'a view, "the successor of the Prophet of Islam must be one who not only rules over the community in justice but also is able to interpret the Divine Law and its esoteric meaning" (Tabatabai, 1981, p. 10). The Sunni-Shi'a difference over the successors to the Prophet is resolved if one separates the administering of Divine Law from interpreting its inner mysteries. Ali accepted the previous caliphs in the Sunni sense of caliphate, that is the ruler and the administrator of the *shari'at,* but confined the function of *walayat* (revealing and interpreting Islam's inner mysteries) to himself. Therefore, Ali is considered Imam in the Shi'a sense and caliph in the Sunni sense. The Shi'a-Sunni differences are well captured in the words of Allamah Tabatabai:

> The five principles of religion (*usul al-din*) as stated by Shi'ism include: *tawhid* or belief in Divine Unity; *nubuwwah* or prophecy; *ma'ad* or resurrection; *imamah* or the Imamate, belief in the Imams as successors of the

Prophet; and *adl* or Divine Justice. In the three basic principles—unity, prophecy, and resurrection—Sunnism and Shi'ism agree. It is only in the other two that they differ. In the question of the Imamate, it is the insistence on the esoteric function of the Imam that distinguishes the Shi'ite perspective from the Sunni; in the question of justice it is the emphasis placed upon this attribute as an intrinsic quality of the Divine Nature that is particular to Shi'ism. (Tabatabai, p. 11)

There is neither time nor space in this book to dwell at any length on the evolution and differences of the Islamic political thought. Suffice it to say that the differences arise over the varying methodologies of jurisprudence, rather than the fundamental tenets of Islam. Otherwise, all Islamic schools of thought are united on the fundamental principles of the faith and the sources, which are the Quran, the *shari'ah* (tradition and canonical law), and the *hadith* (the recorded sayings of the Prophet and the Imams).

A look at history reveals that Islam did not divorce itself from Judaism, but rather perceived its own revelations as a product of religious evolution. In effect, Jewish and Christian traditions were integrated and enhanced in the common idiom of Islam. The underlying link among these religions allowed Islam to emerge as a pivotal force comprising large territories from the Byzantine Empire that succeeded the Romans. Greek influence also prevailed among the peoples of the Asia Minor and Egyptian territories. Along with adoption of the territories of Asia Minor, the Muslims gained much from both Roman and Greek philosophy and the prior civilization of the region. Despite differences over the interpretation of certain ideas, Islam familiarized itself with Western culture through Judaic tradition and Greek learning (Quareshi, 1978, pp. 237-247).

Hence, geographical factors served to enhance the historical evolution and unifying aspects of Islam. In particular, the Mediterranean Sea, which touches the shores of Europe, North Africa, and Asia Minor, served as a communication link among these different territories. Several islands, including the Balearics, Corsica, Sardinia, Crete, trajectories such as Italy and Greece, and waterways such as Gibraltar and the Bosporus, facilitated navigation. The peoples of Europe and Islam could then engage in cultural exchange while also maintaining individual development. On a less positive note, these factors bore the channels of communication that also allowed for more organized states who competed with one another for regional influence.

Several conquests and incursions marked Muslim history and had a profound impact on communication linkages and integration of the Islamic state. Under Genghis Khan (1167-1227) and later his grandson, Hulagu Khan (1217-1265) of Mongolia, the Muslim territories established throughout Central and West Asia over the course of six centuries were invaded and ravaged. Although Europeans boast of their victory over the Muslims, they fail to acknowledge that the Muslim defeat perpetuated the Dark Ages in Europe for seven centuries. Due to the internal conflicts of the Moorish Empire in the Iberian Peninsula, three centuries of remarkable contributions to art, architecture, medicine, social sciences, and learning yielded to the conquests of the Spaniards, beginning in 1085 with Toledo and extending to 1492, when Ferdinand and Isabella seized the Muslim city of Granada.

This Moorish defeat fed the Spanish power and promoted Columbus's trek toward India, which inadvertently led to the discovery of America by Europe. This discovery propelled the Portuguese to sail around Africa, with the guidance of a Muslim pilot, in 1498. The Portuguese use and piracy of the Persian Gulf and the Arabian Sea diminished the political, economic, and intellectual development of the Muslim peoples. Prior to Portuguese supremacy, Muslims peacefully controlled international communication and the maritime activities of the Indian Ocean, thus maintaining strong trade relations with the East Indian archipelago and China. In effect, this domination by the Portuguese weakened the economic viability of the Muslim East. The affluent and far-reaching empires of the Ottomans, Persians, Uzbeks, and Mughuls could not compensate for this loss. In short, the European powers continually attempted to squelch the development of a strong Islamic government and the state.

It is ironic that there is so little written on the importance of the communication and culture of the Islamic history. Although the cultural impact of the Moors in Spain is accepted, little credit has been given to the intellectual contributions of the Muslims to Italy. The Ottoman Turks conquered the Byzantine Empire at the eastern end of the Mediterranean. This conquest of European territories led to the eventual seizure of Adrianople in 1365, Constantinople in 1453, and large areas of the Balkans. Most Western scholars reduced the influence of the Ottoman Empire to that of a turning point whereby the Western modern age began and Islamic traditions were abandoned (Quareshi, 1978, p. 240).[1]

As the modern West emerged in the early 19th century, the Islamic world instinctively rejected any interaction or adoption of ideas or products of the West. This resulted, for instance, in delaying the introduction of modern communication technologies, including the printing press, to the Middle East and a number of other Islamic lands. The modern world was largely imposed on Islam without respect for its geographical, historical, and spiritual heritage. Over time, some secular and Western-oriented groups of Muslims divorced themselves from all aspects of Muslim culture and religion so that they could embrace Western ways of life in its entirety. Others, or the so-called reformists, observing the decline of the Islamic world, maintained a strong faith in tradition, and attempted to acquire modern science and technology from the West. One aspect of this reform movement originated in the scholarly and the political works of Iranian Jamal al-Din Asadabadi (known as Al-Afghani) and his Egyptian disciples Muhammad Abduh, Rashid Rida, and others.[2] Their proposition involved a balance between the adoption of useful aspects of Western civilization and the retention of Islam. However, these 19th-century leaders and scholars deferred in their implementation of this reformist idea.

The Turkish state, as the governing force over Islam during the Ottoman Empire, provides a model of Muslim reaction to Europe in the late 19th century. During their *tanzimat* era (the reform movement) of 1839-1876, the young Ottomans criticized the initial trend toward Europeanization. In turn, three reactions to Europe prevailed throughout the Islamic world. Critics in Iran and a number of Arab countries perceived the influence of Europe as a threat to the *shari'ah,* but others, primarily in the Indian subcontinent, advocated a balance between European modernity and Islamic tradition. A third group, led by Mustafa Kemal Ataturk of Turkey, called for a total embrace of Europe and secularization of the Turkish state, divorced from Islamic rule. Those who claimed the middle ground integrated elements of pan-Arabism, which partially derived from the elements of radical social policies, to form an Arab nationalist movement that could resist Western imperialism. In particular, the Arab nationalists, as prior subjects of the Ottoman Empire, rejoiced at the abolition of the caliphate that had monopolized religious power for so long. Muhammad Iqbal, an influential Islamic modernist in India, supported Turkish secularism and made an attempt to reconstruct Islamic religious thought in light of development in Europe (Iqbal, 1982).

Hence, different religious viewpoints surfaced with Turkey's move toward secularization. On the one hand, the modernists or Muslim revisionists perceived the abolition of the caliphate as an auspicious event marking the overthrow of an old and corrupt hierarchy. On the other, for the more orthodox Muslims, the Turkish and modernist trend toward Western thought and secular practice reinforced the traditional view that Islam must be preserved as an all-encompassing way of life guiding moral, political, and social actions. Thus, the traditionalists regarded Turkey and its supporters as compromising Islamic integrity. During the 20th century, the ideological and cultural differences between those who embraced modern Western ways and those who retained traditional Islamic thought became increasingly pronounced. The birth of new Islamic movements during the closing decades of the 20th century to a large degree can be attributed to the fact that the rise of the nation-state system and the promotion of the brands of nationalism of the Arab, Iranian, Turkish, and Pakistani nature did not lead to any unity of Islamic countries.

Today, those who oppose nationalism and question the basic notion of the nation-state system in Islamic lands propose that foreign encroachment can be resisted through spiritual, moral, and ethical principles of Islam that serve to mobilize Muslims for their cultural autonomy.[3] In the universalistic realm of Islam, patriotic and national views can be transcended through the new principle of *al-watan al-Islami* (the Islamic homeland), or *ummah,* once perceived as the abode of Islam.

Crisis of Legitimacy:
The Case of Iran

Iranian history provides an excellent laboratory for the study of the intricate intermingling of the state and communication in an Islamic country. Until the 1978-1979 Islamic Revolution, during which the monarch was overthrown in one of the most popular uprisings of contemporary history, the state represented successions of a series of dynasties that governed Iran for more than 2,000 years. These rulers and the states, representing a hybrid of pre- and post-Islamic history, justified their legitimacy by a mixed package of Iranian nationalism based on ancient Persian empire, language, race (non-Arab but Arian), and a series of post-Islamic developments described earlier. The men who lifted themselves into history and became "Shahanshah" (King of Kings), "Shadow of the Almighty," "Vice-Regent of God," and "Center of the Universe" came mostly from various tribal groups and legitimized their state by unifying various factions and ethnic groups in light of internal disorders and by using Islam, and especially Shi'a ethos, as a pretext for their political goals.

It must be recalled that the Shi'a school of thought flourished mostly in Iran, Iraq, Lebanon, and Kuwait, although there are considerable numbers of Shi'a population in other Islamic regions, such as Syria, Afghanistan, Saudi Arabia, Pakistan, Central Asia, and India. The rest of the Islamic world is predominantly Sunni. In Iran, the two lines of authorities, the *ulama,* representing the religion and community at large, and the king, representing the government and the state, always remained precarious at best. Several factors could be identified in determining the *ulama*'s attitude or approach toward the state. One factor is the Shi'a belief that secular power is illegitimate and, therefore, only a religious Imam can hold true authority. The efficacy of this belief became tempered by the declaration of the Iranian Safavid state (1502-1736), in which the monarch claimed, but did not prove, his descent from Imams and in which Sufi and mystic philosophies became incorporated. Moreover, a separate Shi'a *ulama* group attained prominence in the state through a de facto authority. The interregnum by the Qajar state (1795-1924) led to the demise of the Safavid system in the late 18th century, which further allowed the Shi'a *ulama* to infuse the state with their illegitimate power. This insurgency prompted the development of two additional factors that characterized the *ulama*'s attitude toward the state. The first was the evolution of the Shi'a jurisprudence (*fiqh*), which supported the *ulama* in directing and ruling the Muslim community. The second was the establishment of Qajar rule that paralleled the characteristics of the Safavid state but with even less legitimacy. Although the Qajars formally claimed a quasi-religious authority in being the "Shadow of God," no practical effort to secure the support of the citizens was made. In the face of these circumstances, the *ulama* could not exercise all the duties delegated to them under Islamic law but instead could only demand some adherence to religious principles within the state (Algar, 1969, pp. 257-258).

The Qajar period was characterized as one when the state controlled the channels of communication through its bureaucracy while the *ulama* maintained control over social communication through their influence in educational institutions (*madrasah*), mosques, bazaar, and community circles. With the public denouncement of Qajar legitimacy, the *ulama* were pressured to act independently of the state. As a result, the monarch isolated himself from his citizenry.

Introduction of Mass Media

The introduction of modern mass media institutions in Iran sharpened the differences between the state and community.[4] Printing was not a social force for about 50 years after its regular and widespread establishment in Iran in the first decade of the 19th century. However, beginning around 1860, under the Qajar king Nasser-u-Din Shah, the press became a matter of kingly concern, for that ruler was noted for his attempt to grasp all possible power. Newspaper publishing was already a monopoly of the state. Because the first newspaper, in 1837, was essentially an official court paper, it may be said that it was licensed. Its successors enjoyed no popularity but were forced on government employees, landowners, and officers of the state, from whose salaries subscriptions were deducted.

The religious disputes, the literary movement, contact with Europe, and changing social conditions were beginning to make the public more interested in events beyond the local sphere. A literary black market in books and pamphlets was starting to supply forbidden information and entertainment. Should the avenues reaching the individual citizen be operated directly by the state and the Shah; should they be semi-independent instruments subject to surveillance by the state; or should they be open to all who, by either past performance or present inclination, indicate that they are not likely to interfere with or openly oppose government policies? The autocratic regime of Nasser-u-Din Shah answered this question with a newspaper monopoly and strict control and censorship over the printing houses in Iran.

A system of strict surveillance over the publishing business required a bureaucracy to make it effective, and in 1863, there was a royal decree appointing a superintendent of the state printing press to guide and control the production of all printing houses within the country. Faced with a multiplicity of voices from both within and without the country, the regime adopted a policy of actively entering the mass communication field. Lack of communication facilities was a main obstacle in the dissemination of information. In the mid-19th century, little improvement could be seen in Iran after the decay of Safavid power in the early part of the 18th century; almost nothing was done to improve the transportation system of the country. Under the Qajars, roads were allowed to fall to ruin, and when, in the latter part of the 19th century, trade began to increase, Iran found itself without sufficient transportation infrastructure. Before the introduction of electronic communication, there was little effective control by the central government over the distant provinces. Much of the history of this period consists of revolts by pretenders and tribal chiefs.

Telegraph. It was in the early years of the 1860s that the introduction of telegraphic communication changed all this considerably, enabling news of provincial events to reach the government on a daily basis. This decade marked a significant change in the nature of communication and in the early media expansion of Iran. Lying on the highway of the nations, Iran is like a bridge in the crossroads between Europe and Asia. British imperialism was a major factor in the expansion of telegraphic lines in

Iran because of Iran's advantageous position as a link between Europe and India.

Internationally, the telegraphic lines linked Iran to the rest of the world and accelerated the transformation of ideas and reform from Europe to the country. Locally, it strengthened central government, because the news of local happenings could now reach Teheran daily and the government had control over local authorities. As for the press, it increased the amount of national and international news.

Interestingly, the *bast,* or sanctuary system, of protest called *tahhasun,* a peculiar Iranian tradition that has managed to survive even the 20th-century enactment of modern codes of law, finally became associated with the Morse invention, the telegraph. The wires were popularly believed to end at the foot of the throne in the royal palace, and on this account, the telegraphic offices became *bast* (sanctuaries) and thus provided an outlet for *tahhasun,* a certain defense against oppression. Ever since, telecommunication offices, the parliament, the shrines, the *ulamas'* residences where communication centers are supposed to be located, have become sanctuaries for the expression of *tahhasun* or opposition to the state. The Iranian constitution of 1906 was granted after the people had taken sanctuary in telegraph offices throughout the country—that is, congregated there, refusing to leave until their demands had been granted. Even newspaper editors whose papers were censored or confiscated by the state took *bast* at these centers, sending wires to the authorities and demanding freedom. Thus, at the end of the 19th century, two important channels of modern communications, the press and telegraphic service, were both a monopoly of the state.

Imperialist Penetration From the West

The Anglo-Russian rivalry was a prominent feature of the 19th-century political scene in Iran. Each side sought to prevent the other from controlling the Iranian government or absorbing pieces of Iranian territory. This rivalry also took the form of economic penetration. The fast-growing industries of the West demanded both access to raw materials and new markets for manufactured products, and countries such as Iran and India were markets for economic penetration by the European powers, necessitating some degree of political intervention on the part of colonial powers. Although Iran was never officially colonized by the European powers, this policy found one application in the struggle for concessions. In fact, the 19th century became a buyers' market for commercial concessions as the shahs discovered that their extravaganzas could be financed in this fashion. The communication institutions had to be used to advance the policies of the government in power so that the state could achieve its objectives.

In 1872, a British banker, Baron Julius de Reuter, whose scheme involved the floating of several companies to work the vast enterprise, obtained an extensive concession from the Shah. In fact, Reuter was more than just a banker; he was the founder of the Reuters News Agency. Detailed in more than 20 articles, the concession gave Reuter the right to construct railways and streetcar lines, to exploit minerals and oil for a period of 70 years, and to manage the customs services for 24 years. The agreement between Reuter and the Shah was signed in an atmosphere where no opposition voices could be heard. The feeling of Iranians was against the surrender to Europeans of such far-reaching control. On this occasion, public opinion was mobilized by opposition political and religious leaders and ultimately blocked the award of this concession to Reuter.

The 19th century was an age of great railway construction. The Baghdad Railway, the Chinese Eastern and South Manchurian Railway, and Cecil Rhodes's Cape to Cairo scheme were typical of the connection between communication, colonialism, and the state. Iran was an arena of one of the most intense imperialistic competitions. Soon after the defeat of the concession given to Reuter in 1872, Russia's first concrete attempt to build a railway took place. Every concession brought new demands from rival parties. The rivalry and the race for economic penetration continued as the shahs played their role of retailers.

Power of the Media in Exile

It was under this restrictive censorship that the publication of newspapers from exile by Iranians in Turkey, France, England, India, and Egypt increased. The history of the Iranian press in the closing decades of the 19th century is the history of the press in exile (Mowlana, 1991, pp. 37-54). It was precisely during this period that such a prominent Islamic leader as Jamal-u-Din Asadabadi (Afghani) launched his campaign and crusade against both secularism and imperialism from Iran and later Egypt, Turkey, and India. He disseminated his ideas through his newspaper, *Al-Urvatul Vosgha (The Indissoluble Link)*, which was published in Paris and disseminated throughout the Islamic world.

The newly mobilized public opinion led by the *ulama* and the exiled media met their first challenge during the year of 1892, when the Shah

gave a tobacco monopoly to a British concern. The ill-judged concession gave full control over the production, sale, and export of all tobacco
in Iran. The concession affected the position of tobacco growers, sellers,
and smokers alike. It was at this point that the grand Ayatollah Hajji Mirza
Hassan Shirazi asked every citizen to boycott smoking, forcing the can-
cellation of the concession and laying the ground for the Constitutional
Revolution 10 years later.

The growing lines of communication in Iran, both in mass media and
at traditional levels, combined with the state's submission to foreign
influence, not only crystallized the despotic nature of the Qajar regime
but also mobilized the public behind the community leaders who were
seeking constitutional reform. The challenge to the state and the European
imperialism in Iran came first from the *ulama* and later from the secular
liberal groups who were inspired by the parliamentary systems of France
and Britain. This led to the Constitutional Revolution of 1905-1906, and
eventually to the demise of the Qajar state in 1925. The resistance of the
ulama to becoming mere instruments of the state, and correlating division
between religious and secular leadership, triggered this eventual revolution. While the Qajars secured their state rulership, the *ulama* internalized
the doctrines and the duties of Shi'a theology with more tenacity than
before. Although the Qajar monarchs suppressed religious activity on the
governmental level, they failed to prevent the *ulama* from being active on
the community level.

The Constitutional Revolution led to the establishment of *Majlis,* the
National Consultative Assembly, where religious members were given the
power to veto any enactment of any legislative nature that would be
contrary to *shari'ah.* The constitution also guaranteed the freedom of the
press and assembly. For a short period, Iran witnessed a remarkable growth
of the press representing various voices within the country; the nature and
the boundaries of the new state, however, had yet to be resolved. Iran had
removed a despotic regime but had not yet succeeded in establishing an
Islamic state. It had acquired a liberal constitution but had not yet abolished the monarchy and the hereditary system of royalty. This contradiction, which lasted until the 1978-1979 Islamic Revolution, could be seen
clearly in the 1908 Press Law, adopted by *Majlis* 2 years after the
Constitutional Revolution.

Although it guaranteed freedom of the press and of expression, the law
attempted to find a happy medium between Islam and secular monarchy.
Criminal penalties of imprisonment for 3 months to 1 year were provided for the offense of libel against the Shah, and 1 month to 2 years for

publishing anything against the Islamic religions. Furthermore, as time passed, the constitutional provision allowing the *ulama* to review the legislative process and pass judgment on the laws approved by the *Majlis* was ignored. The Constitutional Revolution, at best, had become constitutional reform, having been pressured by foreign interventions, especially by Britain and Russia, and having been influenced by secular leaders inspired by European liberalism and Soviet socialism.

From Nationalism to
the Islamic Revolution

During the next 70 years, Iran paid dearly for the contradiction between a secular state tailored on European models and an Islamic state based on *ummah*. From 1925, when the Iranian monarchy was handed from the Qajars to the Pahlavis, mainly as a result of British instigation and support, until the Islamic Revolution in 1978-1979, an authoritarian secular nation-state was imposed on Iran. The reign of Reza Shah, the founder of the Pahlavi dynasty, was a period of wholesale Westernization. Religion, which had always dominated national life, was subordinated to the interests of the state. Reza Shah undercut religious power in the country in many ways. For example, he took away the judicial authority of the *ulama* and gave it to civil courts. He sent many religious leaders and well-known ayatollahs of the time into exile and, as a result, the state gained considerable influence over its new bureaucracy and much of urban society.

The founder of the new dynasty was a military officer who gained control over the army and the bureaucracy through a coup and, in light of the weakening of the old dynasty, established himself as head of state. Lacking the legitimacy of belonging to a specific tribal group, which previous kings enjoyed, and unable to establish any coalition with the religious authorities over his dynasty, Reza Shah had to rely on coercion as an instrument of state policy. The concept of public communication that developed in his reign was exactly what would be expected in an authoritarian setting. Reza Shah expressed his feeling in the official ideology with which he established and propagated his cult of nationalism through government-controlled or -owned newspapers, radio stations, and schools. His nationalism taught love of king and country. Under the rigorous censorship of his regime, freedom of thought, of speech, and of the press were suspended. Any discussion of political topics, let alone criticism of the state, was unthinkable and dangerous, even in private conversation. No party was formed during his reign. The parliament was not even a debating society, and the constitution meant very little. A reliable secret police, such as the country had not seen since Nasser-u-Din Shah in the 19th century, was created. The Muslim conquest of Iran was presented in the press and schools as a national calamity.

Although there was no wireless licensing fee, anyone owning a radio set had to declare it to the Ministry of Posts and Telegraphs and the Central Police Station. In 1934, Reza Shah established the first state news agency, named Pars, which was operated as a service of the Ministry of Foreign Affairs until 1941, when it became part of the Department of Propaganda and Publications. In short, as Iran moved into a modern nation-state system and as communication technologies were introduced into the country, the state established a monopoly of ownership over public communication, except for a few privately owned newspapers that also continued to carry the official ideology.

Reza Shah's official ideology did not survive the fiasco of 1941, when British and Russian troops marched into Iran during World War II, thus resulting in his abdication. However, the concept of public communication that he had laid out continued under his son, Mohammad Reza Shah, except for several short periods of relaxation in which religious authorities and secular liberals succeeded in challenging the state's dominance of political discourse and its monopoly of communication. Two decades of Reza Shah's rule had not succeeded in separating religion from politics to the degree that it was carried out under Kemal Ataturk in Turkey.

From 1951 to 1953, a combination of religious and secular movements occurred. Ayatollah Sayied Abul-ghasem Kashani and the nationalist liberal Mohammad Mossadegh, who had become prime minister, waged an anti-imperialist war against the British. He nationalized Iranian oil companies, nearly toppling the regime of Mohammad Reza Shah, who had fled the country after an unsuccessful attempt against this religio-political coalition. However, a coup instigated by the American Central Intelligence Agency (CIA) in August 1953 ended this short period of religio-political expansion and convergence and restored Mohammad Reza to power. The second challenge to the state's power came a decade later. In 1963, Imam Ayatollah Ruhollah Khomeini mobilized the population behind religious authorities and used traditional channels of public communication—such as the mosques, bazaars, and religious colleges (*hozah*)—to wage a campaign against the Shah's authoritarian regime and Western model of development. This resulted in Khomeini's exile, first to Turkey and then to Iraq.

It was important both politically and in terms of leadership that Shi'a religious leaders or *ulama* could maintain their independence from the semisecular or monarchical states that had come into power in the past. In the Sunni-tradition countries, such as Egypt and Saudi Arabia, religious leaders' power was consolidated within the existing political structure, leaving *ulama* little autonomy. It was precisely this power of checks and balances between the *ulama* and the state or monarchs in Iran that allowed Imam Khomeini—and others before him—to be at the center of power when disputes arose. Mohammad Reza sought wholesale Westernization through his so-called White Revolution. His attempt to make Iran a modern nation-state system modeled after Europe did not succeed. This was due in large measure not only to his propensity to rely on the United States and certain European powers but also the systematic intrusion of foreign powers in the internal affairs of Iran, which further eroded the legitimacy of the state on which his power was based (Mowlana, 1979b, 1984a, 1984b). Indeed, it was the publication of an article against religious authority, placed by the Shah's regime in the leading Teheran daily newspaper, *Ettella'at,* on January 7, 1978, that quickened the revolutionary uprising, accelerated the outburst of popular anger, and finally led to the overthrow of the Pahlavi dynasty in February 1979.

In sum, three major elements underscored the process of communication and the state before the Islamic Revolution of 1978-1979. First, the concept of a secular nation-state was never fully realized in Iran because of the contradiction it generated with Islamic notions of the state and community. Second, two lines of contradictory and competing communication channels were created, one directed by the state and the other rooted in the Iranian religio-political tradition. The state, by its modernization attempts, generated specific lines of communication along with the development of bureaucracy, university systems, military and telecommunication systems, mass media, and managerial systems. Meanwhile, the community leaders and the *ulama* maintained control over vast, highly complex, and sophisticated cultural and communication systems, never yielding to the authority of the state. As long as the state bureaucracy and infrastructure remained fairly small, it was possible to control and socialize its members along the state party line. With the growth of population and the expansion of education and bureaucratic and information communication systems, however, the process of secularization was indeed difficult to sustain. In other words, control of political power in Iran requires control over the traditional channels of communication rather than the mass media alone. It is the power of traditional authorities that determines the legitimacy of the modern media, rather than the other way around. The integration of the two infrastructures of modern and traditional channels of communication is a prerequisite to any system of state in Iran that seeks legitimacy and cultural authenticity. Third, systematic interference by foreign powers, in both communication and state affairs of Iran, further eroded the legitimacy of governments in power and deliberately blocked any attempt to establish a religio-political state that might have served as a model for the Islamic community in general.

Communication and the State
in an Islamic Context

It was at the height of these developments that the Islamic Revolution overthrew the monarchy and attempted to restructure a new state and a new concept of public communication. Imam Khomeini, who led the revolution, argued that monarchy and hereditary succession contradict Islam and therefore cannot rightfully exist. He emphasized that to avoid laws that contradict social values, Islam has invoked an executive power to monitor established laws. He stated that the laws of the *shari'ah* as a whole addressed the needs of a complete social system: interactions with neighbors, fellow citizens, children and relatives, husbands and wives, individuals, war and peace, and interactions with other nations, as well as penal and commercial codes and regulations concerning trade and agriculture. Although the religious jurists (*fughaha*) are the "trustees of the Prophets," according to Imam Khomeini, they are not confined to judicial opinion alone. More important, he argued, the *fughaha* (scholars of the Islamic religious science, especially jurisprudence) must go forth to establish a just social system guided by the principles of Islam. (Khomeini, 1981, pp. 28-39)

Equitable and compassionate social relations can only be ensured through the establishment of an Islamic state, whether by the Prophet or his followers; hence, all the duties practiced by the Prophet must be carried on by his successor, with utmost respect to the ordinances of Islamic law. He commented that, "It is not that the exercise and function of government bestow spiritual rank and privilege on a man; on the contrary, spiritual rank and privilege qualify a man for the assumption of government and social responsibilities" (Khomeini, 1981, p. 83). He put heavy emphasis on the role of communication and *tabligh* (propagation). To establish an Islamic government, Imam Khomeini advocated the propagation of the

Islamic cause; another prerequisite to such a government is instruction of the people in true Islamic teachings. He advocated the reform of the religious teaching institutions to present Islam properly to the people.

The Constitution of the Islamic Republic of Iran establishes a concept of *Velayate-Faqih,* the leadership of the state and community. Whenever any Islamic jurists meets the conditions set forth in Article Five of the Constitution, and according to a decisive majority of the people is recognized as the leader, that person will be the Leader of the state and community, as was the case with Imam Khomeini, the founder of the Islamic Republic of Iran.[5] The duties and responsibilities of Leadership include nomination of the jurisprudence of the Guardianship Council, which oversees the legislative laws, appointment of the highest judicial authority of the country, commander-in-chief of the armed forces, the establishment of a Supreme National Defense Council, and the declaration of war and peace.

According to the Constitution, two additional bodies play an important role in the conduct of the state: *Majlis-e-Khubragan* (The Assembly of Experts), who propose the Leader or the Leadership Council and are themselves elected by the people, and *Shuray-e-Negahban* (The Council of Guardians), a group of 12 *fughaha* and jurists (6 appointed by the Leader and 6 elected by the Islamic Consultative Assembly from among the Muslim jurists presented to it by the Supreme Judicial Council), whose task is to protect the ordinances of Islam and the Constitution by assuring that the legislation passed by the Islamic Consultative Assembly does not conflict with them.[6] As stated in the Introduction to the Constitution,

> The mass communication media, radio and television, must serve the diffusion of Islamic culture to aid the further development of the Islamic Republic. To this end, there is benefit in the healthy encounter of differing viewpoints, but the media must strictly refrain from the diffusion of propagation of destructive and anti-Islamic qualities. (p. 24)

Article 24 of the Constitution states that "Publications and the press are free to present all matters except those that are detrimental to the fundamental principles of Islam or the rights of the public" (p. 37). The Constitution also guarantees the formation of political and professional parties, associations, and societies (Article 26) and forbids any form of torture for the purpose of extracting confessions or gaining information (Article 38).

The Role of the Mass Media:
Radio and Television

The unique role played by radio and television in the process of individual and group socialization was well recognized by the founders of the Islamic Revolution in Iran. Indeed, by recognizing the importance of the electronic media in the process of political, cultural, religious, and economic mobilization, Iran became the first country to include in its fundamental laws specific constitutional provisions in regard to the electronic media. Whereas the operation of the national news agency IRNA (The Islamic Republic News Agency) and the regulations governing the press, including newspapers, magazines, books, and films, are within the jurisdiction of the Ministry of Islamic Culture and Guidance, the organization and operation of radio and television as an independent entity is under the supervision of the republic's leadership.

This importance attached to radio and television as means of Islamic propagation and cultural transmission was well documented in Article 175 of the Constitution of the Islamic Republic of Iran. By proclaiming that "Freedom of publicity and propaganda in the mass media—radio and television—shall be insured on the basis of Islamic principle," the new constitution gave it an independent organization outside any single ministry, placing it under the joint supervision of the Judiciary (High Judiciary Council), legislative, and executive branches. According to the revised and supplementary constitution, the radio and television organization remains under the supervision of a council composed of two members from each of these three branches, and the power of the Leader of the Revolution (or members of the Leadership Council) to appoint the director of the organization for radio and television has been clearly stated. Thus, special Islamic legal experts are appointed to the boards of the press and broadcasting organizations to advise the staff on Islamic law. News, information, and documentaries are prepared within the framework of Islamic interest. Commercial advertising is not allowed; entertainment and information are recognized as social items and not as neutral manufactured commodities.

In addition, over the past 16 years, the revolutionary leaders in Iran, schooled in traditional communication, have in many cases consolidated the mass media channels in an integrative and convergent manner with the old, such as the mosque, Friday prayer, and hundreds of other traditional channels peculiar to Iran and Islam. For example, the Friday prayer ceremony, a forum for both religious and political topics attended by millions nationwide, is broadcast by radio and television and covered extensively in the press. Correspondingly, mass media contents are discussed in the bazaar and scores of other traditional institutions of social communication, such as *doreh* (group circles), *takyeh* (religious centers for public speech and ceremonies), and *madrassah* (traditional education centers).

It is at this point that it becomes difficult to determine the effects of television without first tracing its sources and legitimacy to the input and output of the traditional means of communication at its roots. The role of traditional channels has been examined vis-à-vis the modern media in the process of political and religious mobilization in Iran. Close examination of Iranian television structure, operation, and contents reveals a surprising blend of modern technology and tradition in the process of political and cultural change (Mowlana, 1989; Mowlana & Mohsenian, 1990). The technological infrastructure of television has remained intact throughout the revolution and postrevolutionary years, but its symbolic and cultural contexts have been altered institutionally. Print media remains a mixture of individual, institutional, and public ownership. For example, major independently operated daily newspapers are under supervision of public foundations, though various ministries and individuals are able to publish their magazines and journals. Book publishing and filmmaking operate as a mixture of both private and public enterprise, and telecommunications remains a state monopoly.

In his last will and testament, made public immediately after his death, Ayatollah Khomeini wrote,

> Television films depicting Eastern or Western products made young men and women stray from the normal course of their work, throwing life and industry into oblivion in respect of themselves and their personalities. It also produced pessimism vis-à-vis their own being, their country, and culture and about highly valuable works of arts and literature, many of which found their way into the art galleries and libraries of the East and West through the treachery of the collectors. . . .
>
> My advice to the Islamic Consultative Assembly [Parliament], to the Guardianship Council, to the Supreme Judicial Council, and to the government now and in the future is to maintain the news agencies, the press, and the magazines in the service to Islam and in the interest of the country. We must all know that the Western style freedom degenerates the youth, is condemned in Islam's view and by reason and intellect. ("Imam Khomeini's Last Will and Testament," 1989, p. 6)

As a spiritual and political leader, as well as a propagator of the Islamic Revolution, Khomeini always recognized the importance of *tabligh* (propagation). In fact, his will and testament emphasized its role through the media, including television, at least 15 times in regard to domestic and foreign policies.

As Islamic Iran enters its second decade of revolution, there is no doubt that it has succeeded in the Islamization and institutionalization of many of its political, economic, military, educational, cultural, and media sectors. Whether it has created sufficient organizational and managerial infrastructure to implement the policies articulated remains to be seen. Communications infrastructure, especially telecommunications, television, and radio broadcasting, will doubtless be given high priority, especially in light of the economic problems confronting Iran during the war. These postrevolutionary and postwar reconstruction years will be a crucial period of full-scale implementation of the Islamic policies.

As described above, the geography of Iran and the Middle East has not changed much over the past century, but the geopolitical and socioeconomic dimensions of the area, in the struggle for cultural, military, security, economic, and ideological dominance, were altered during the closing decades of the 20th century by a number of important events. These included the Islamic Revolution in Iran and the resurgence of political-cultural movements in the region; the erosion of monarchical, military, and secular regimes and the inability of Arab nationalism to respond to the problems confronting the area. Added to this is the increasing dependency of many countries in the region on the superpowers and the technological shift in human ability to build, destroy, transport, and communicate. In other words, geopolitics of information wrapped in modern communication technology have now become a crucial and decisive element in the international relations of the area, making this region one of the most sophisticated centers of modern military networks in the world.

Thus, the fragmented nature of political systems in Iran, the desire to accelerate the process of modernization, combined with transitions in Eastern Europe and the demise of the Soviet Union, have all contributed to the quest for alternative visions of state, community, and leadership in the Middle East and elsewhere.

Dualism of the State:
The Challenges Ahead

Simplification and mystification in international politics since World War II has been best illustrated by the dualism of contemporary ideologies. It is apparent in the relations and the discourse of the great powers, through the use of such reductive terms as *capitalism* versus *socialism, liberalism* versus *authoritarianism, dependency* versus *interdependence,* and *internationalism* versus *nationalism.*

What then are the vital and preeminent items best describing the global landscape of international relations? Major factors involving communication and the state include the following:

- Changing pattern of human values
- Growing gap between haves and have nots
- Demographic landscape and the growth of population
- Vital and nonrenewable resources, such as oil
- Technology of communication
- Financial resources, control of market, and access to labor
- Control of political systems
- Contending public and private virtues

To this dualism can be added two major developments, discussed in the previous chapter, that now characterize the state of international communication and international relations as we approach the 21st century. First is the emergence of a new global order based on The Information Society Paradigm. This new order is that of the advanced industrialized nations, which has evolved as a result of a number of economic, political, and technological developments. It is evident now that the world is also witnessing a second development—a desire, indeed a quest, for a new cultural order that goes beyond the simple dualism of state and community, of communication and information. The quest for The Islamic Community Paradigm is a manifestation of such a development. This dualism demands new discourse and international and worldwide debate and makes communication and information concepts subservient to the broader notions of culture and social interactions. Indeed, attempts to alter the global information and communication structure to a new form, without first explaining that form, are premature. It is the examination of the nature, direction, and development of the images and realities of what might be called a grand cultural ecology, discussed in the next chapter, that will determine the parameters of global actors and participants. It will be the source and determinants of power transformation as well as the future struggles within the international system.

Although the many powers speak a similar language about the new world order, they do not mean to distribute and equalize power. Instead, they seek national and international stability at the top of the global hierarchy, with inequality of power below. For this reason, "issue definition" such as trade, monetary systems, population growth, disarmament, food, environmental problems, security, war, and peace will remain the areas of negotiation, cooperation, and conflict among the nation-states and institutions. In this manner, therefore, the present dominant cultural ecology or paradigm—through its international communication network and intellectual-cultural power—is determined to keep the centrality of the United States and a few European powers at the top in political, military, and economic affairs. This has necessitated the maintenance of inequality below in such cultural systems as Islam and others in the South.

The East versus West Cold War may be over, but the South versus North Cold War is an emerging system. The Eastern socialist systems have crumbled, yet the alternative models for them are embryonic. Concurrently, the centrality of the North is increasing as secular transcontinental Europe and North American form a cultural ecology over the southern half of the world. The demands for a new world order by the North, and the demands for change and redistribution of resources and power by the South, have cultural contexts and stem from different notions of politics and culture. Thus, as the economic and political power of the former Soviet Union declines, and as the Central and Eastern European nations are incorporated into the global market economy, the centuries-old cultural ties between Europe and America are bound to find new alliances and common ground. This is not simply a matter of economics and technology but has its roots in powerful epistemological, ontological, linguistic, and cultural experiences of the past.

As the dominant powers monopolize the ability to create the norms and institutions of the international economic and political systems, the so-called retribalized and nomadic politics of other cultures, in the form of nation-states, institutions, and groups, will be released in response to submerged cultural tendencies in changing societies. Today, nation-states no longer are the sole political and economic actors in the world. Other groups, such as national elite structures and transnational institutions, exert parallel, if not identical, influence over the international system and its cultural ecology. And it is precisely here that the relationships among political strategy, culture, and communication become evident.

In this context, the case of Islam and the Middle East is highly useful. Similar to what has occurred in many countries in the West, communication through the print and electronic cultures helped to concentrate power in the hands of a few in the capitalist and nation-state-oriented systems of the Middle East and to contribute to the centralization of the state apparatus. The traditional mode of communication under an Islamic paradigm helped to decentralize and diffuse the power of the state in these societies and to establish a counterbalance of authority in the hands of those who were grounded in the Islamic sociopolitical tradition. The individuals maintained their ability to communicate within their own community and beyond, despite the influence of state propaganda and modern institutions. The resurgence of Islam and the political and revolutionary movements within the Islamic countries led by traditional authorities, such as the *ulama,* are but one example of the potential use of culture and communication and the confrontation with the nation-state system inherited from the West.

Since the demise of Western-style development in Iran and the Islamic Revolution of 1978-1979, the mass media in the region have developed a new awareness of the outside world and at the same time a great degree of Islamic self-consciousness. If the substance and strategy of the revolution in Iran were new, so too was the realization that, in Islamic societies of the Middle East such as Iran, control of modern communication media does not guarantee political control. Under the Islamic system, the state's involvement in communication institutions seems natural and even necessary as long as there is no demarcation between the state and the *ummah;* under the present nation-state and economic system, however, the state's interference in public communication is being challenged. Unless the contradictions outlined here in some detail are not intellectually, politically, and practically resolved in the Middle East, the crisis of political legitimacy will continue to underline the relationship between communication and the state. These problems will be even more compounded as the countries in this region face the global development and the penetration and influence of outside institutions and powers.

Notes

1. For a more extensive review of Islamic civilization, see Arnold and Guillaurne (1960); Bosworth (1967); Enan (1940); Holt, Lambton, and Lewis (1970); Sarton (1950); Sherwani (1955); Von Grunebaum (1953).
2. For example, see Algar (1978, pp. 285-296); Enayat (1982, pp. 69-139); Halabi (1976); Keddie (1968); Kerr (1968).
3. For example, see the writings of Ayatullah Murtaza Mutahhari (1985, 1986); Ali Shari'ati (1979, 1980); Muhammad Baqir as-Sadr (1982).
4. For a history of the press and media communication in Iran, see Mowlana (1979a).

5. *Constitution of the Islamic Republic of Iran* (1980, p. 32). However, if outstanding capacity for leadership in a certain *marja* (an Islamic religious authority and jurist whose authoritative guidance is followed in matters of Islamic practice and law) is not available, according to article 107 of the Constitution, experts elected by the people will review and consult among themselves and will appoint either three or five *marjas* possessing the necessary qualifications for leadership and present them as members of the Leadership Council. The current Leader of the Islamic Republic of Iran is Ayatullah Seyyed Ali Khamene'i. Although there are separate executive, legislative, and judiciary powers vested in such offices as the President and *Majlis Shuriyeh Islami* (Islamic Consultative Assembly or Parliament), the position of Leader is unique.

6. Article 13 of the Constitution states that "Zoroastrian, Jewish, and Christian Iranians are the only recognized religious minorities with the right freely to perform their religious ceremonies within the limits of the law and to act according to their own customs in matters of personal status and religious education" (p. 18). Their elected representatives are members of the Islamic Consultative Assembly. Although the official religion of Iran is Islam and the *Twelver J'afari* school of *Shi'a* thought, other Islamic schools of thought, including the *Hanafi, Shafi'i, Maliki, Hanbah,* and *Yazdi* schools, are to be accorded full respect, and their followers are free to act in accordance with their own jurisprudence in performing their religious devotions.

8

Communication as Cultural Ecology

The last decades of the 20th century have shaken the foundations of our thinking. The world has shuddered under seismic forces of change that are welling up in not only the symbolic but also the daily and mundane structures of society. For example, ideological notions of capitalism and socialism have converged in meaning; history is now instantaneous and tele-communicated; economic and political liberalism have encountered crises in legitimacy.

Simply put, history cracked open. A quest for new ideologies began. Leaders, whose demise was unthinkable, have been lost. New leaders and followers have emerged, dark surprises for some and the lights of hope for others. American politics, Islamic culture, Japanese technology, to cite a few, ventured into what some people thought would be experimental regions of new enlightenment while others feared, instead, only quagmires of disillusionment.

These decades also were pivotal. They produced vivid theaters of operations: Vietnam, Iran, Lebanon, Afghanistan, Nicaragua, Panama, Chile, China, South Africa, Kuwait, Iraq, and, of course, Eastern Europe and the Soviet Union, not to mention the developments from Kashmir to Algeria and from Northern Ireland to South Africa. A spirit of change has seemed to pervade the political, economic, and cultural climates of the world.

Some events took nearly all the American and European international relations experts and social scientists by surprise. In a pattern well established immediately after World War II, millions of dollars were spent on social science research to learn just how the political and communication systems worked in such lands as the Soviet Union, Eastern Europe, and the Middle East. Yet, in the spring of 1989, almost no one in the West entertained, let alone predicted, the unraveling of the Communist regimes, the fall of the Berlin Wall, and the unification of Germany.

Similarly, a decade earlier, nearly no one in the West foretold the resurgence of Islam and its consequences in the Middle East and around the world. Furthermore, virtually no one in mainstream social science, the government, or the media could have guessed that Mohammad Reza Pahlavi, the Shah of Iran and close friend of the West, would be overthrown by Ayatollah Ruhollah Imam Khomeini, a man then relatively unknown to the West. In addition, no one could have guessed the resilience of the Iranian people in the 1980s to withstand 8 years of a war imposed by Iraq. Equally astonishing has been the alignment of the West and the conservative states of the Persian Gulf with Saddam Hussein of Iraq in the 1980s, and the realignment against him following his subsequent invasion of Kuwait in the 1990s.

What went wrong? Why did the observers neither prophesy nor delineate the communication, political, and cultural landscapes that prevail today? Was this because they paid too much heed to those elements in modern life that characterize formal institutions and formal ideologies? Or, did they simply misconstrue the processes of social change taking place in our time? Were they misled by their cultural bias and the pattern of discourse that had dominated their social interactions? How critical were their "critical" methodologies?

To understand this complex ecology of new and old issues, we must turn to the study of international communication in the context of cultural aspects of global affairs. Explicit and implicit in this task of understanding culture is an understanding of the value and belief systems that both give unity and diversity and provide an environment for national, regional, and even global institutions. In the past, in the area of international and intercultural communication, cultural and human components have been overshadowed by technical, political, and economic aspects of the field. What matters most today are the specific value and belief systems embedded in the cultural and human dimensions of international and societal relations.

Prevention of war, respect for human dignity, and recognition of diverse cultural values, religions, and traditions different from our own are the areas that must be promoted and publicized internationally. In addition, one of the most profound developments of the past two decades has been that of both *communication* and *communications,* that is, interactions in both human and technological dimensions. The human dimension of communication has become increasingly pivotal and central to understanding economic and political issues as well as cultural, belief, and value systems. The issue of technological hardware, of innovations in telecommunications, must be viewed as facilitating rather than dominating the human or software communication process. The question becomes, then, how we can understand this phenomenon in light of new thinking, concepts, and ideas?

The goal here is to develop the idea of international communication as a window on the multidimensionality of what can be called *cultural ecology*. By this is meant an integrative topology that emphasizes the less tangible, less formal, less measurable, more human components of international society.

Transformation in International Relations

The profound changes occurring in the global scene over the past several years, the disappearance of one of the major super nation-state systems, and the emergence of at least a dozen or more new sovereign participants in global politics have permanently altered the process of international relations both quantitatively and qualitatively. To understand these quantitative and qualitative changes, it is now necessary to look at global political and economic affairs at a more comprehensive and integrative level, which includes the dynamics of economic, technical, political, and sociocultural developments taking place.

A central indicator of the transformation taking place in the international system has been the rise in level of uncertainty and unpredictability of international interactions. Looking from the present back to the 1970s, to the Iranian Revolution, even to the war in Vietnam, it would have been impossible to predict who would be in charge, who the real leaders might be. Even with the benefit of hindsight, we have entered a new age in which no one is able to define a clear course in international affairs.

Now, a number of decades have elapsed. What then appeared to be impossible to many already is a fact. We now are witnessing an unprecedented phenomenon of social transformation everywhere that cannot be explained merely by orthodox political economic theories of social change. The world we have known for four decades since World War II could not go on forever. We have entered a challenging and yet chaotic era of transformation in which human relations and international politics are being converted into a complex and uncertain world.

The result is a redefinition of international politics in terms of communication and cultural activities. The unpredictability of international events and the insecurity dominating the major powers are included in this, as are the increasing demands of smaller nations and groups for change, and the erosion of the legitimacy of the nation-state system. It is neither an "end of ideology," as one American sociologist predicted some years ago, nor "the end of history" that one conservative commentator had recently told us. History clearly is open; quests for new ideologies and world order have begun.

Communication and Culture and the Quest for a New World Order

Two major developments have characterized the state of international communication and intercultural relations in recent decades. First, a new global information and communication order has been in the making. The emerging order is now replacing the old regime of information and communication, and it is fundamentally different in both substance and form from the one demanded two decades ago by the group of nonaligned nations and the Third World generally known as NWICO (New World Information and Communication Order). It is the new order of the advanced industrialized nations that has quintessentially evolved as a result of a number of economic, political, and technological developments, the least of which was to limit and block the original demands put forward by the Third World.

Second, since the MacBride Commission Report (International Commission for the Study of Communication Problems) in 1980, the world has also witnessed a second fundamental development—a desire, indeed a quest, for a new cultural order that goes beyond the simple notion of communication and information. This new discourse, which has a potential for a major international and worldwide debate, makes communication and information concepts subservient to the broader notion of culture and social ecology. This discourse proceeds with the notion that although the early advocators of NWICO rightly recognized and acknowledged the interrelationship between information and culture, they nevertheless made technological, economic, and political factors the foci of their demands. The underlying assumption was that once the nation-states and the peoples acquire independence, sovereignty, and communication infrastructure on some equal basis, the cultural questions that were being debated would automatically be resolved. Not so, say the new proponents of a new world cultural order.[1] The notion that information and communication are, in fact, culturally neutral is the greatest myth of our time. The assumption that the global information and communication structure can or should be altered to a new form without first explaining that form and its cultural ecology is indeed premature.

The resounding quest throughout the past 30 years has been for a new world order. In contemporary international relations, this quest is not new; what is new is the nature of such a demand and, more important, its participants. Two decades ago, the quests for a New International Economic Order (NIEO) and a New World Information and Communication Order (NWICO) were the hallmark of international debate in the United Nations and its specialized agencies as well as among the nongovernmental organizations, especially in the fields of economics and the media. As we know, the main protagonists and promoters of that debate were members of the Nonaligned Movement (NAM) and the Third World. They were asking for an equitable and fair share of the world's economic and communication resources, but their demands, at least in part, became victims of the Cold War and of superpower rivalries; they were met by a great deal of hostility from the United States and the West.

The NWICO debate, which dominated the 1970s, had a number of major features that demonstrated both its strengths and its weaknesses. The debate was mainly state-centric and a North versus South issue, with the United States and the capitalist countries at the center of the controversies (International Commission for the Study of Communication Problems, 1981; International Organization of Journalists, 1986; Smith, 1980). One of the major aspects of the debate was the so-called balance-imbalance equation in the flow of information globally, which gave a high premium to the analyses of means of production and distribution. Underlying the position of the Third World countries were the important assumptions that NWICO is related to the New International Economic Order (NIEO) debate, not independent of it (Pavlic & Hamelink, 1985). This development was a result of the increasing realization that the imbalances perceived in the economic field were also prevalent in the information or communication field and needed equal redressing. It underlined Western domination of radio, television, advertising, book publishing, film, and satellite communication. The demands of the South included a more equal distribution of the world's limited radio frequencies; reduced international postal rates for magazines, books, and newspapers; preferential telecommunications tariffs for developing countries; less restrictive copyright laws; protection against possible direct broadcast satellites; and a score of other issues.

One of the elements in the debate was the fact that *information* was assumed to be a universally understood term with an agreed-on meaning, which was not in fact the case; communication, and at times not necessarily the outcome of it, was emphasized. Furthermore, media and journalism were emphasized heavily, with traditional infrastructures and developing communication technologies taking a secondary role in the public discussion. In short, the debate, as is well outlined by others, had a number of distinct features that separated it from the global issues that followed in the 1980s. Perhaps more than any other element, the debate was mainly a political process that had not reached its economic, military, and technological dimensions by the time the MacBride Report was produced.

The NWICO debate went through a number of evolutionary stages often associated with the work of international organizations, such as agenda setting, coalition of various elements, and declarations of intentions, but it rarely reached the negotiation and bargaining stages. Thus, the debate could be explained as merely infrastructural, legal, regulatory, and procedural in its nature and goals. This is by no means to minimize the number of declarations, treatises, and dissertations written, articulating the nature, objectives, and plans of this debate. Rather, this is to argue that the realities of contemporary international relations demonstrate the vital aspects of this discourse interlocking it with the broader issue of culture. Indeed, the creation of the International Program for the Development of Communication that marked the final stage of the MacBride Report was so cosmetic, technical, and polarized that it received very minimal financial and public support.

The change in the personnel as well as the debates of this nature in international organizations over the past decade also is illuminating, for it parallels the many international relations developments that followed in the 1980s ("UNESCO: Why?," 1984). After the United States and the United Kingdom's withdrawal of their representations from UNESCO, and a long but sluggish period of instability and uncertainty, this international body entered its new phase, to eliminate many of the programs opposed by Western countries. UNESCO was not the only beleaguered organization. The entire body of the United Nations suffered tremendously from the lack of financial aid, which was delayed by the United States and its policy of disengagement. The West succeeded in preventing the continuation of the debate on information-communication and economic orders that had been originated by a number of nonaligned Third World countries a decade earlier.

In short, the concept of a new world order was put on the back burner, only to be used later, in the 1990s, when it suited the interests of the great powers. The United Nations was now being used to mobilize new alliances and legitimize the new world political order that was taking form as a result of transformation in global economic and political scenes.

In the field of information and communication, for example, the debate resulted in the withdrawal of the United States and the United Kingdom from UNESCO. The debate also became very distorted in the mainstream media of the Western world, who often saw a coincidence between their philosophy of the media, their own commercial self-interest, and the appropriate direction for world communication. The lessons learned from that global debate were clear: (a) The major economic and political actors in the world will resist any genuine changes in the global order if it threatens their dominance over the world's vital resources; (b) the state-centric debate, which mainly characterized the polemics of the 1970s and 1980s, by itself is not a sufficient ingredient for such an order; and (c) nongovernmental groups and citizens' mobilization and participation are vital elements for any world order that seeks legitimacy and thus the ability to cope with the realities of our complex global interactions.

At the center of all these stand at least two unclear and yet visible notions of a new world order. One is the official and publicized version of a new world order expressed by the United States and a number of European and highly industrialized countries. This world order envisions total unrestricted market economy, globalization of information by dominant Western transnational firms, and military and political coalitions of a handful of states. No role exists in this order for the developing countries of Africa, Asia, and Latin America, except to view this process as a fait accompli. The second is an unofficial, unpublicized, often desperate call for a new world order by the less fortunate groups, nations, and citizens who are often seen in grassroots activities yet are unable to strike any bargain with the powerful because of their lack of resources and to the divisions created among them.

It is precisely at this juncture that the reconceptualization of global development by those who claim to represent the nonaligned movement can make a difference. The political-economic divisions of this planet into three distinct worlds was never scientific and correct, and its reconceptualization into a single world is proving to be no better. The so-called Third World is divided, as the Persian Gulf war and other events proved; the Second World and the Soviet Union have disappeared; and the United States and the remainder of the First World are becoming increasingly irrelevant to the rest.

With the rise in preeminence of culture, values, and belief systems, traditional economic and political models are no longer totally reliable; political and economic issues are compounding, preempting international agenda and global relations. To appreciate the transformation and the complexity of global politics and relations, an integrated framework and indeed both a destructuring and a restructuring of international relations concepts are needed.

The World Since the MacBride Report

The major developments that have occurred since the MacBride Report, in 1980, can be explained in two major categories: information and communication developments and their impact over the past 10 years, and the political-economic events taking place on the international scene during this period.

The developments in the information technology area included the following (see Mowlana, 1993):

- The increasing flow of information, data, and related services among the industrialized countries as well as between the industrialized and the Third World nations
- The growing political, economic, and strategic aspects of information and related products and services, particularly as they affected the balance of trade and military powers
- The increasing importance of cultural, especially religious and social, factors not only in the relations among nations but also in how they are able to use the existing communication technology
- The emergence of new information-based products and services without regulatory and legal protection and for which new institutional and organizational structures are needed, particularly at the international level
- The growing magnitude of technological development in the information and communication field that poses challenges to the existing arrangements of the international system and threatens the status quo of international relations and the world order

Research and writings over the past several years provide valuable data on interlocking elements of each of the factors cited (see Mowlana, 1986; Schiller, 1984). The data generated are initiating a number of plausible hypotheses on the many issues and questions that confront us today. Indeed, such debated areas as national sovereignty, individual privacy, intellectual property rights, standardization, deregulation, and trade deficits are but a few examples of the interrelationships between information technology and political-economic sectors.

On the international relations scene, the world has also witnessed a number of developments that have had a profound bearing on the emergence of this new global information and communication order as well as stimulating discourse on the cultural ecology of our globe. Included in the staggering number of major international events within the past decade are the following:

- The worldwide resurgence of Islam as an alternative ideology and a new world order
- The Nicaraguan revolution, the subsequent intervention of the United States in that country and Panama, and the quest for more participatory regimes in Latin America
- Civil war in Lebanon and the intervention of foreign powers leading to major international crises, from kidnapping to hijacking and from internal factional fights to external interventions and invasions
- The Iraqi invasion of Kuwait and the ensuing Persian Gulf war, with the United States as a major participant
- Intifada and general uprisings by the Palestinians in the territories occupied by Israel
- Trends toward neoconservatism in the United States, the United Kingdom, and a number of other Western industrialized countries
- Transnationalization of markets, privatization of industry, and the economic integration of the European Community
- Ecological disasters and environmental crises in almost every major geographical area of the world, crises often associated with the development of modern science and technology
- Demise of the Soviet Union and transformation of East European countries under such terms as independence, democracy, and market economy
- The struggle for cultural and political identities from Kashmir to South Africa
- The decline of superpower economies and the rise of First World and Third World debt
- The emergence of the Pacific Basin as a major economic center, with Japan as a super economic power
- The systematic increase in large-scale corruption in the major industrialized world, accompanied by irregularities in the existing system of international finance
- The increasing incidence of terrorism and political crises worldwide
- National and international problems in health, safety, and security, such as the worldwide epidemic of AIDS and regional disasters in agriculture and nutrition leading to famine

The Ecological Dimensions of International
Relations and Global Communication

The process of information and technological innovations, as it relates to communication between human beings and their environment and among the peoples and nations, is demanding new explanations. One way to conceptualize the world in an integrated way is to look at world communication as a cultural ecology composed of international dimensions. Culture conceived as a symbolic interaction underlying world politics may help explain such phenomena as the growing multiplicity of nation-states, the rise of ethnicity, the diversity of national developmental goals and needs, the incredible diffusion of technology by national and transnational actors, and the simultaneous entry of many nations into the industrial-technological age and the communication and information age.

Culture and communication as value systems can be better understood, therefore, under ecological models that incorporate the complexity of contemporary affairs. The purpose is to give students of international relations a conceptual framework with which to see culture, world politics, and international communication in an integrative manner.

It now seems more imperative than ever to discuss the global tension not only in terms of explicitly economic, geopolitical, and military structures but also equally in the context of cultural communication and information struggles. To suggest that culture and communication are crucial for analyses of international relations is not to view these areas as exclusive territories of the idealist approach to world politics, which so often characterized the Wilsonian era of international politics and the more normative discourse of war and peace literature that followed the years immediately after the first and second world wars. The post-Cold War era, I believe, will bring the cultural dimensions of world politics to its most prominent position.

For one, the reductionism of the conservative school of realpolitik and that of radical political economy, which dominated the scholarly and policy fields for more than four decades, proved incomplete in answering the many questions regarding developments around the world. Furthermore, the epistemological tradition of research, in which the realm of ideas was separated from that of matter, was not only historically specific to the tradition of Western philosophy and science but also created a dualism that impeded the formulation of concepts and theories of a practical nature. Most important of all, the erosion of state legitimacy and the political development that followed the events of Eastern Europe and the Soviet

Union, combined with the economic crisis in the West and challenges emanating from the non-Western culture, made the inevitable conduct of human affairs by the Western powers more problematic.

Today, as the West moves toward the so-called information society, the concepts of justice, derived from civil society by the intellectual elites of the 19th and 20th centuries, have run into trouble. On the international level, the conventional argument was popularized that if one wants peace, one should prepare for war. The systems of autonomous nation-states had little sense of community but strived for power and divergent interests under pluralism. For much of humankind, at national and international levels, culture increasingly became something that arrived in cans. Indeed, a contradiction was developed between nationalism of the small powers and integration of the big powers. Thus, hegemony in the name of universalism was asserted by the big powers as small nations struggled against domination. Both realism and historical materialism directed attention to conflict. On the national and societal level, the line between civil rights and state rights became blurred.

The Unitary Theory of Communication as Ecology

For some time now, I have argued that the process of information and technological innovations, as it relates to communication between human beings and their environment and among peoples and nations, can be explained under what could be termed *the unitary theory of communication as ecology* (Bell, 1960). I use the term *ecology* here in a broad sense to include all the symbolic environments in which human and technological communication takes place.

The major dimensions of this ecological terrain include the following:

- Ecology of goods and commodities, such as industrial and manufacturing items
- Ecology of services, which includes banking, insurance, education
- Ecology of warfare, meaning all the military and security hardware, software, and infrastructure therein
- Ecology of information, encompassing such processes as cultural industries and mass media
- Ecology of habitat, comprising such areas as demography, housing, physical environment, and pollution

- Ecology of ethics and morality, referring to specific normative discourse such as religion, mores, laws, and social contracts

Ecology of Goods and Commodities, Such as Industrial and Manufacturing Items. The thesis that industrialization brings progress is now being tested with ecological problems of global scale, such as the warming of the earth, the threat to the ozone, the attack from the sky in the form of acid rain, and the loss of the forests. The industrial culture in which we produce and distribute goods and commodities and the economic system under which it is nourished determine the quality of this ecological terrain. Ever since the air became an overcrowded garbage dump for industrial waste and the internal combustion engine, it has become easier for us to turn off our sense of communication with the natural environment than to keep it functioning. Our ability to produce a variety of goods and commodities also is mixed with consumerism and environmental repression.

Ecology of Services, Which Includes Banking, Insurance, and Education. The manner and systems by which we arrange the acquisition and delivery of such services as education, health, travel, finance, banking, and child care determine the direction and quality of our communication. For example, the banking sector is changing shape in many countries as the increased use of credit cards for retail payments has altered the traditional relationship between the banks and the shops. At the same time, traditional barriers between markets and countries are crumbling. There are profound changes in our cultural ecology being created by the ability to communicate cheaply and conveniently, the change in the locus of educational experience within and across institutions, and the blurring of boundaries between educational and other institutions, such as entertainment and education, education and work. In many instances, education is moving from self-discovery to a service-oriented institution and toward taking on aspects of a goods-oriented industry.

Ecology of Warfare, Meaning All the Military and Security Hardware, Software, and Infrastructure Therein. With the advent of nuclear weapons and the development of sophisticated chemical and biological deterrents since World War II, the ecology of warfare has been in the forefront of international communication. Both Cold War and the so-called post-Cold War world have produced ecological dimensions of their own in terms of psychological propaganda, low-intensity war, public mobilization, national security, disarmament, peace movements, and a score of other militarily related phenomena. The environmental destruction resulting from such wars as Vietnam and the Persian Gulf, combined with the symbolic environment created to justify the actions of international actors, constitute a special ecological terrain in which communication and culture are interwoven.

Ecology of Information, Encompassing Processes Such as Cultural Industries and Mass Media. Linked together, communication and information technology, including mass media and advertising, not only lead to new distribution in time and space of the individual and society but also create a symbolic environment that determines the mood and the climate of actions. Communication and information media have the potential of both polluting the symbolic environment we breath and crystallizing and clarifying issues. The degree of noise created by modern media and the amount of space taken by information-related technologies, from television to computers and from videocassettes to music, has profoundly affected the arrangements of space and time in our daily lives. In examining the terrain of information and media ecology, these questions remain: How can we learn to use the media when negative conditioning, in terms of the excessive focus on violence and commercialism, limits our confidence and approach to life? How can we make information systems accessible and useful to everyone without creating information haves and have nots? Who owns information and communication space? What distinguishes private from public spheres in information ecology? Is the individual enriched or impoverished, master or servant?

Ecology of Habitat, Comprising Areas Such as Demography, Housing, Physical Environment, and Pollution. Population growth, urbanization, architecture, city planning, urban renewal, and the flow of persons across national and cultural boundaries, in the form of immigrants or refugees, constitute a sphere of ecology that determines our territory and underline one of the most profound ways we come to interact and communicate with one another. In short, social and personal use of space creates a kind of ecology, which determines some of the most important cores of culture and communication.

Ecology of Politics, Ethics, Law, and Morality, Referring to Specific Normative Discourse, Such as Religion, Mores, Laws, and Social Contracts. Our individual and collective perceptions regarding the relationships between politics and ethics, between law and morality, between religion and the state create one of the most important ecological terrains of our time. This specific ecological terrain determines the climate and mood of national, international, and community actions; it not only determines our understanding of such phraseology and ideologies as *democracy, progress, justice, egalitarianism, freedom,* and *good society* and helps to legitimize the directions of governmental and public policies but also creates dissent, protest, division, and even revolution. What is politics? Should it be separated from ethics? What is religion? Should religion or church be separated from politics? What is sovereignty? To whom does it belong? Does the government have responsibility to narrow the gap between rich and poor? Or should inequality be defended as a source of productivity, economic growth, and individual striving for excellence? What are the attributes of a good society or a good community? Is the real nature of a human being the totality of his or her social relations? In short, the ecological terrain that constitutes our collective understanding and faith in the nature of religion, community, laws, politics, and the state alters our social vision. This in turn interacts with other ecological dimensions, cited above, and ultimately accounts for the process of change at national and global levels.

These six ecological terrains are not spatial but relational and integrative. That is, not only do we interact with these environments on separate and one-on-one bases but the integrative interactions of these six terrains, among themselves and with human beings, also characterize the unique aspect of our civilization. Our cultural, economic, and political environments cannot be understood completely unless we turn our attention to this unitary phenomenon in terms of communication and culture. Thus, our notion of self, society, and universe is very much shaped by this ecological view and the way we perceive language, literacy, arts, sciences, and, in short, reality.

Our worldview, in such an integrated ecological perspective, is shaped by at least three distinct actors and participants: the state, groups and institutions, and individuals. For example, the link between ecology of goods and commodities and ecology of services has created an environment of international economic and financial complexity. In the same way, the network of ecology of goods and commodities, when intersected with the ecology of warfare, produces the so-called military-industrial complex. International propaganda and political discourse are as much the result of the linkages between the ecology of warfare and the ecology of information as the mass media and cultural industry complex are in major part the result of the ecology of information and that of ethics and morality.

Take, for example, the perception and the relationship of such phrases as *democracy* and *individual rights* with that of the automotive industry in a number of highly industrialized countries. Here, the automobile not only is the means of transportation and mobility, and even prestige and wealth, but also, in a very quintessential way, is perceived as the individual's freedom of action as well as rights. In the same manner, ecology terrains are created when military is linked to security, private space to public space, data to knowledge, dependency to interdependency, and progress to decay.

Quest for a New Cultural Order

It is precisely in this environment that cultural forces come into play globally. As international relations expand into a multitude of diverse interests and structures, ranging from military to political, from economic to cultural spheres, the question of communication ecology, and the environment in which a new structure is taking root, occupies a prominent role. The growth in recent years of both fora and literature in the area of ethical and moral dimensions of international relations illustrates the centrality of value systems and the attention given to the symbolic environment created by information technology. The ideological, religious, and spiritual struggles of the past 10 years highlight both the urgency and the depth of cultural clashes in international relations.

Embedded in the rhetoric and conduct of international politics over this period is convincing evidence of the interlocking of ideology and technology—and with this, a direct or indirect call on the part of individuals and even nation-states for a new information ecology with culture at its center. Nowhere is this better illustrated than by both the events in the Middle East and the United States' involvement in that part of the world over the past several decades. Although the strategy of information dominance and high technology enabled the United States to gain victory over the secular and unpopular regime of Iraq, Washington's persistent effort to keep the Shah of Iran in power and prevent the Islamic Revolution was indeed a major defeat. Thus, any discussion of a new world order must take into account not only the broader ecological-communication context outlined earlier but also the diversities of global culture. Whose information? Which civilization? What global order?

Long before Canadian Marshall McLuhan's phrase *the global village* became popular, American Wendell Willkie, with an enthusiasm touched off by modern air transport, popularized the phrase *one world.* The complex feelings and ideas now generally associated with these phrases, however, were not originally Willkie's or McLuhan's discourse. These phrases have a long history. The fact that the world is one in an astronomical or a technological sense, as a single planet located in the gravitational field of a definite star, is not of political, economic, and cultural importance. Historical geography depends on an Einsteinian rather than a Newtonian function. Despite technological and scientific development, including the tremendous growth of communication and information hardware and software over the past several decades, the large majority of residents of this global village live in undignified conditions of illiteracy, disease, hunger, unemployment, and malnutrition and are still deprived of the basic tools of modern communication information and knowledge.

The irony is well captured by an Indian writer:

> If there were 100 residents in this global village, only one would get the opportunity for education beyond school level, 70 would be unable to read and write. Over 50 would be suffering from malnutrition, and over 80 would live in sub-standard housing. Six of the 100 would hold off the entire income of the village. How would these six live in peace with their neighbours without arming themselves to the teeth and supplying arms to those willing to fight their side? (Vilanilam, 1989, pp. 171-173)

For example, with the coming of the so-called information explosion and information society, among the most crucial questions facing Islamic societies have to do with both the ultimate control of information processing and technology in the contemporary electronic age and the gradual disappearance of oral or traditional culture that has been a major resistance force in the face of cultural domination. The concept of secular society was introduced into the complex life of Islamic lands at a time when the forces of resistance were at a minimum. With the new awareness and the degree of mobilization and cultural resurgence that we have witnessed during the past decades in Islamic communities around the world, the introduction of the information revolution and the entry into the information society seem to land on rocky soil.

The crucial question for the Islamic societies is whether the emerging global information communication community is a moral and ethical community—or just another stage in the unfolding picture of a transformation in which the West is the center and the Islamic world the periphery. Throughout Islamic history, especially in the early centuries, information was not a commodity but a moral and ethical imperative. Is the information society a kind of network community where a new rationalism is likely to impose a policy of radical instrumentation under which social problems will be treated as technical problems and citizens will be replaced by experts? Will the new technologies of information encourage the centralization of decision making and the fragmentation of society, leading to the replacement of forms of community life with an exasperated individualism? Is the information society in a position to produce qualitative changes in traditional forms of communication and eventually transform social structures, and will such new structures require new ethics? Thus, it seems that the discourse and concepts of global order now at the center of world politics both celebrate the arrival of a new communication ecology and hold the key to greater information control.

Note

1. The Islamic movement around the world has been the most outspoken voice for a new world cultural order, especially since the Islamic Revolution in Iran in 1978-1979. For example, see Khomeini (1981).

9

Shapes of the Future: International Communication in the 21st Century

With the end of the twentieth century and the turn of a new millennium, the global arena and the field of international communication are undergoing significant changes. Looking back on the field, both the international order and many international communication topics stemmed from the post-World War II order and the Cold War. With the collapse of the Soviet Union the shadow of the Cold War has lifted to reveal shifting political, economic, and cultural alliances and conflicts spanning from Eastern Europe, to the Middle East, to the Pacific Basin. The increasing importance of these currents, especially in the cultural sphere, demands a reconsideration of the nature of the international communication field within the rubric of international relations.

This chapter will specifically address these changes and their implications for study within the field through the discussion of ten major points, eight of which are current phenomena in international and global systems and two of which are underlying methodological and epistemological elements of the field. These shifts may be the result of long periods of gestation which are now coming to the surface, and furthermore, may have their roots in several different areas. Some focus on the need to reformulate categories and terminologies used in the field to deal with the listed global changes of an economic, political, technological, and cultural nature. Furthermore, it must be noted that these changes cannot be considered as mutually exclusive, for example, the changing nature of the nation-state crosses many themes from the rise of alternative actors to the redistribution of some traditionally state-owned powers.

In short, the ten dynamics occurring within the field of international communication are the following:

1. The move from considering international communication in the classical sense to a vision of global communication

2. The realization that this new global conception, which recognises new communicative actors, is not universal
3. The increase of conflict arising along the lines of culture and civilisation
4. A recognition of two opposing trends in the international arena, positing a rise of nationalism and ethnicity against a resurgent universalism
5. A move toward regionalism primarily within an economic framework reflecting emerging technologies and productive processes
6. The decline of the power of the nation-state as the predominant international actor, and the rise of new entities, which I labeled "ghetto states"
7. The erosion of national sovereignty and traditional forms of state power and the rise of transnationals
8. The reassertion of the so-called dominant paradigm as a paradigm of dominance in forms of neo-modernism, post-modernism, neo-conservatism, and neo-liberalism
9. The reconsideration of the epistemological basis of the field
10. The necessary reconceptualization of our methodological tools in terms of our categories and levels of analysis

I will attempt to illustrate these changes through the implicit theme of a need for reconceptualization of the field's definition given the emergence of new actors, the growing importance of cultural factors, the decline of state power, and finally a shift in the categories and theoretical approaches used within the field.

1. The Move Toward Global Communication

During the past few years, the term globalization has become a common buzzword within both academia and politics. Unfortunately, the word has assumed expansive connotations and has been reified as a process in and of itself (Featherstone, 1990). In relation to the field of international communication, it is necessary to clarify this "global" process and to illustrate the underlying flows and actors that are global and those who are not. In today's world the classical sense of international communication as interactions among states or policy-making elites can no longer be considered the sole dimension of communication studies. The rise of non-state actors, their subversion of traditionally sovereign domains of action, the increase in economic and interpersonal interactions at the global level, as well as the changing nature of diplomacy and propaganda all reveal the expanding conception of what *international* means for this field, as well as for international relations in general.

This significant rise in non-state actors, such as corporations, non-governmental organizations, and social movements, within the past few decades has extended interactions beyond the state to state level. Communicative dimensions have expanded economically, politically, and interpersonally, creating new supra- and sub-state movements in communication (Mowlana, 1986). Tourism, migration, and business contacts have all risen dramatically with the improvements in technologies and affordability of travel. This move toward sub-statism is especially evident in the growth of international business entities from multinational corporations with their headquarters in one state and branches in others to transnational corporations with a decentralized, essentially global decision-making process. At the supra-state level both governmental organizations, such as the United Nations, as well as non-governmental organizations, such as human rights and environmental groups, communicate with individual nations at the state level, with the goal to create institutions, regimes, and laws operating above the state. Thus, for the field, the term inter-national is too restrictive in its focus on state actors, and we need to reconceptualize our terminology to reflect the global nature of contemporary communications.

Equally important in this period of seemingly international or global actions is the inability of the so-called developing countries or small nations to influence the process of current world development at any significant level. Thus, communications in certain arenas have been globalized representing a fundamental change in the classical sense of international relations and communication. But, this global shift to new actors and new levels does not mean that there are no restrictions or limitations on communications. International communication has become world communication and this process has global dimensions. Certainly, something is happening and it may be a new meaning of communication, but we know little about it.

2. Global Communication Is Not Universal Communication

What is globalization? How does it function? Who or what controls globalization, and for what purpose? Is the process of globalization now under way producing qualitative changes in traditional forms of communication, and eventually to the transformation of social structure? What are the new ethics of such structures? Whose interests are served by the emergence of globalization?

The Club of Rome considers the development of advanced technology as one of the major forces of globalization which is responsible for the emergence of a new society. Put simply, the information society, according to this view, must then be the end result of globalization or the global revolution. According to the report by the Council of the Club of Rome,

> The global revolution has no ideological basis. It is being shaped by an unprecedented mixture of geostrategic earthquakes and of social, economic, technological, cultural and ethical factors. Combinations of these factors lead to unpredictable situations. In this transitional period, humanity is therefore facing a double challenge: having to grope its way towards an understanding of the new world with so many as yet hidden facets and also, in the mists of uncertainty, to learn how to manage the new world and not be managed by it (King & Schneider, 1991, p. xxiii).

Yet, the Club of Rome's description and explanation of the process of globalization are somewhat superficial and indeed partial at best, because they constrain our ability to systematically ascertain and analyze such a phenomenon. To render globalization as "ideology-less" is to imply that globalization is a force without agency. To attach a degree of unpredictability to it is to imply that globalization is not only without vision but also void of structure. As such, the Club of Rome's desire to help humanity by calling for long term policies to establish some semblance of stability in the midst of unpredictability without fully exploring and analyzing the process of globalization. At best this would only result in further confusion, but at worst, it succeeds in restructuring society according to concealed visions/perceptions of that which ought to constitute a global society or community.

The uncritical and restricted perception and analysis of information technology is playing a major role in the first global revolution, and consequently, the emergence of an information society has been paralleled by yet another highly publicized phenomenon: the post-modern perspective. The view that exclusively imparts to information technologies the power to restructure society cannot help but subordinate culture to information technology. Criticism of information technology would, then, paradoxically rest on the very ground that information technology is established on, for example, instrumental rationality. The inclusion and application of concepts such as morality and agency are effectively neglected in this approach; therefore, it is no wonder that the global revolution can be considered as having no ideological basis.

Anthony Giddens provides us with an analysis of how under modernity and postmodernity change is global. According to him a primary result of modernity is globalization:

> This is more than a diffusion of Western institutions across the world in which other cultures are crushed. Globalisation . . . which is a process of uneven development that fragments as it coordinates . . . introduces new forms of world interdependence in which, once again there are no "Others." (Giddens, 1990, p. 175)

However as Ziauddin Sardar has expressed, Giddens' argument is inherently self-defeating:

> If globalisation is fundamental to modernity, and if the globalisation of Western culture produces an interdependent world where "there are no Others," how then can non-Western cultures contribute to shaping modernity? Moreover if, as Giddens acknowledges, modernity is "inherently future-oriented" and "anticipation of the future becomes part of the present, thereby rebounding on how the future actually develops," the future is effectively colonised. Modernity not only ensures a firm Western hold on the present, it also has an equally secure grip on the future. (Sardar, 1992, p. 497)

There is, however, a proposition in the literature dealing with globalization to move beyond the oppositional thinking of global versus local—that global constitutes and is constituted by the local and thus the global and the local interpenetrate. But what constitutes "local" or "locality" if the term of locality is relative and is related to such concepts as space and time? How does it relate to globalization? Implicit in this argument is the notion of "consciousness" that globalization and localization refer to subjectivity and inter-subjectivity. The way in which we define ourselves, and in relation to others, the way in which we organize ourselves and that of others, are constituted by and constitute the interpretation of the global and local conditions. The argument is based on Hobsbawm and others that the current level of globalization is reinventing tradition but this new tradition does not have a basis so much in the past as it does in the synthesis of past and present (Hobsbawm and Ranger, 1983). Is the current process of globalization similar to Benedict Anderson's hypothesis in which the invention of the printing press—print capitalism—created and creates the notion of imagined communities? (Anderson, 1990) What role does communication play in the interpretation of the global and the local—in terms of the kind of consciousness that is being discussed?

If groups of human beings are far from being globalized, then what are the indicators of globalization? A cursory examination of popular and academic literature points to the globalization of technology, communication, food production, insurance, and legal and financial services (Warf, 1989, pp. 257-271; Handy, 1990, pp. 1-5; Reid, 1991, pp. 92-93; Duffy, 1991, pp. 366-380; and Moran, 1990, pp. 57-99, and 1989, pp. 315-336). In short, that which appears to be in the process of globalization are forces of production, distribution/delivery, and consumption of goods and services. It is important to stress that although the consumption of goods and services (i.e., behavior of consumers) may indicate a pattern of homogeneity —for example, the consumption of Western products, edibles such as Coca-Cola, Pepsi, and pizza, and non-edibles such as television programs. This does not in any way imply that consumers across the globe are homogeneous in terms of values, attitudes, and morals. Phrased differently, the behaviorist approach and objectives of producers (i.e., changing behavior patterns to bring about changes in values) may be indicative of a desire to fundamentally alter the consumer in such a way so as to create lifestyles in accordance with the wholesale acceptance and increased demand for the latter's goods and services. Thus, generally speaking globalization may be said to be a process of structuration that encompasses homogenization and heterogenization—a process in which agencies operating under different temporal sequences interact to connect and alter varying structures of social existence to create a structurally oligarchic, but interconnected, world. The paths or flows of globalization can be multi-directional and multi-dimensional; they cut across vertical (individual, clan, group, state, international levels) and horizontal (law, economics, politics, culture, education) organizations of human life.

It is here that the behaviors and objectives of transnational corporations served as an initial catalyst for the processes of globalization. Indeed, the establishment, growth and expansion of transnational corporate power and wealth (and not the presence of technology per se) have infiltrated into the servicing of nearly every aspect of human needs and wants (Schiller, 1989). However, this is not to say that transnational corporations either acted alone, acted unopposed or even acted out of an initial desire to re-create the world. Rather, the thrust of capital expansion and control of market share initiated a series of "domino-like ripples" that have produced that which are now discerned as manifestations of globalization (i.e., the prevailing perception that the world is becoming one because of increased contact among peoples, institutions, cultures, etc.) (see Rhinesmith, 1991, pp. 22-29; Peterson, 1990, pp. 527-530; Karpinski, 1991, pp. 8-9; Sherman, 1991, p. 19; and Cooper, 1990, pp. 52-54).

Put simply, nation-states need to construct a new vision or new reality to encompass difference and diversity without losing ground to the forces of globalization. In fact, seen from this perspective the New World Information and Communication Order and the New International Economic Order are not as functionally dead as believed. As I have argued elsewhere, the process of globalization has indeed revived at least modified versions of NWICO and NIEO, among the developed countries and will continue to be on the agenda of the global scene in the decades to come (Mowlana, 1993).

One perspective in the field of international communication supports humanistic values of universalism, the ability for all people to communicate, both receiving and distributing their messages. Norms such as the right to communicate and freedom of speech are embodiments of human rights declarations. Even technically and institutionally there has been a long desire to establish such universal systems as the postal union and to strive for universal services in such sectors as telecommunication. However, what is "global" is not universal and we must keep in mind that global communication does not mean universal communication. Although the distribution of information has become global, the actors controlling it are few. Thus, while information reception might be universal in nature, the capacity for distributing messages is severely limited and centralized.

The trend toward oligarchy is clearly evident in the flurry of mergers between telephone and cable companies in the United States and the vertical integration of consumer electronic and audio/visual software companies by the Japanese. At the political level, the "great powers" continue to be the dominant voices in all international forums ranging from the United Nations to GATT. Thus, political issues have become global in their impact, but the agenda setters for those problems can hardly be considered global, let alone universal. For example, the United Nations Security Council is central to decision making regarding United Nations activities, yet it is controlled by a small portion of the international community. These economic and political entities continue to obstruct the establishment of universal communication, while the gaps between rich and poor are increasing at all levels.

3. Conflicts Revolve Around Cultures and Civilizations

In the field of international communication the phenomena of communication and culture history has been the subject of many discussions and debates during the last several decades. Although numerous studies have been carried out in this somewhat general and prolific area, the comparative aspect of this concern has remained fairly underdeveloped, particularly by the students of communication theories. In the field of international mass communication and information technology, the subject of culture has only been dealt with in the realm of cultural industries and their impact on society and as part of broader cultural studies. In the area of inter-cultural and cross-cultural communication the theme of culture has been treated on levels of interpersonal and group communication, isolated from the international and global phenomena as though inter-cultural communication takes place in a world without political, economic, and technological boundaries.

There are a number of distinct reasons for this neglect, among them, lack of conceptual clarity, epistemological and disciplinary rigidities, insufficient amounts of skill in language and cultural studies, a high level of ethnocentrism and parochialism, and ideological biases. Consequently, our knowledge of communication, cultural and social systems, is provincial rather than universal.

In the past the field of international relations has viewed power, the nation-state, and political economy as central to the dynamics of the global system. But now that orientation is shifting in a fundamental way as culture, ethnicity, and religion enter the picture. Previously, both international relations and international communication scholars assumed that these factors played little roles, as states merely contended via balance of power, power politics, rational decision making, and political economy. But now these cultural aspects are becoming pivotal determinants for international relations as recognized by the changing positions of traditionally realist scholars. For example, Samuel Huntington (1993), known for his work in political modernization, recently wrote that conflicts between civilizations will be the central focus of the new world "disorder." John Mearsheimer's claim that nationalism will become the new threat to Europe following the Cold War is opening up the black box of the state and is looking at internal cultural affinities, not power politics, as realists generally assume (Mearsheimer, 1990). Indeed in the closing decade of the 20th century, there are serious reflections among the group called "strategic thinkers" that there must be more to international relations and international communication than simple military diplomatic situations and complex information and communication technologies.

Cold War theorists subordinated the influences of culture and civilization to geopolitical and economic factors and framed conflict along ideological lines. While cultural determinants and tensions always existed, they have once again resurfaced as a principal concern for both policy-makers and academics. Cross-cultural clashes can be seen in the dissolution of Yugoslavia, ethnic strife throughout the former Soviet empire, migration problems in Western Europe, and even within the cultural orientation of trade and business between the West and the East. Within many of these struggles religion provides a fundamental stimulus; Islam, Orthodox Christianity, Judaism, Shintoism, Confucianism, and Western Protestantism/Calvinism are resurfacing as central to defining identities.

For example, consider a study of social systems and value systems within an Islamic context. A social system is a process of interaction of individuals within a larger unit called society, which exhibits the property that Ibn Khaldun, an Islamic thinker of the 14th century, called solidarity (*assabieh*), a term employed later by Durkheim in his works. As Kroeber and Parsons have noted, a social system is not the value itself, but a system of values and actions of individuals that are associated in terms of symbolic meaning. On the other hand, values are instruments of maintaining the cultural integrity and cohesion of society, serving to legitimize the modes of more concrete action. Here, we are concerned with the question of cultural systems and how they interact with problems of conceptualization, theorization, and practices of information and communication. What impact do cultural settings have on the studies of communication? What communication theories and practices do they foster?

4. Nationalism Versus Universalism

With the end of the bipolar world and the ideological conflict centered around the Cold War, the international system is reorienting itself in new ways. Central to these changes are two opposing trends: increased nationalism and a resurgent universalism.

The conflict in the former Yugoslavia between Croats, Bosnians, and Serbs; the division of Czechoslovakia into Czech and Slovak states; the fall of the Soviet Union and the consequent rise of ethnic conflicts in Georgia, Armenia, Azerbaijan, the Baltic states, and Russia itself; and even the resistance of significant portions of the population of Western European states like England, France, and Norway to ratifying the political, economic, and military commitments to the European Community, all point to a renewed concern with national and ethnic identities. Centered around Europe many of these conflicts can be seen as accruing to the end of the Cold War and the disintegration of the U.S.S.R.

In addition, the end of the Cold War has removed the ideological divisions that divided different social groups. Most obviously the reunification of the two Germany's symbolizes this national reunion. At a larger level, separated communities in the East and West can now associate with greater ease and less stigma. Religious, linguistic, and national groups can now assert the common bonds previously divided by the superpower conflict. In essence the Berlin Wall was a cultural as well as an ideological barrier.

While the unification of Europe has allowed for the emergence of a variety of old identities, there has been a movement in the opposite direction toward Islamic unification in the non-Western world. Ever since the Islamic Revolution in Iran there has been a renewed faith in the creation of a general Islamic community. With the collapse of the U.S.S.R. and the birth and instability of new Central Asian states with significant Muslim populations, this desire has been reinforced. The impetus behind the Islamic resurgence is to create a single Islamic community, which supersedes state and national divisions. Evidence of this can be found in movements in Iran, Egypt, Morocco, Sudan, and the conflict in Algeria.

A crucial factor for the future will be how these two processes interact. Currently, the situation in the former Yugoslavia does not provide a reassuring case. As the Islamic Revolution in Iran in 1979 crystallized the demise of the dominant paradigm of development and communication in an Islamic country, the genocide in Bosnia-Herzegovina demystifies the thesis of the so-called "global village." Genocide is being carried out on television before the world audience every day, and yet it is clear that the world leaders who have access to money, organisations, power, and the military have decided to allow "ethnic cleansing" to continue. Bosnia is not Nazi Germany, where the world pretended it did not see the atrocities.

What is clear is that the collapse of Soviet communism is neither the end of history nor the end of the Cold War. The Berlin Wall has disappeared but the ethnic walls are emerging and fundamental conflicts will continue to pattern global relations. The U.S.-Soviet Cold War has ended but we are at the threshold of a new cold war; it has already begun and in my opinion will continue as long as the current international system in its political and economic framework constitutes the global scene. Indeed, international communication has entered a new phase; whereas the superpower conflict highlighted the threat of nuclear annihilation, the current focus on interstate and inter-ethnic relations makes international communication more complex and challenging.

5. Move Toward Economic and Technological Regionalism

In looking at the economic trends shaping international trade, significant emphasis is being placed on the formation of regional trading arrangements. Thus, the European Community, the North American Free Trade Agreement, and the internal developments within the Pacific Basin, all point to regionally based economic clusters. This move toward economic regionalism replaces the geopolitical/military regionalism that dominated the Cold War (e.g., NATO, SEATO, CENTO, and the Warsaw Pact). The trend toward regionalism at an economic level does run counter to many of the separatist/fragmentary national movements as well as to the notions of globalism and universalism, which are occurring at a more cultural level.

Yet, the growing regionalism of these areas also points to the concern of external actors. What is to be the fate of Latin America, Africa, the Middle East, and Central Asia given this stress on regionalism in the industrialized world? Will they regionalize as well? Furthermore, what is the relationship between these regional entities and globalization? Are they supra-state building blocks that will assist in the creation of a globalized world? Or are they divisive fragments that hinder the process of globalization?

Indeed the amount and patterns of investment by the Western world in Central and Eastern European, as well as in Central Asian, telecommunication systems ever since the collapse of the Soviet Union, illustrate the type of competition between the North American and Western European economic blocs. Furthermore, given the fact that major research and development in the field of telecommunication is taking place within these three regional systems, the diffusion and adaptation of any new forms of telecommunication systems in others parts of world, including such vast geographical areas as Russia, China, and India, will be determined by the type of communication and technological research under way in the three advanced regional systems. The history of HDTV development over the last decade illustrates this phenomenon, as well as the extreme competition among these industrialized blocs on this specific technology. Furthermore, the three industrial regions will be in a position to determine both the outcome of the politics of standardization and the debate under way on the new international information and communication order in a variety of international inter-governmental organizations.

Plus, these countries will receive the primary financial and technological advantages for their economies and industrial bases.

However, on both the political and cultural level, the process of regionalism will run into several different obstacles and questions. To what extent will national systems be willing to delegate their political and cultural sovereignty to gain economic and social benefits? Certainly, the experience of political integration in Europe with strong reservations against the Maastricht Treaty expressed by smaller countries like Denmark, is illustrative of the sensitivity of national systems when the question of economic integration is put before them. To what extent will the Canadians and Mexicans feel the cultural domination of the United States, as they have expressed on many occasions in the past? Strong arguments can even be made in regards to Europe, given the ferment of culture and nationalism between France, Germany, and England.

On the other hand, one may consider the implications of the emerging regionalism in the industrial world and its impact on the less developed countries. It is possible that by the beginning of the 21st century, for a variety of political and economic reasons, that we may witness the formulation of new regional economic, technological, and even information systems based on cultural commonalities. For example, there is tremendous potential in the Islamic world, especially with the emergence of new nations in Central Asia and the resurgence of Islam in North Africa and the Middle East, for an Islamic regional system beyond its current loose structure.

6. Nation-States and Ghetto States

If we accept the definition of globalization described earlier, we can then appreciate the changes that are taking place in the world economy and in international communication with profound implications for sovereign states and the people who live in them. The legitimacy of the modern nation-state always hinged on its role as guarantor of social space and as a protector of a national economy. The state patroled the borders of the nation, gave security to its citizens, and represented their interest. However, global capitalist consumerism has gone beyond national boundaries and through the networks of modern international communications, the national government is being by-passed in almost all of its traditional responsibilities. Transnational corporations, for example, are becoming increasingly adept at finding ways to circumvent national borders in their search for cheap labor, thanks to modern transportation and communication systems. In short, the nation-state is increasingly unable to serve as champion against transnationalism and globalization. The rise of transnational corporations and the changing pattern of international communication between all levels of actors has limited and altered the traditional role of the state.

As the certainty of nationhood comes under question and as the modern nation-state fails to deliver the security and services desired by citizens, a sense of anchorlessness is developed. Cultural identity, ethnic reassertion, and modern tribalism are indications of phenomena seeking local political reflection.

On the political map, with the fall of the Soviet Union, the disintegration of Yugoslavia, and the move into the new world there has been a dramatic increase in the number of supposed independent states. From Central and Eastern Europe to the heart of Central Asia we have witnessed the resurgence of new states. Furthermore, the ethnic divisions in these regions reflect a changing conception of the notions of statehood, independence, and sovereignty in general. Indeed, the post-Cold War era has added a new dimension in the array of political systems in international relations, which I have called "ghetto states." These "ghetto states" do not enjoy the same sovereignty, legal rights, and international representation entitled to legitimate states. Bosnia Herzegovina and Somalia have become examples of such states; Palestine with its small pocket of territory being negotiated for limited authority is another case in point.

These territorial and national collectivities are divided, dismembered, and have now become disunited islands or so-called "safe havens" within a sea of states. In addition no one is assuming responsibility for them and for assistance with the principal conflicts that divide them. The United Nations has extended its role beyond the traditional limits of state to state relations into the domestic affairs of small states. The traditional task of the United Nations of peace keeping has now become nation-building, as the world's dominant actors, like the United States and the major European powers, cannot assert a cohesive and consistent policy toward these issues.

The parallel between the end of World War II and the demise of the Cold War between the United States and the former Soviet Union[1] is one appropriate analogy for understanding the challenges facing the emerging international communication regime. Today the former republics of the Soviet Union as well as of Eastern and Central European states are in a similar position to the developing countries of Asia, Africa, and Latin America immediately after gaining their independence. They are entering the new international system with a colonial legacy and under the conditions of marginality from the centres of world power where economic and communication frameworks are already set for them. These issues have broad implications for the conduct of political and economic communication at the state to ghetto state level, as well as at the national level in terms of social development and cultural identity reformulation. With the changes taking place, many so-called nation-states will be reduced to handling local, personal concerns, leaving economic and communication rule-making to regional, transnational, or international bodies.

7. The Erosion of Nation-State Sovereignty

With the increasing trends in economic globalization and communication flows at numerous levels, the state is losing control over its traditionally sanctified notion of sovereignty (Nordenstreng & Schiller, 1993). The rise of international governmental organizations and non-governmental organizations has been well documented. For example, many of these entities perform and/or advocate management and regulatory functions for environmental causes, human rights, economic trading (GATT), and communications (ITU). This reflects an increased functionalism at the interstate level. What this also means is that the state is voluntarily and involuntarily losing some of its traditional claims to sovereignty. States may have representation in many of these bodies, but they no longer have sole control over how outputs will affect themselves. The growing functionalism of international organizations and the reassertion of political and military dominance by the state in certain regions affect the concept of sovereignty. For the field of international communication, increasing concern must be paid to looking at how functional organisations operate in relation to the state and to each other as well as to the possible persistence of dominant actors in the political realm.

At the same time that states in general are losing sovereign rights (often at the point where they have just obtained the independence to utilize them) some states will maintain the ability to violate others' sovereignty, whether voluntarily or involuntarily. Thus, the United States can selectively intervene in Somalia or Haiti for the interests of democracy and peace. Similarly in the Persian Gulf War, the United States entered the fray to preserve the political orders of such states as Kuwait, Saudi Arabia, and Israel. In fact the United States was welcomed, which reveals the extent to which the state system has created its own dependencies thereby contradicting the notion of sovereignty. Thus, arises the interesting dilemma of a state inviting the violation of its national sovereignty in order to preserve it.

8. The (Re-)Emergence of the Paradigm of Dominance

With the end of the Cold War, American policymakers and academics alike have declared the victory of liberalism through democracy and capitalism. The decline of the socialist system and the insignificance of other alternatives have given rise to a rejuvenated world system based on liberal economics.

This recent trend parallels the post-World War II era when the United States sought to extend its democratic and capitalist ideals to Europe and Japan through development aid provided by the Marshall Plan. Such financial aid was supplemented by the growth of U.S. created "international" institutions like the International Monetary Fund, the World Bank, and the Bretton Woods system, in order to help manage capitalist development. This development ethic was then extended to the Third World in order to compete with a rising Soviet threat. This gave rise to the large concentration on modernization, Westernization, and Industrialization theories: the so-called dominant paradigms of development.

While the late 1960s and the 1970s provided a brief respite as the Non-Aligned Movement and the Group of 77 asserted their individual political and economic rights for autonomy and equity within the system, these alternative movements have faded away in the last decade. The "rise" of the dominant paradigm was indeed real, but its reported decline was only a myth. Now, with the euphoria of a victory in the Cold War, liberalism and capitalism are again trumpeted as the optimal strategy for economic growth. The trends in globalization speak to this fact at a number of levels (increased interdependence, transnational corporations, segmentation and distribution of the production process, and expanded information flows). Furthermore, the relative decline of American economic strength combined with the end of the Cold War have reduced efforts for development assistance. These trends have also reinvigorated a belief in U.S. economic conservatism as both competition and the stakes thereof rise in high-technology industries. Discussions reflecting this move toward a post-industrial or information society hinge on the perpetuation of this paradigm of neo-modernization, both domestically and internationally.

The field of international communication needs to understand these underlying dynamics and their political, economic, cultural, and ethical implications. Thus, discussions of information highways and cyberspace should be cognizant of the assumptive framework of a neo-modernization paradigm. Furthermore, the centrality of the topic of post-industrialization should be kept in perspective. Any discussion of a new world order must take into account the broader ecological/communicative context as well as the diversities of a global culture. Will the new world order be introduced internationally in such a way that developing countries become increasingly dependent? Can we handle the "information revolution" better than we handled the industrial revolution? Neo-modernization is hardly global and past trends in modernization and Westernization still meet resistance in non-Western cultures. Therefore, it is necessary to maintain a global perspective paying attention to comparative cultural approaches, which entails a deeper expansion of our epistemological and methodological views toward the field.

9. The Need for Epistemological Reorientation

As I have outlined elsewhere (Mowlana, 1993, and 1994), the reductionism of the conservative school of realpolitik and that of radical political economy, which have dominated the scholarly and policy fields around the world for over four decades proved incomplete in answering the many questions regarding developments around the world. Furthermore, the epistemological tradition of research, in which the realm of ideas was separated from that of matter, was not only historically specific to the tradition of Western philosophy and science, but also created a dualism that impeded the formulation of concepts and theories of practical nature.

Traditionally, research in the field of international communication has stemmed from the two distinct traditions of the Western intellectual inquiry. Evolving in the post-World War II era the first trend centers on the application of a number of disparate fields like functional sociology, political science, and social psychology to aspects of administrative research (audience analysis, elite to elite communications, etc.). In the United States especially, these interdisciplinary approaches adopted a behaviorist format in existing attempts to scientize the social sciences. The other dominant trend in communication research arose from efforts to refute the growth of logical positivism. The Frankfurt School represents this line of critical research which adopts both past and present theorists of the Marxist line. While extensive calls have been made to expand the theoretical and epistemological basis of the field, these two fields are still the dominant theoretical approaches to international communication.

An examination of the recent survey of the discipline by the *Journal of Communication* ("Future of the Field," 1993) reveals the existing myopia of the field to alternative views. While attempting to identify the advances and set-backs in the field since its last survey a decade ago ("Ferment in the Field," 1983), the issue still limits its views to the works and prospects for administrative and critical research. For example, Karl Rosengren uses Burrell and Morgan's (1979) schema for describing communication research, which aptly separates the critical trend (radical humanism and radical functionalism) from the administrative trends (interpretive and functional sociology). The only distinguishing character of their taxonomy is the objective/subjective axis cutting through both schools of thought. Rosengren's analysis might be that the field has fragmented, not fermented, but the reality is that this fragmentation has occurred within the two dominant schools. Finally, although calling for the inclusion of humanistic/qualitative approaches to the field, Rosengren still posits the need to base them on formal models and empirical data, thereby reasserting the positivist project.

Other authors in the volume also conduct their discussions within the rubric of the aforementioned trends. While they debate the issues of theory and practice (Craig), empiricism and hermeneutics (Fitzpatrick), and the history of objectivist and constructivist foundations (Krippendorff) they do not expand their approaches beyond the limits of the field's dominant schools. Even O'Keefe who discusses the need to account for culture, remains within the Western foundations of positivism, critical theory, and post-modernism. For a field recognizing the inputs of different disciplines, it is now necessary to recognize the contributions of different cultural and intellectual approaches.

The field of international communication has recently realized the importance of culture as a social conception. But, communication scholars currently approach culture from an ethnocentric epistemological approach. True inter-cultural understanding will not come until theoretical approaches to the field accept the viability of other intellectual schools. Thus the need for understanding culture exists at both the topical, substantive level as well as at the epistemological level.

Another general critique of the current intellectual tradition within the field of international communication centers around its notions of how theoretical discourse should be conducted and validated. Discourse relies on the citation of established fundamentals and exemplar scholars within the field, thereby necessitating a synthesis of past with present. While there might be a perception of intellectual freedom within the field, even those diverging from the common discourse have to substantiate their claims by invalidating those of their contemporaries and/or predecessors. Furthermore, the accepted terminology and topics within the field place further limits on the intellectual tolerance of international communication. What is necessary is an open, universal discourse among communications scholars that deliberately seeks to extend beyond the bounds of culture and language to create a truly comparative and global approach to the field. Alternatively, one of the intellectual strengths of the field of international communication has been its reluctance to allow itself to be dominated by a single discipline.

Indeed an examination of the philosophical and political disciplines within the non-Western traditions provides a vast depository of knowledge on which international and comparative communication studies could benefit. For example, Islamic thought views reason as a means to an end. With positive value being attached to names, as the conceptual and symbolic representation of reality, reason serves the purpose of allowing the wilful person to come to self-knowledge, which leads to knowledge of God (Mutahhari, 1985; Shari'ati, 1979, and 1980; and Ha'iri Yazdi, 1992). Here we see the "eye of contemplation" at work. Indian thought is positioned at the extreme toward this issue. Both experience and reason belong to the illusory world of phenomena (Copleston, 1980, p. 20). The relationship between the ground of reality and knowledge of reality renders the individual a passive vehicle for the expression of truth. Knowledge is contemplation, by which *Atman* (self) comes in contact with absolute, *Brahman*. Reason does not even serve as a means to an end. In short, Indian philosophy views perception—sensory and non-sensory—as a source of knowledge. In Chinese thought, both reason and experience are real, as they are expressions of the flowing wholeness of the Tao (Creel, 1953; Copleston, 1982; and Capra, 1975). The eye of contemplation seems to be emphasized in Taoist thought, while respect for tradition is emphasized in Confucian thought (Nakamura, 1964, and Wilbur, 1977 and 1983).

The second parameter we can examine is on the different approaches to knowledge and on the relationship between being and becoming. For example, from an Islamic perspective the world view of science is a knowledge of the past, not the whole, and thus hypothesis and experiment have a provisional value. The principles of epistemology in Islamic tradition are based on two kinds of sciences, namely *Aghli,* or creative sciences, and *Naghli,* or transmitted sciences. Whereas transmitted sciences are exoteric, creative sciences are esoteric and need to be intellectually and empirically understood. These two traditions of knowledge did not develop in isolation from each other. From the tenth century and the beginning of the so-called "Islamic Golden Age," the methodologies developed by creative sciences and the transmitted sciences benefited each other. Although the Greeks systematized, generalized and theorized about knowledge, the systematic investigation and scientific methods, prolonged observation and quantitative measurement belonged to the Islamic era of information and knowledge. What we know as modern science (astronomy, medicine, physics, demography, political economy) arose in Europe as a result of this new spirit of inquiry which was introduced by Muslim scientists before the period of Renaissance. Islam underlined reason and experience and put emphasis on nature and history as sources of human knowledge.

10. Reconsidering Categories and Methodological Concepts

Given the present drives for reorienting the field in view of the new developments in the international system and the aforementioned need to open the intellectual boundaries to research, it is also necessary to reconceptualize the dominating categorizations in the field.

The notion of levels of analysis has always been central to the discussion of international relations. Within that field the notion of levels was based traditionally on perspectives toward the causes of war. Some of the seminal works outlined the different perspectives of the individual, the state, and the structure/system. However, within the field of international communication the discussion of levels of analysis has been muted. First and foremost, this is due to the fact that in international communication more than in the field of international relations, the categories dealt with are more of an individual, institutional, and non-state character. That is to say, that more individuals and institutions are involved directly in the day to day phenomena of international communication than of international relations. The diversity of these topics discussed in communication literature points to the diversity of actors operating within the field. Yet, the importance, centrality, and the changing influence of the state in the conduct of international communication cannot be denied. Furthermore, movement between levels is more apparent in international communication due to the distribution of impacts to a variety of levels (individual, cultural, developmental, etc.) from different stimuli (information flows, technological growth, elite actions, etc.) Thus movement from macro to micro, micro to macro, and in between are easier given the global nature of communication and the variety of central actors to the field.

Connected with this issue is the need to re-evaluate the field's traditional categorizations of actors. For example, the notion of an international arena divided into the first, second, and third worlds is no longer accurate in the advent of the Cold War. Politically and economically much has changed since this terminology was originally introduced, therefore, it is necessary to rethink the basis for how we approach these actors. An alternative to this approach based on political and economic criteria is a framework based on cultural spheres. If the conflicts of the new world are to be defined by relations between cultures and civilizations, then it is necessary to reconceptualize our terminology along these lines. As such we may develop categories like the Islamic, Confucian, North-American, or West European zones. These divisions reflect both the cultural and the geographical importance of communications in today's world.

And perhaps most important of all are the methodological tools with which the reliability and the validity of data at hand are determined. International and comparative communication studies and research will benefit greatly by exploring alternative methodological tools to the ones currently available to students and researchers, especially when dealing with communication modes and practices in the old and non-Western societies.

Again, an example from the Islamic tradition can illustrate the rich and diverse sources of discourse analysis and its database. In the realm of Islamic philosophy and epistemology one may identify at least 9 categories of data, each category accounting for a specific validity criteria of contents (Sheikh, 1970). Such alternative methodological and conceptual tools can provide a different and valuable perspective on issues for international communication. And as we increase the study of our field globally, these new approaches will be able to play an ever increasing and contributing role.

The first survey of the state of international communication between 1850 and 1960, which I undertook over two decades ago, demonstrated two major themes. One was the overwhelming amount of literature on propaganda, public opinion, mass media, persuasion, journalistic techniques, and communication and development, with little work in such areas as cultural analysis, the political economy of communication, discourse analysis, and comparative studies. Some new areas received no more than a few pages of bibliographic references due to their newness (e.g. space communication and infomatics/telematics). The second main conclusion of that survey was the direct correlation between the areas of research and publishing and the United States' military, political, and economic involvement around the world (Mowlana, 1971 and 1973).

A quarter century later, one is overwhelmed by the amount and extent of research output in international communication with diverse areas of inquiry and highly specialized streams of research. However, this impressive accumulation of data and information that now accounts for our aggregate knowledge in the field is in my opinion still primarily the accumulation of works in the United States and in a number of highly industrialized countries of Europe with a comparatively small portion of research coming from the non-American and non-European sources or from the scientific and philosophical basis of other cultures. The old correlations may still exist in regards to the quantity and quality of research vis-à-vis the political and economic actors considering the profound changes taking place in international relations: the ascent of Europe and Japan, and the demise of the former Soviet Union.

We should not be deceived by an illusion of the diversity of the subject matter and the vastness of the literature. We need to concentrate on promoting the diversity of cultural views and our ability to make the field more interesting and challenging by exploring new avenues and voices of knowledge. If we do not watch for these potential sources, we may go on for another long generation or decades without really making any effort that may account for a true shift in our thinking and our research paradigms.

References

Algar, H. (1969). *Religion and state in Iran, 1785-1906: The role of the Ulama in the Qajar period.* Berkeley: University of California Press.

Algar, H. (1978). Islam and the intellectual challenge of modern civilization. In A. Guahar (Ed.), *The challenge of Islam* (pp. 285-296). London: Islamic Council of Europe.

Anderson, B. (1990). *Imagined communities.* London: Verso.

Arnold, T., & Guillaurne, A. (1960). *The legacy of Islam.* New York: Oxford University Press.

Aronson, J. D., & Cowhey, P. F. (1988). *When countries talk: International trade in telecommunications service.* Cambridge, MA: Ballinger.

Astroff, R. (1992). The politics and political economy of language. *Media Development, 1,* p. 3.

Baqir as-Sadr, M. (1982). *Iqtisaduna* [Our economics] (2 vols.). Teheran: World Organization for Islamic Service.

Bell, D. (1960). *The end of ideology.* New York: Free Press.

Bernstein, R. J. (1976). *The restructuring of social and political theory.* Philadelphia: University of Pennsylvania Press.

Bosworth, C. E. (1967). *The Islamic dynasties.* Edinburgh: Edinburgh University Press.

Bredemeier, B. B. (Ed.). (1956, Spring). *Public Opinion Quarterly, 20,*(1) [Special Issue].

Bruce, R. R., Cunard, J. P., & Director, M. D. (1986). *From telecommunications to electronic services: A global spectrum of definitions, boundary lines, and structures.* Boston: Butterworth.

Burrell, G., & Morgan, G. (1979). *Sociological paradigms and organizational analysis.* London: Heinemann.

Capra, F. (1975). *The tao of physics.* New York: Bantam.

Center for International Studies, MIT. (1953). *Research in international communication: An advisory report of the planning committee.* Cambridge: Author.

Chay, J. (Ed.). (1990). *Culture and international relations.* New York: Praeger.

Cherry, C. (1961). *On human communication.* Cambridge: MIT Press.

Commission of the European Communities. (1988, February 9). *Toward a competitive community-wide telecommunications market in 1992: Implementing the green paper on the development of the common market for the telecommunications services and equipment* (Com (88) 48 Final). Brussels: Author.

Constitution of the Islamic republic of Iran (H. Algar, Trans.). (1980). Berkeley: Mizan.

Cooper, M. (1990). Global Goliath: Coke conquers the world. *U.S. News & World Report, 109,* pp. 52-54.

Copleston, F. (1980). *Philosophies and cultures.* Oxford, UK: Oxford University Press.

Copleston, F. (1982). *Religion and the one: Philosophies east and west.* New York: Crossroad.

214

Creel, H. (1953). *Chinese thought: From Confucius to Mao Tse Tung.* Chicago: University of Chicago Press.

Deutsch, K. (1966). *The nerves of government: Models of political communication and control.* New York: Free Press.

Duffy, H. (1991). Globalization fever grips insurers. *Site Selection and Industrial Development, 36.*

Edelstein, A., Bowes, J. E., & Hersel, S. M. (Eds.). (1978). *Information societies: Comparing the Japanese and American experiences.* Seattle: University of Washington Press.

EEC. (1990, May 4). Programa de acción para estimular el desarrollo de la industria audiovisual europea [Program of action to promote the development of the audiovisual industry of Europe] (Com (90) 132). In *Media: 1991-1995.* Brussels: EEC.

Ellul, J. (1965). *Propaganda: The formation of men's attitudes.* New York: Vintage.

Enan, M. A. (1940). *Decisive moments in the history of Islam.* Lahore: SH. Muhammad Ashraf.

Enayat, H. (1982). *Modern Islamic political thought.* Austin: University of Texas Press.

Featherstone, M. (Ed.). (1990). *Global culture: Nationalism, globalization and modernity.* London: Sage.

Feketekuty, G. (1988). *International trade in services: An overview and blueprint for services.* Cambridge, MA: Ballinger.

Feldstein, M. (Ed.). (1988). *The United States in the world economy.* Chicago: University of Chicago Press.

Ferment in the field [Special issue]. (1983). *Journal of Communication, 33*(3).

Future of the field [Special issue]. (1993). *Journal of Communication, 43*(3).

Garitaonandia, C. (1990). *La comunicación en el pais vasco* [The communication in the Basque country]. Unpublished working paper.

Gerbner, G., & Siefert, M. (Eds.). (1983). *World communication: A handbook.* White Plains, NY: Longman.

Giddens, A. (1990). *The consequences of modernity.* Cambridge, UK: Polity.

Giving power to the people through language [Editorial]. (1992, January). *Media Development, 39,* 1.

Guahar, A. (1978). Islam and secularism. In A. Guahar (Ed.), *The challenge of Islam.* London: Islamic Council of Europe.

Ha'iri Yazdi, M. (1992). *The principles of epistemology in Islamic philosophy: Knowledge by presence.* Albany: State University of New York Press.

Halabi, A. A. (1976). *Zendegi vs safarahaye Sayyid Jamal-ad-Din Asadabadi* [The life and travels of Sayyid Jamal-ad-Din Asadabadi]. Teheran: Zavar.

Handy, C. (1990). The globalization of food marketing. *National Food Review, 13.*

Hellman, H., Nordenstreng, K., & Varis, T. (1980, August 26-29). *Idealism, aggression, apology, and criticism: The four traditions of research on "international communication."* Paper prepared for the XII Congress of the International Association for Mass Communication Research (IAMCR), Caracas.

Hills, J. (1986). *Deregulating Telecom: Competition and control in the U.S., Japan, and Britain.* London: Frances Pinter.

Hobsbawm, E. J., & Ranger, T. O. (1983). *The invention of tradition.* Cambridge, UK: Cambridge University Press.

Holt, P. M., Lambton, A.K.S., & Lewis, B. (Eds.). (1970). *The Cambridge history of Islam* (2 vols.). London: Cambridge University Press.

Huntington, S. (1993). The clash of civilizations. *Foreign Affairs, 72.*

Ibn Khaldun, A. (1957). *Mugaddimah* (Vol I) [M. P. Gonabadi, Trans.]. Teheran: Bongahe Tarjumeh va Nashreh Ketab.

Ibn Khaldun, A. (1967). *The introduction to history: The Mugaddimah* 4[F. Rosenthal, Trans., N. J. Dowood, Ed.]. London: Routledge & Kegan Paul.

Imam Khomeini's last will and testament. (1989, June 24). *Khayan International, 10*(2446).

International Commission for the Study of Communication Problems. (1981). *Many voices, one world*. London: Kogan Page.

International Organization of Journalists. (1986). *New international information and communication order sourcebook*. Prague: Author.

Iqbal, M. (1982). *The reconstruction of religious thought in Islam*. Lahore: SH. Muhammad Ashraf.

Karpinski, R. (1991). AT&T asks Tobias to lead globalization. *Telephony, 221*.

Keddie, N. R. (1968). *An Islamic response to imperialism: Political and religious writings of Sayyid Jamal ad-Din "Al Afghani."* Berkeley: University of California Press.

Kerr, M. (1968). *Islamic reform: The political and legal theories of Muhammad Abduh*. Berkeley: University of California Press.

Khomeini, R. (1361-1365). *Sahifeh noor: Majmoe rahnemood ha'i Imam Khomeini* [Collected speeches and letters] (18 vols.). Teheran: Vezarate Ershad Islami.

Khomeini, R. (1981). *Islam and revolution: Writings and declarations of Imam Khomeini* (H. Algar, Trans.). Berkeley: Mizan.

King, A., & Schneider, B. (1991). *The first global revolution: A report by the council of the club of Rome*. New York: Pantheon.

Kirschenmann, P. P. (1970). *Information and reflection: On some problems of cybernetics and how contemporary dialectical materialism copes with them*. Dordrecht, Holland: D. Reidel.

Laponce, J. A. (1987). Language and communication: The rise of the monolingual state. *Communication and interaction in global politics*. Beverly Hills, CA: Sage.

Lasswell, H. D. (1942). Communication research and politics. In D. Waples (Ed.), *Print, radio, and film in a democracy* (p. 106). Chicago: University of Chicago Press.

Lasswell, H. D., Lerner, D., & Speier, H. (Eds.). (1980). *Propaganda and communication in world history* (3 vols.). Honolulu: University of Hawaii Press.

Lenin, V. I. (1935-1939). *Selected works II* [J. Fineberg, Ed.). New York: Macmillan.

Louw, E. (1992). Language and national unity in post-apartheid South Africa. *Media Development, 1*, 8.

Machiavelli, N. (1980). *The prince*. New York: NAL Penguin.

Markham, J. W. (Ed.). (1969, March). International communication as a field of study. *Reports and Papers from the Wingspread Symposium on Education and Research in International and Comparative Communication*, Racine, Wisconsin. Iowa City: University of Iowa Publications Department.

Mattelart, A. (1990). *Communication and class struggle, 3: New historical subjects*. New York: International General.

Mearsheimer, J. (1990). Why we will soon miss the cold war. *Atlantic Monthly, 266*.

Merritt, R. L. (Ed.). (1972). *Communication in international politics*. Chicago: University of Illinois Press.

Moran, T. (1989). The globalization of stock markets and foreign listing requirements. *Journal of International Business Studies, 20*.

Moran, T. (1990). The globalization of America's defense industries. *International Security, 15*.

Morgenthau, H. (1985). *Politics among nations: The struggle for power and peace* (6th ed.). New York: Knopf.

Mosco, V., & Waski, J. (Eds.). (1988). *The political economy of information.* Madison: University of Wisconsin Press.

Mowlana, H. (1971). *International communication: A selected bibliography.* Dubuque, IA: Kendall/Hunt.

Mowlana, H. (1973). Trends in research on international communication in the United States. *Gazette: International Journal for Mass Communication Studies, 19*(2).

Mowlana, H. (1979a). *Sey-re ertebatate ejtemai dar Iran* [Social communication in Iran]. Teheran: College of Social Communication Publications, Gilan Press.

Mowlana, H. (1979b). Technology versus tradition: Communication in the Iranian revolution. *Journal of Communication, 29,*(3), 107-112.

Mowlana, H. (1984a). Communication for political change: The Iranian revolution. In G. Gerbner & M. Siefert (Eds.), *World communication: A handbook* (pp. 294-301). White Plains, NY: Longman.

Mowlana, H. (1984b). The role of the media in the U.S.-Iranian conflict. In A. Arno & W. Dissanayake (Eds.), *The news media in national and international conflict* (pp. 71-99). Boulder, CO: Westview.

Mowlana, H. (1986). *Global information and world communication: New frontiers in international relations.* White Plains, NY: Longman.

Mowlana, H. (1988). Mass media systems and communication. In M. Adams (Ed.), *The Middle East: A handbook.* London: Muller, Blond and White.

Mowlana, H. (1989, October-November). The Islamization of Iranian television. *Inter Media, 17*(5), 35-39.

Mowlana, H. (1990, Spring). Geopolitics of communications and the strategic aspect of the Persian Gulf. *The Iranian Journal of International Affairs, 11*(1), 85-106.

Mowlana, H. (1991). Opposition media outside national boundaries: From constitutionalism to the Islamic revolution. In A. Fathi (Ed.), *Iranian refugees and exiles since Khomeini* (pp. 37-54). Costa Mesa, CA: Mazda.

Mowlana, H. (1993). From technology to culture. In G. Gerbner, H. Mowlana, & K. Nordenstreng (Eds.), *The global media debate: Its rise, fall, and renewal.* Norwood, NJ: Ablex.

Mowlana, H. (1994). International communication research in the 21st century: From functionalism to postmodernism and beyond. In C. Hamelink and O. Linne (Eds.), *Mass communication research: On problems and policies.* Norwood, NJ: Ablex.

Mowlana, H., & Mohsenian, M. (1990, August 26-31). *Japanese programs on Iranian television: A study in international flow of information.* Paper presented at the 17th World Congress of the International Association for Mass Communication Research, Lake Bled, Yugoslavia.

Mowlana, H., & Wilson, L. J. (1990). *The passing of modernity: Communication and the transformation of society.* White Plains, NY: Longman.

Mutahhari, M. (1977). *Nahjul Balagha: Sermons, letters and saying of Hazrat Ali* [S.M.A. Jafery, Trans.]. Elmhurst, NY: Tahrike Tarsile Quran.

Mutahhari, M. (1982). *Majmoe ghoftara* [Collection of speeches]. Teheran: Sadra.

Mutahhari, M. (1985). *Fundamentals of Islamic thought: God, man and the Universe* [R. Campbell, Trans.]. Berkeley: Mizan.

Mutahhari, M. (1986). *Social and historical changes: An Islamic perspective.* Berkeley: Mizan.

Nakamura, H. (1964). *Ways of thinking of eastern peoples.* Honolulu: East-West Center Press.

Nordenstreng, K., & Schiller, H. I. (Eds.). (1993). *Beyond national sovereignty: International communication in the 1990's.* Norwood, NJ: Ablex.

Nye, J. S., Jr. (1990a). *Bound to lead: The changing nature of American power.* New York: Basic Books.

Nye, J. S., Jr. (1990b). Soft power. *Foreign Policy, 80,* 153-171.

Pavelic, B., & Hamelink, C. J. (1985). The new international economic order: Links between economics and communications (Reports and papers on mass communication, No. 98). Paris: UNESCO.

Peterson, D. (1990). Globalization and telecommunication leadership. *Vital Speeches of the Day, 56.*

Quareshi, I. H. (1978). Islam and the west—Past, present, and future. In A. Guahar (Ed.), *The challenge of Islam* (pp. 237-247). London: Islamic Council of Europe.

Reid, P. (1991). The globalization of technology. *Issues in Science and Technology, 7.*

Rhinesmith, S. H. (1991). An agenda for globalization. *Training and Development Journal, 45.*

Sardar, Z. (1992, June). Terminator 2: Modernity, postmodernism and the "other." *Futures.*

Sarton, G. (1950). *Introduction to the history of science* (Vols. I-III). Baltimore: William and Wilkins.

Schiller, H. I. (1984). *Information and the crisis economy.* Norwood, NJ: Ablex.

Schiller, H. I. (1989). *Culture, inc.: The corporate takeover of public expression.* New York: Oxford University Press.

Schlesinger, P. (1990, November). *Media, the political order and national identity: A perspective from Scotland.* Paper presented to the International Symposium, "Public Communication, Cultural Identity and Cross-Cultural Relations," Barcelona.

Shannon, C. E., & Weaver, W. (1961). *The mathematical theory of communication.* Urbana: University of Illinois Press.

Shapiro, M. J. (1981). *Language and political understanding.* New Haven: Yale University Press.

Shari'ati, A. (1979). *On the sociology of Islam.* Berkeley: Mizan.

Shari'ati, A. (1980). *Marxism and other western fallacies: An Islamic critique.* Berkeley: Mizan.

Sheikh, M. S. (1970). *A dictionary of Muslim philosophy.* Lahore: Institute of Islamic Culture.

Sherman, S. (1991). Houghton Mifflin CEO hopes to globalize. *Publisher's Weekly, 238.*

Sherwani, H. K. (1955). *Muslim colonies in France, Northern Italy and Switzerland.* Lahore: SH. Muhammad Ashraf.

Simpson, C. (1993). U.S. mass communication research, counterinsurgency, and scientific "reality." In William S. Solomon & Robert W. McChensey (Eds.), *Ruthless criticism: New perspectives and in U.S. communication history.* Minneapolis: University of Minnesota Press.

Simpson, C. (1994). *Science of coercion: Communication research and psychology warfare, 1945-1960.* New York: Oxford University Press.

Smith, A. (1980). *The geopolitics of information: How western culture dominates the world.* New York: Oxford University Press.

Smith, G. (1992). *Tourism, telecommunications, and transnational banking: A study in international interactions.* Doctoral dissertation, School of International Service, The American University.

Smythe, D. W. (1981). *Dependency road: Communications, capitalism, consciousness, and Canada.* Norwood, NJ: Ablex.

Strange, S. (1986). *Casino capitalism.* New York: Basil Blackwell.

Strong, T. B. (1984). Language and nihilism. In M. Shapiro (Ed.), *Language and politics* (p. 82). New York: New York University Press.

Tabatabai, S.M.H. (1981). *Shi'a.* Qum: Ansariyan.

Tunstall, J. (1986). *Communications deregulation: The unleashing of America's communication industry.* New York: Blackwell.

UNESCO: Why? A world forum [Editorial]. (1984, Autumn). *Journal of Communication, 34*(4).

Universal Esperanto Association. (1978, December). *Language problems: Communication problems.* Paris: UNESCO.

Van Dinh, T. (1987). *Independence, liberation, revolution: An approach to the understanding of the third world.* Norwood, NJ: Ablex.

Vilanilam, J. V. (1989). *Reporting a revolution: The Iranian revolution and the NICO debate.* New Delhi: Sage.

Von Grunebaum, G. E. (1953). *Medieval Islam.* Chicago: University of Chicago Press.

Walker, R.B.J. (Ed.). (1984). *Culture, ideology, and world order.* Boulder, CO: Westview.

Warf, B. (1989). Telecommunications and the globalization of financial services. *The Professional Geographer, 41.*

Wiener, N. (1961). *Cybernetics, or control and communication in animal and the machine.* Cambridge: MIT Press.

Wiener, N. (1967). *The human use of human beings: Cybernetics and society.* New York: Avon.

Wilber, K. (1977). *The spectrum of consciousness.* Wheaton, IL: Theosophical Publishing House.

Wilber, K. (1983). *Eye to eye: The quest for the new paradigm.* Garden City, NJ: Anchor.

Author Index

Subject Index

222

catalyst for processes of, 198
definition of, 198
modernity and, 197
of communication, 198
of food production, 198
of insurance, 198
of legal and financial services, 198
of technology, 198
Global village, 190-191, 202
Goodsell, Charles T., 36
Grotius, Hugo, 143, 144
Group of 77, 207

Hafiz, 135
Haitham, al, 136
HDTV, history of development of, 203
Hegel, Georg, 77
Heidegger, Martin, 110
High-definition television, 39-40
Human rights, ix
Husserl, Edmund, 110
Hyman, Herbert, 20

Ibn Arabi, 135
Ibn Bajjah, 138
Ibn Rushd, 118, 138
Ibn Sina, 118, 136
Ibn Tufayl, 138
Ideology, 77-78
Indian philosophy, 210
Inference method, 30
Informatics, 4
    and need for new policy-making, 41
    definition of, 40-41
    IBI definition of, 41
    See also National informatics policy
Informatics age, 39
Information, international flow of:
    awareness of imbalance in, 5
    awareness of inequality in, 5
Information, private industry of, 87-88
Information Age, 58
Information economics, 59, 94
Information economy, 56-58
Information services, U.S.:
    export of, 55

Information society, xii, 92, 186, 191, 196
    and Islamic society, 128, 129
Information Society Paradigm, 140, 144, 172
    as service-based, 132
    characteristics of, 132
    description of, 131-132
    versus Islamic Community Paradigm, 131-135, 142
Information technology, 200
Integrated Services Digital Networks (ISDN), 4, 57, 70
Intellectual property organizations, international:
    U.S. participation in, 55
Intellectual property rights, 5, 40, 183
Inter-American Development Bank (IDB), 63
Intergovernmental Bureau of Informatics (IBI), 41
International broadcasting, rise of, 5
International Business Machines (IBM), 60
    private data system of, 58
International communication, 8
    aggressive phase of, 37-38
    apology phase of, 38
    critical phase of, 38
    definition of, 9
    dynamics, 194-213
    increased number of nation-states in, 5
    international relations and, 31
    realism phase of, 38
    strategic impact of, 4
International Communication as a Field of Study. See Markham volume
International communication issues,
    increased political legitimacy of, 5
International communication phenomena,
    language-based, 107-111
International communication research:
    development of diplomacy and, 3
    development of international organizations and, 3
    development of new communication technologies and, 3
    disregard of language issues in, 103
    formalization of, 35-37
    international conflict and, 3

About the Author

Dr. **Hamid Mowlana** is Professor of International Relations and the founding director of the International Communication Program at the School of International Service, American University, Washington, DC. He has been on the faculty of American University since 1968, and has served as visiting professor and guest scholar in Europe, the Middle East, Africa, Asia, and Latin America. He received his Ph.D. from Northwestern University, Evanston, Illinois, in 1963. He has received a number of awards, among them American University Faculty Award for Outstanding Scholarship, Research, and Other Professional Contributions.

An advisor and consultant to a number of international organizations, he has worked for UNESCO in Paris and has written extensively on international communication, cultural and psychological aspects of international relations, and socioeconomic development. He is president of the International Association for Mass Communication Research (IAMCR).

He is the author and editor of numerous works, among them: *Global Information and World Communication: New Frontiers in International Relations*; *Mass Media in the Middle East: A Comprehensive Handbook*, with Yahya R. Kamalipour; *The Global Media Debate: Its Rise, Fall, and Renewal*, with George Gerbner and Kaarle Nordenstreng; *Triumph of the Image: The Media's War in the Persian Gulf*, with George Gerbner and Herbert I. Schiller; *The Passing of Modernity: Communication and the Transformation of Society*; and *Communication Technology and Development*, with Laurie J. Wilson. He also has chapters in books and anthologies, including *International Encyclopedia of Communication* and *The Oxford Encyclopedia of the Modern Islamic World*. He is on the editorial board of numerous scholarly journals.